The Psych

The Psycho File

*A Comprehensive Guide
to Hitchcock's Classic Shocker*

Joseph W. Smith III

McFarland & Company, Inc., Publishers
Jefferson, North Carolina, and London

LIBRARY OF CONGRESS CATALOGUING-IN-PUBLICATION DATA

Smith, Joseph W., 1960–
  The Psycho file : a comprehensive guide to Hitchcock's classic shocker / Joseph W. Smith III.
    p. cm.
  Includes bibliographical references and index.

  ISBN 978-0-7864-4487-8
  softcover : 50# alkaline paper ∞

  1. Psycho (Motion picture : 1960) I. Title.
PN1997.P79S65 2009
791.43'72 — dc22   2009028947

British Library cataloguing data are available

On the cover: Hitchcock chatting with a crew member in front of the Bates mansion (©Universal Pictures; courtesy of Universal Pictures–Photofest); *inset* Edward Theodore Gein, November 23, 1957; shower drain ©2009 Shutterstock

Manufactured in the United States of America

McFarland & Company, Inc., Publishers
 Box 611, Jefferson, North Carolina 28640
  www.mcfarlandpub.com

For my parents,
who instilled in me
at a very young age
a love for movies
and a tireless curiosity

Acknowledgments

Writing is lonely work — but publishing is not. As I gradually finished my manuscript and emerged from the black hole surrounding my laptop, I became increasingly aware of just how collaborative a book really is — and of why so many authors make a point of acknowledging their debts to others.

I am grateful to:

Philip J. Skerry for his help and encouragement — even though I borrowed a lot of his material; Stephen Rebello and his agent, Mary Evans, for permission to quote so liberally from his excellent book; Derek Davidson and Ron Mandelbaum at Photofest (their amazing collection — and their ability to grab frames at will — is an invaluable resource for those seeking movie stills); my former student Tony Cupiccia for providing the quotation that begins Chapter 16; Matt Reitz and Rodney Easton for contributing memories for Chapter 19; and my two proofreaders, Dr. John Kelsey and my wife, Mona Chang — the latter, as always, my sagest critic and ally.

Naturally, I am considerably in debt to the writers who have gone before me in examining *Psycho* and its many themes, ironies, and symbols.

"Thank God for giving knowledge to Man, who could then create film so generations to come could enjoy and reap the benefits provided by the greats of the past."
—*Janet Leigh*

Table of Contents

Part 3. And That Still Wasn't Enough: Aftermath

Part 1.
Before Committing Yourself:
A Few Preliminaries

Introduction

We All Go a Little Mad Sometimes

Psycho has surely generated more written material than any motion picture in history. In addition to books by Janet Leigh and Stephen Rebello on how the film was actually made, Hitchcock's classic shocker has inspired hundreds of pages of insightful analysis in magazines, journals, anthologies, and book-length treatments.

In his book on the shower scene, for example, Philip J. Skerry points out that Mother is right-handed — while Norman is left-handed.

Bill Krohn, in *Hitchcock at Work*, notes that the shower scene's only shot of penetration occurs at Marion's womb, near her navel — and thus Norman is attacking the symbol of attachment to one's mother.

And as Raymond Durgnat observes, Marion's narrative begins by looking into a hotel window and ends by looking out of one.

It seems to me that these brilliant insights ought to be together in one volume. And that's the idea behind this book. Its intent is to pull together the most salient material on a work that continues to captivate viewers after 50 years: background on real-life serial killer Ed Gein, who was the basis for Norman Bates; discussion of Robert Bloch's original novel, on which the movie is based; various details on the mechanics of how *Psycho* was filmed; the movie's effect on first-time viewers in 1960; and its three sequels — as well as Gus Van Sant's controversial 1998 shot-for-shot remake.

As you may already have noted, the brunt of the text is taken up with a minutely detailed analysis of the actual film — scene by scene, shot by shot, line by line. This section examines the film the way one might dissect a work by Shakespeare, Dickens, or Dostoyevsky — concentrating on literary devices such as irony, symbol, image, foil, and motif; psychological motives and movements; patterns in the storyline's structure; moral and ethical implications; and the combined effect these devices have on viewers.

Of the eight different books on *Psycho*, you are holding the only one that brings all this material together in one place.

In addition to building on the work of others, I also offer several of my own original insights on the film — gleaned from watching, studying, teaching, and discussing *Psycho* for more than 20 years. Most of this occurred in the high-school classes I've taught in Pennsylvania and New Jersey, where hundreds of bright young minds offered many keen insights — much more willingly, I might add, than they do when approaching *The Scarlet Letter* or *Macbeth*. Most of the "new" insights here are mine, but some are theirs. For their inventive and enthusiastic response to *Psycho*, I owe a debt of gratitude that I cannot repay.

Readers who don't share the widespread obsession with *Psycho* may be skeptical about the meticulous detail in this text. They are likely to react as my students often do: "That stuff can't all be there on purpose! You've seen this film too many times — you're reading too much into it!"

My response to such objections is to cue up the scene right after Marion's car sinks into the bog. We are in Sam's hardware store, and the first thing we see is Sam's letter to Marion, laced with deliberate and painful ironies. For example, he calls her "right-as-always," when she has in fact stolen $40,000; and he agrees to marry her if she "still hasn't come to her senses," when in fact she will never come to her senses again — because she's dead.

Even more heartbreaking is the fact that in the letter, Sam at last declares his willingness to wed Marion, a change from his previous resistance due to financial woes. Since she stole the money to help "persuade" him, this essentially means that she never had to commit the theft in the first place, a revelation that gives devastating resonance to Marion's already tragic death.

This emotion-laden letter is onscreen for mere seconds — and most viewers never even get to read it; yet Hitchcock has apparently paid careful attention to its every word and phrase.

Furthermore, as the camera then pulls back from Sam, we see a customer at the counter worrying whether a certain insecticide will hurt the bugs; her insistence that "death should always be painless" provides a bitterly ironic contrast to the shattering death we just witnessed.

To remind us of that, as the woman speaks we can clearly see a display of knives in the background. And of course, we must try to remember that this is not a *real* hardware store; it's one constructed specifically for the movie, and thus all these items had to be carefully placed on the set by Hitchcock's crew. In fact, the knives in this scene are specifically called for in Joseph Stefano's script.

And if that still doesn't do it, I mention a story Donald Spoto used to tell in his Hitchcock classes at Manhattan's New School in the 1980s. During a visit to the set of *Family Plot*, Spoto watched Hitchcock instruct cameraman Leonard J. South to change his angle slightly, lest a glare from the overhead chandelier ruin the shot. South checked the shot, noted the glare, and made the change, yet Hitchcock had foreseen this problem without himself looking through the camera. According to Rebello, nearly the exact same thing happened during the *Psycho* shoot; without looking through the camera, Hitchcock was sure that one of the set's arc lights was visible in a nighttime shot in front of the Bates Motel. Cameraman John L. Russell assured him that the light was not in the frame, but subsequent dailies proved Hitchcock right, and the footage had to be reshot.

Along these lines, Rebello cites a *TV Guide* interview in which Hitchcock angrily reacted to the suggestion that something in *Psycho* was "unconscious": "The stupid idiots! As if I don't *know* what I'm doing. My technique is serious. I am *consciously* aware of what I am doing in *all* my work" (175).

The simple fact is that Sir Alfred the Great, who made 53 feature films, two documentaries, and 20 shorter television films; whose career began with black-and-white silents and then proceeded to sound, color, and 3-D; who made horror, romance, comedy, thrillers, and docudramas; who inspired more books, studies, and analyses than any other director you can name — this man knows *exactly* what we're hearing and seeing in every frame. And it's always important.

Psycho, of course, has generated not only reams of analysis but also hundreds of cultural allusions and tributes. Such a list might include several "Far Side" cartoons, episodes of *The Simpsons*, numerous pop songs (e.g., Landscape's "My Name Is Norman Bates"), various scenes from subsequent horror films (Brian De Palma, *High Anxiety*), and even the marvelous DiGiorno commercial that features Mom and Norman "splitting" a pizza.

In compiling material on the film, however, I could not bring myself to attempt a compendium of these numerous references. Such a list would be long, dry, and tedious, and would inevitably overlook many examples ("What — you mean he forgot to include ... ?"). In addition, most of these need to be seen or heard for their full effect, something that can't be done in print.

A few final notes on my approach: In re-reading the literature on *Psycho*, I was struck by how much of it consists of plot summary — something that is avoided here. I have simply assumed that anyone who chooses to read this book has already seen the film — probably several times — and doesn't need me to reiterate what happens in each scene. My approach has been, in fact, to cram as much material as possible into every page and paragraph, and not to go into excessive detail.

Readers may also note several references to younger viewers, including a few personal anecdotes from classroom showings of the film. Having screened *Psycho* for more than 1700 high school students since 1988, I feel not only qualified but also compelled to provide some record of its reception among modern teens, a perspective that receives virtually no attention in the widespread writings on the film. It has been my goal to approach *Psycho* with half an eye on younger viewers, and thus to help "preserve" it for future generations, while at the same time showing how and why it still works for gore-glutted teens raised on *Scream*, *The Ring*, and *Saw*.

With this in mind, I have tried to preserve an informal, conversational tone to make the book accessible to younger readers and to those unfamiliar with film terminology and Hitchcock scholarship. My apologies to film students and professors who will have to tolerate an occasional explanation of something they already know, such as the 180-degree rule, the Hitchcock cameos, or the Production Code. And to keep it user-friendly, I have pledged not to use the words "filmic," "diegetical," or "subsegmentation" anywhere in this book. (For the record, my word processing program red-lined those last two words; apparently, even computer programs object to such unnecessary jargon.)

In a similar vein, avid Hitchcock scholars will note that my approach is rather old-fashioned, and does not pay much heed to some of the more recent writings on his work (e.g., Laura Mulvey, Slavoj Zizek) or to more recent literary theory. The reason for this is simple: I don't think the average reader finds this material particularly interesting, convincing, or even — in some cases — comprehensible. Some of the more trendy studies of film and literature seem to be retreating into a rarefied atmosphere that is of little interest to the general populace. Hitchcock, however, was an intensely *popular* filmmaker, and studies of his work should be similarly sensitive to popular tastes.

In other words: No, this book does not offer any exciting new approach to the film, no new slant that will make it groundbreaking or revolutionary. It isn't going to interpret the film from a postmodern viewpoint, from a Marxist viewpoint, from an existentialist viewpoint, or with any specific intellectual agenda. In fact, a friend recently asked what my thesis was, and I told him quite simply: "*Psycho* is a fascinating film." To put it another way: I don't want readers to react by thinking, "Wow, what a great piece of writing!" but rather by exclaiming, "This film is amazing! I'm going to have to watch it again."

And if I send you back to the film, or running for the other writers I have cited, then I will have done my job.

If, on the other hand, you're inclined to find me overly obsessed with the film, my response would be Norman's: "We all go a little mad sometimes."

Haven't you?

1

He Stole Her Corpse
Gein and Bloch

Alfred Hitchcock once said, "*Psycho* all came from Robert Bloch's book."

He was talking, of course, about the 1959 novel on which the film is based. Yet even Bloch's original *Psycho* doesn't give us the actual genesis of Norman Bates.

Yes, Bloch's lurid little shocker supplied the movie's characters and storyline; but just as the film was based on the book, the book was in turn based on something even earlier — a real-life American crime case that, in the words of Harold Schechter, makes *Psycho* look "as reassuring as a fairy tale" (xi).

In his later autobiographical writings, Bloch himself claimed that folks often asked him where he got such "perfectly *dreadful* ideas" for his many horror stories and thrillers; his response was to "shrug and point to the map" ("Shambles" 224).

In the case of *Psycho*, it would be a map of rural Plainfield, Wisconsin, where in November 1957 police first entered the appalling homestead of a 51-year-old recluse named Ed Gein. They were looking for a missing hardware store owner named Bernice Worden, and they found her — hung upside down in a shed by the kitchen, headless and gutted, like a freshly killed deer.

Gein — rhymes with "mean" — was eventually implicated in Worden's death, and in the murder of local barmaid Mary Hogan three years earlier. Some suspect that Gein also had a hand in the death of his own brother many years before that — a death that occurred under suspicious circumstances while the two men were fighting a brush fire.

In any event, the greatest shock in the Gein case lay not in the murders, nor even in Worden's desecrated corpse, but rather in what police found when they made their way into the house itself. Scattered throughout the filthy, cluttered home were ten human skulls — including two hung decoratively on

Gein's bedposts. Several had been sawn off at the top, their rounded caps turned upside down and fashioned into crude soup bowls that had clearly been used for meals.

Other grisly discoveries made by police: human organs wrapped and carefully preserved in the freezer; a human heart in a stove-top pot; a cup of noses; death-masks made from the facial skin of women (some hung on walls, some made up with rouge); chairs, lampshades, and a wastebasket upholstered with human skin, as well as other horrors made from human flesh — bracelets, a knife sheath, a belt, a shade-pull adorned with lips.

Perhaps most shocking of all were nine sets of carefully removed and preserved female genitalia. Not to mention the pair of leggings and a vest, complete with breasts — all made with peeled-off human flesh.

Despite initial impressions to the contrary, these horrific items were not by-products of additional murders; rather, they came from a series of night-time grave-robbing episodes to which Gein eventually confessed. Over a period of several years starting in 1947, Gein had plundered perhaps as many as 15 burial plots in two or three local cemeteries — most in the same Plainfield graveyard where his own mother was interred. Later psychological examination revealed that Gein was obsessed with his mother (and with female anatomy in general), and that he actually wore some of his grisly handmade items, in an attempt to understand what it felt like to be a woman.

Though many of these details did not become widely known till later, the case caught the attention of Robert Bloch, a young horror writer who lived in Wisconsin only 35 miles away.

Bloch wrote more than 20 novels and 400-plus short stories — including the frequently anthologized "Yours Truly, Jack the Ripper" and the Hugo-winning "That Hell-Bound Train"; he also penned several screenplays — including William Castle's *Strait-Jacket* (1964), starring Joan Crawford — and three episodes of the original *Star Trek* TV series.

Though much of this work came after *Psycho*, Bloch was already well-established in the thriller genre when Gein's case planted the idea for a book with which his name would forever be associated.

Remarkably, Bloch claimed that at the time he wrote *Psycho*, he was unaware of Gein's transvestitism and obsession with his mother — that he knew no details of the case and virtually nothing about the fiend himself until much later, when he began research for his essay on Gein in Anthony Boucher's true-crime anthology *The Quality of Murder* (1962).

"I based my story on the *situation* rather than on any person," Bloch wrote in his delightful memoir *Once Around the Bloch: An Unauthorized Autobiography*. When he first conceived *Psycho*, Bloch was simply interested in the idea that "the man next door may be a monster"—and with this in mind, he set out to create his character "from whole cloth" (228).

If this is true, the numerous parallels between Gein and Norman Bates are downright uncanny.

Gein's first victim was named Mary, just like the woman in Bloch's book (Hitchcock's crew changed the name to Marion when they learned that a real "Mary Crane" was living in Phoenix); and Gein's final victim ran a hardware store—just like Mary's boyfriend, Sam.

According to Gein biographer Harold Schechter, Eddie's mother was strict and domineering—a "domestic tyrant" (13) who expounded on "the wickedness of modern women" and made her boys swear they would "keep themselves uncontaminated" from such "tainted, fallen creatures" (25–26). All of this sounds much like the shrewish and puritanical Mrs. Bates, who also rules her son with an iron fist, scolds him bitterly, and in the film finds it "disgusting" that he wants to have "strange young women" in for supper.

More parallels with Norman Bates: After the untimely deaths of his father and older brother, Gein lived alone with his mother in an isolated home on a lonely road many miles from town. As Schechter writes, when Augusta Gein died in 1945, Eddie lost "his only friend and one true love. And he was absolutely alone in the world" (36)—though he later told psychiatrists that, like Norman, he sometimes heard his mother's voice speaking to him.

After her death, Gein boarded off those parts of the house that had been his mother's domain (principally her bedroom and the downstairs parlor), maintaining them as a sort of shrine. Schechter tells us that when police entered the home more than a decade later, these rooms were "in a state of absolute tidiness," with everything "in perfect order" (91), including women's clothes folded carefully away in dresser drawers—once again comprising an uncanny precursor to Mother's pristine bedroom in *Psycho*.

Well—*almost* pristine. After all, the bedroom was also where Norman kept his mother's ten-year-old corpse. The film's psychiatrist tells us that Norman had "treated" this cadaver to "keep it as well as it would keep"—and similarly, many of the artifacts in Gein's home were found to have been sprinkled with salt or rubbed with oil to delay putrefaction. One 1957 psychological examiner described Gein's fetish for corpses in a way that could easily be applied to Norman as well: He had "a desire for a substitute for his mother in the form of a replica or body that could be kept indefinitely" (quoted in Schechter 217). Or consider this summary of expert testimony at Gein's first hearing in 1958—another passage that describes Norman almost as well as it does Gein: He was "a chronic schizophrenic who had been lost in 'his own little world' of fantasy and delusion since the death of his mother twelve years before" (Schechter 229).

According to the fine Internet article on Gein by Rachael Bell and Marilyn Bardsley, Gein had a love-hate relationship toward women resulting from attitudes his mother had instilled. In Schechter's words, Gein developed "violently divided feelings for his mother — with murderous hatred coexisting alongside worshipful love..." (153). Again, this sounds appallingly like Norman, who in the film tells Marion that he can't put his mother in an institution because "if you love someone, you don't do that to them, even if you hate them."

Or consider this conclusion from a 1957 article in *Time* magazine: Gein was "the victim of a common conflict: while consciously he loved his mother and hated other women, unconsciously he hated her and loved others" (quoted in Schechter 206).

The film reflects this in Norman's attitude toward Marion, which veers between attraction and guilt, with concomitant rebellion and submission directed toward his mother. In the concluding words of Dr. Richmond, when Norman met Marion, "he was touched by her — aroused by her. He wanted her. That set off the jealous mother, and Mother killed the girl."

The Richmond scene, in fact, cites two "unsolved missing-persons cases" — both "young girls" who may have been killed by Norman. As it turns out, in the Plainfield area two young girls had also disappeared earlier without a trace, one leaving behind signs of a bloody struggle. Gein was never implicated in either case — but of course, he didn't preserve his victims in a bog.

Yet another uncanny similarity is the vast discrepancy between each man's public and private personae. Despite the monstrous secrets in his life, Norman comes across as shy and bumbling, especially around the attractive Marion Crane. Gein, who often did various chores for neighbors — including quite a bit of babysitting — was dubbed "shy" by nearly everyone who met him, even *after* his arrest. Friends and neighbors called him "a very nice fellow," insisting that "you'd never believe he'd be the kind of guy to do such a thing.... Others emphasized Eddie's social backwardness — his 'shyness,' 'meekness,' and awkwardness around women" (Schechter 115–29).

Even Gein's hometown — Plainfield — sounds much like *Psycho*'s Fairvale.

Perhaps most disturbing of all: In Bloch's first chapter, Norman is fascinated by a book on the Incas, who have fashioned a drum from a human cadaver by stretching the skin on its stomach (sounds come out the mouth); as it turns out, Gein's premises had also yielded a tom-tom made with human skin.

"In inventing my character I had come very close to the actual persona of Ed Gein," Bloch later reflected. "It horrified me how I could think of such things. As a result, I spent the next two years shaving with my eyes shut. I didn't want to look in the mirror" (Rebello 13).

Bloch may have had particular justification for being disturbed by Gein's deeds; found among the countless magazines stacked in Gein's house were issues of pulp magazines like *Startling Detective, Unknown Worlds,* and *Marvel Tales*—some of which contained stories written by Bloch.

As for the original case, Gein was eventually found not guilty by reason of insanity and spent the rest of his life in a mental institution. He died in

Forerunner to the Bates homestead: the Wisconsin house of grave-robber Ed Gein, boarded up after the grisly discoveries inside. Only months after Gein was arrested for murder in 1957, the place burned to the ground, probably torched by Plainfield residents tired of crowds driving through every weekend to gawk at it. (Courtesy Photofest)

1984 and was buried in the same cemetery he himself had robbed more than 30 years earlier — right beside his own mother, in fact.

Yet the case has always fascinated America.

During the days and weeks following the gruesome discoveries in Gein's home, police stood guard on the house around the clock "to discourage curiosity seekers, including groups of fraternity boys from the University of Wisconsin bent on throwing beer parties in the infamous 'house of horror'" (Schechter 167). Carloads of rubber-neckers poured through the town — perhaps as many as 4,000 families just on the Sunday following Gein's arrest. A few months later, a crowd of 20,000 descended on Plainfield when Gein's property was opened to the public before its sale by auction. But by then, there wasn't much to see; only three days earlier, the Gein house had burned to the ground, probably torched by local residents irritated over the hordes of gawkers — and by their town's sullied reputation.

As recently as 2005, the Gein farmstead appeared briefly as a sale item on eBay; though the listing was quickly removed due to ethical objections, owner Mike Fisher said he got 10,000 hits during his one-day posting.

Two full-length books have studied the Gein case (Schechter's *Deviant* and *Ed Gein — Psycho!* by Paul Anthony Woods) — along with a graphic 2004 documentary and a fictionalized feature film (the latter was 2000's cheesy *Ed Gein*, a.k.a. *In the Light of the Moon*, starring Steve Railsback).

Details of the case also found their way into Tobe Hooper's 1974 gorefest *The Texas Chain Saw Massacre*, as well as lesser-known shockers like *Deranged* (also 1974) and the picturesquely titled *Three on a Meathook* (1972). In addition, as many horror fans know, Gein's fixation with corpses and female anatomy was the explicit inspiration for Buffalo Bill in *The Silence of the Lambs* (1991).

But first, of course, there was Alfred Hitchcock...

2

Do You Mind If I Look at Your Book?
Stefano and Hitchcock

With 46 feature films behind him — including the just-released hit *North by Northwest*— Hitchcock was once again on the prowl for new material. In the spring of 1959 he and his assistant, Peggy Robertson, noticed a rave review of Bloch's book in Anthony Boucher's regular *New York Times* feature "Criminals at Large." Hitchcock spent a weekend with the book in his Bel Air home.

What he found, in the words of Stephen Rebello, was that "Bloch had sexed-up and Freudianized the Gothic, revitalizing such creaky elements as the rattletrap Old Dark House, the stormy night, and the crackpot madwoman locked in the dank basement" (12).

Or as Hitchcock biographer Patrick McGilligan puts it:

> Hitchcock liked to boast about playing the emotions of audiences as though they were notes on an organ, but when he read *Psycho* he must have recognized his own inner music surging through him. It was ... a phantasmagoria with a scary mansion, stairwell, and dark basement; it was a Peeping Tom and a screaming Jane; it was the world's worst bathroom nightmare, mingling nudity and blood.... It is no exaggeration to say that Hitchcock had been waiting for *Psycho*—working up to it — all his life [579].

Using an agent, Hitchcock made a "blind bid" of $7500, which Bloch and his agent negotiated up to $9000. Only afterward did Bloch learn that he had sold *Psycho*'s rights — with no provision for future royalties — to the most famous film director in the world.

Ironically, advance copies of *Psycho* had already circulated at several Hollywood studios. One script reader had long ago told Hitchcock's studio (Paramount) that Bloch's book was "shocking," "too repulsive," and "impossible for films" (Rebello 13).

Hitchcock got a similar reaction when he presented the idea to Paramount moneymen; in Rebello's words, they went into "executive apoplexy" over the sordid material (23). They refused to finance the picture; they wouldn't even let Hitchcock film it on their lot.

Some of Hitchcock's own people were likewise alarmed. Production assistant Joan Harrison reportedly told the director, "This time you're going too far" (Rebello 30) — and assistant director Herbert Coleman, who had worked on six Hitchcock films in seven years, left for his own career, claiming that he "didn't much care for the sort of movie that it was shaping up to be" (Spoto, *Dark* 417).

In a rare move, the fiscally conservative Hitchcock decided to finance the picture himself — and to film it at Universal, if Paramount would distribute it. Hitchcock deferred his usual $250,000 director's fee in exchange for an initial 60 percent ownership and a deal in which all rights and revenues would revert to him after a predetermined profit for Paramount.

According to biographer Donald Spoto, this savvy deal eventually made Hitchcock a millionaire 20 times over.

In the meantime, a screenplay had been penned by television writer James P. Cavanagh, who had also written "One More Mile to Go" for *Alfred Hitchcock Presents*. Aired in 1957, "Mile" is one of the teleplays Hitchcock himself actually directed, and its storyline — about a husband who murders his wife and drives off with her body in the trunk, after which he is hounded by a well-intentioned highway cop — bears marked similarities to *Psycho*.

Though Cavanagh's draft included many elements that wound up in the film — Marion's drive, her conversation with Norman, and much of the shower murder and cleanup — Hitchcock found it unacceptable. As Peggy Robertson later noted, "It took some kind of genius to make that story dull, but Cavanagh managed to do it!" (Leigh, *Psycho* 10). The director turned instead to a 38-year-old lyricist and composer named Joseph Stefano, who had written the movie *The Black Orchid* for producer Carlo Ponti.

Bloch's novel contains some terrific moments, especially at the end; and like Hitchcock's film, it's laced with tasty irony for those who know that Norman and Mom are the same person: During an early conversation with his mother, Norman thinks, "The things she was saying were the things he had told himself" (11); later he reflects, "If she's a little odd now, it's my fault" (32–33); and toward the end: "He had to protect Mother. It meant protecting himself as well, but it was really Mother he was thinking about" (101).

Nevertheless, we can easily understand Stefano's puzzlement when he read what James Naremore has called "a pretty vulgar piece of writing" (23). It seemed a strange project for the man who had given the world such colorful, larger-than-life films as *Rear Window*, *Vertigo*, and *North by Northwest*.

In particular, Stefano disliked Norman — a pudgy, balding, bespectacled drinker who is introduced in the book's first chapter. Finding that he couldn't sympathize with Norman, Stefano wanted to start *Psycho* off with Marion; to be specific, he told Hitchcock that he wanted to show Marion "shacking up" with Sam while she's supposed to be having lunch.

"The moment I said 'shack up' or anything like that, Hitchcock, being a very salacious man, adored it," Stefano recalled. "I said, 'We'll find out what the girl is all about, see her steal the money and head for Sam....' He thought it was spectacular. I think that idea got me the job" (Rebello 39).

According to Rebello's commentary on the 2008 DVD, Hitchcock was particularly pleased with Stefano's draft of that opening hotel room scene — the first piece of writing he did for the film. Having looked it over, the director indicated his approval in the usual way — by referring to his wife, who had herself done considerable film work as a screenwriter, assistant director, and continuity checker. "Alma loved it," Hitchcock told the young writer.

And when the director mentioned that he was considering the trim, handsome, and likable young Anthony Perkins to play Norman, it was clear that he and Stefano were on the same page.

Except for his very early work in the 1920s and 1930s, Hitchcock was not generally credited as a writer on his films. Nevertheless, the screenplays for most of his movies were developed under Hitchcock's careful supervision, usually involving weeks of conferences between the director and such able screenwriters as John Michael Hayes and Ernest Lehman. For *Psycho*, Stefano spent five weeks meeting daily with Hitchcock and three more weeks writing on his own — producing a script that is radically different from Bloch's book, especially in its treatment of Marion.

Her story occupies only two of the novel's 17 chapters — less than 15 percent of the text. Hitchcock and Stefano expanded this to nearly half of the narrative — lengthening her drive to include a roadside nap, a suspicious highway cop, and an extended car purchase (the latter occupies less than a sentence in the novel). They also fleshed out her character with the hotel room tryst between Sam and Marion. In the book, she and Sam are not sexually active — Mary is a virgin.

Of course, one could write endlessly about Stefano's changes (e.g., Bloch's detective is tall, rangy, and aggressive; he makes two calls to the hardware store instead of one); but the finished script — available at the website The Daily Script (www.dailyscript.com; see *Stefano* in the bibliography) — makes several important alterations that *Psycho* fans may find intriguing:

Bloch's Mary is from Fort Worth, Texas, not Phoenix, Arizona — and rather than driving west to California as in the film, she heads north through Oklahoma to reach Sam in Missouri.

Stiff and unappealing in the movie, Sam is much more sympathetic in the book. Though Stefano's Sam does pen a fondly worded letter to Marion, in the book he is even more articulate and philosophical. In fact, he's the one who provides all the background on Norman at the end — telling it to Lila as he heard it from the doctor.

For her part, Lila is much younger ("the kid sister") — and there is a clear note of blossoming romance between her and Sam. Hitchcock claimed he excised the love interest in order to focus on the solution to the mystery of Marion and Norman — but as Lesley Brill points out in *The Hitchcock Romance, Psycho* posits that "fantasies of domestic happiness are unlikely." Specifically, none of the guy-girl relations in the film promise much "familial warmth or stability" (228) — not Norman and Mom; not Sam and Marion; not the rich man (Cassidy) and his daughter; not even the real-estate secretary (Caroline) and her husband (Teddy). To put it simply, a budding romance between Sam and Lila would seem to offer a sort of hope that has no place in the world of Hitchcock's film.

Besides the characters, another big difference was noted by François Truffaut in his book-length series of interviews with Hitchcock. Specifically, Bloch's third-person narrator often "cheats" by treating Mom as though she were a living, moving person: "Mother had been sleeping in her room" (9); "She was over at the window now, staring out at the rain" (9–10); "Mother opened the door and Mr. Arbogast walked in" (96). Hitchcock certainly tricks us in this regard, but he never cheats — though one must admit this is easier to pull off in his visual medium than it is in Bloch's verbal one.

Another major change occurs near the end: When Sam and Lila explore Mary's motel room, Norman is watching them through his peephole, so he knows that they're looking for Lila's sister. More important, he is aware of Lila's plan to explore the house on the hill. This occurs in Stefano's script as well — but it was excised in the film. (See Chapter 13 for more detail.)

In the novel, this discovery of Sam and Lila's real identity makes Norman angry and unguarded during the ensuing conversation with Sam — and in a crucial difference between book and film, Bloch's Norman suddenly reveals to Sam that he dug up his mother's corpse. Having shared a drink with Sam, he tipsily insists that he brought her back to life — but the reader has little trouble figuring out she's dead, and Bloch thus quashes the element of surprise in the climactic scene.

Hitchcock, significantly, keeps us in the dark about Mom's true identity till our final moments at the Bates homestead — and thus, in the nerve-wracking basement scene, the moment of greatest suspense and the moment of greatest surprise occur at precisely the same time. (More on this in Chapter 14.)

In the book's denouement, there is no hint that Norman killed other young women — whereas in the film, Mom's final speech alludes to "those girls" who were "killed." And Bloch's psychiatrist posits three personalities for Norman (child, man, and mother). Of course, the film adheres to two — using Norman as the keystone for its theme of doubling and split personalities.

More generally, the book uses nonlinear plotting. For example, the first chapter has Norman arguing with Mother as Mary pulls into the motel lot; Chapter 2 then employs a flashback device, giving expository information on Mary and how she wound up at the Bates Motel. Similarly, near the end, after Sam has been knocked out by Norman, he emerges from unconsciousness to hear Lila screaming from the house; the next chapter then backs up to describe Lila's exploration of the house as it leads up to her shriek-inducing visit to the basement. Hitchcock's film, on the other hand, maintains a strictly linear narrative throughout.

Working together, Hitchcock and Stefano took a competent thriller and molded it into the raw material for one of the master's greatest films. Now it was time to transfer that material onto celluloid.

3

The Nuts and Bolts
Hitchcock and His Crew

Two entire books have been written on the making of *Psycho*—and many technical aspects of the film (especially the shower montage) are easier to discuss when considering the specific scenes where they occur. For these reasons, the present section will confine itself to a few key observations that don't fit well into subsequent chapters.

Though Hitchcock sometimes called *Psycho* a "30-day picture," it actually required 42 shooting days, with principal photography beginning on November 30, 1959, and wrapping on February 1, 1960. This is nevertheless an impressively tight schedule—but perhaps not quite as impressive as *Psycho*'s final budget: $806,947.55. (Compare 1959's *North by Northwest*, which cost roughly five times that—or another 1959 film, *Ben-Hur*, whose budget totaled $11 million.)

Hitchcock's determination to keep costs down stemmed partly, of course, from the fact that he was paying for the picture himself; but he seems to have had another motivation as well: matching wits with such companies as Hammer and American International, and such directors as Roger Corman and William Castle.

As the 1950s drew to a close, these folks were cranking out second-rate thrillers like *Macabre*, *The Tingler*, and *The Curse of Frankenstein*—and such films were making plenty of money despite budgets under $1 million. As Leigh's book on the film puts it, Hitchcock wanted "to beat his cheapjack imitators at their own game" (6).

Similarly, he also appears to have been rankled by the success of Henri-Georges Clouzot's *Les Diaboliques* (1955), a terrific low-budget thriller that earned its director a reputation as "the French Hitchcock." In fact, the black-and-white *Diaboliques*, which includes a chilling murder in a bathtub, was screened more than once for Stefano and others on the *Psycho* crew while the film was being made.

In keeping with the low-budget trend of these films, Hitchcock made several important decisions to help curtail costs.

First, he chose black-and-white photography. Not only was this cheaper, but he also felt that red gore would be too repulsive for his viewers. In retrospect, this proved a wise move; the bloody red shower scene in Van Sant's 1998 color remake is all but unwatchable.

Budget considerations aside, *Psycho*'s black-and-white photography greatly enhances its chilling and depressing effect and perfectly matches its sordid, seedy milieu of cheap motels, used-car lots, and low-paying jobs. Unlike the bright and glamourous world of *To Catch a Thief* or *North by Northwest*, the colorless, lifeless, loveless world of *Psycho* is not one we would ever want to live in.

Similarly, before shooting, Hitchcock excised several shots from Stefano's script that were either too costly or slowed the film unduly: Lila's hotel room in Fairvale; exteriors of Marion's neighborhood in Phoenix; a 360-degree pan as Arbogast approaches the Bates Motel; an early scene in which the fleeing Marion stops for fuel but drives off quickly when the gas station phone rings; a lengthy sequence in which Lila and Arbogast, both in cabs, converge on Sam's hardware store; shots of Arbogast's car repeatedly driving past the Bates Motel while checking on Marion's whereabouts; and a sequence of exterior shots drawing the viewer into the courthouse as the final scene begins. In fact, with the exception of the used car scene, a few shots of the highway cop, and second-unit work around Phoenix, Hitchcock was able to film the entire movie on the back lot at Universal.

As with the black-and-white photography, these decisions were made for monetary reasons; yet by limiting exteriors, Hitchcock gave the film a constricted, claustrophobic feel that meshes well with its theme of entrapment. Viewers obsessed with *Psycho* may sometimes wish for deeper glimpses into the world of the film—more of the Bates home, more in Phoenix, more in Fairvale—but as Spoto points out, "[T]here are no crowd scenes, no subjective or objective views of large groups of people or busy situations, and very few outdoor scenes" (364). Hitchcock restricts us to his suffocating, fate-like storyline, which seems to forbid freedom, fresh air, movement, choice, or escape. In the words of William Rothman, "Part of *Psycho*'s myth is that there *is* no world outside its own, that we are fated to be born, live our alienated lives, and die in the very world in which Norman Bates also dwells" (255). This, too, is key to *Psycho*'s unnerving effect.

Another cost-cutting decision involved using the less-expensive crew from TV's *Alfred Hitchcock Presents*, which was then entering its fifth year. The TV personnel handled costumes, hairstyles, makeup, photography, and set design — though Hitchcock did retain several non–TV experts: composer Bernard Herrmann, editor George Tomasini (his greater experience was needed for the shower scene), and pictorial consultant Saul Bass, who created visual designs for the titles, the Bates home, Mom's corpse, and both murders. Bass, who had also done the tasty title designs for *Vertigo* and *North by Northwest*, is the one who suggested the swinging light bulb in the final basement scene — a device that gives a disturbingly lifelike quality to Mother's shriveled skeleton.

As part of his "quick-and-cheap" methodology on *Psycho*, Hitchcock made the decision — unusual for him — to use multiple cameras in filming several scenes. This enabled more coverage and a faster shoot for many of the sequences; the various angles and shots necessary for a single scene could be executed simultaneously. Bill Krohn's careful research in *Hitchcock at Work* shows that on many of the shooting days, the director had rented two, three, and sometimes four cameras.

Hitchcock normally laid out everything in advance for his pictures; for example, as Janet Leigh recalled in her book on *Psycho*, atop Hitchcock's desk at home lay "a scaled model of every set to be used [in the film], complete with miniature furniture, breakaway walls, little dolls for people" (41) — all for the purpose of planning every camera angle before the shoot. But as Krohn notes, *Psycho*'s speedy schedule "seems to have made Hitchcock even more intuitive than usual." Despite careful scripting, "half the time he would have a better idea of how to do the scene by the time he filmed it" (221).

For instance, the script did not originally call for the long rising dolly shot just before Norman carries Mom downstairs; Hitchcock himself rewrote the scene to include this difficult shot. Likewise, in Arbogast's ascent of the staircase (which was actually filmed after the aforementioned dolly shot), Hitchcock once again abandoned the approach that had been storyboarded (showing repeated cuts of Arbogast's hands and feet); instead, he "retook Arbogast going upstairs in one continuous shot" (Krohn 231). As another example, once principal shooting on the shower scene was finished, Hitchcock needed a few additions — and he brought onto the set a Moviola (a portable editing device with a small view-screen) so that he could watch the rough cut into which the new shots would be inserted. Considering Hitchcock's meticulous pre-planning (he once boasted that there were only 100 feet of outtakes on *Rear Window*), this is indeed an "intuitive" method.

What is perhaps most impressive about Hitchcock's pre-production, however, is the careful research — some of it going back to the script stage. For instance, Hitchcock hired a private detective as technical adviser for Stefano, and he had Stefano visit a used car dealership in Santa Monica.

Hitchcock and his crew also did research on taxidermy, local swamps, real estate offices, psychiatric detainment facilities, and Route 99 (the highway Marion takes) — including common rates for motel rooms in that area. According to Rebello, Hitchcock sent the following memo to the studio research department: "What would be the condition of the corpse of a woman who had been poisoned at age forty — embalmed and buried — then, after two months, disinterred and kept in a residence for ten years?" (75).

The answer — provided by a Los Angeles college of mortuary science — helped reassure Production Code censors who were worried about Mother's appearance in the film.

Assistant director Hilton A. Green told Rebello:

> Hitchcock wanted to know things, like *exactly* what a car salesman in a small town in the valley would be wearing when a woman might come in to buy a car. We went up there and photographed some salesmen against a background. He wanted to know what people in Phoenix, Arizona, looked like, how they lived, what kind of people they were. He wanted to know the exact route a woman might take to go from Phoenix to central California. We traced the route and took pictures of every area along the way [56].

Hitchcock even sent workers to low-budget motels in the area and had them examine the décor, look in the drawers, and photograph the furniture, in order to make the film's *mise-en-scène* as authentic as possible.

Furthermore, as wardrobe supervisor Helen Colvig recalled, "In Phoenix, he'd found a girl like Marion, went into her home, photographed everything from her closet, her bureau drawers, her suitcases" (Rebello 71).

"It was the practice at that time for the wardrobe to be custom-made," Leigh recalled in her book on the film, "but Mr. Hitchcock insisted we [Leigh and costumer Rita Riggs] shop in a regular ready-to-wear store." In other words — no fancy dresses for the movie's big-name star. "He asked us to buy Marion's two dresses off the rack and only pay what a secretary could afford" (43).

Somewhat less realistically, Riggs also recalled how much trouble she had finding old ladies' lace-up shoes in a woman's size ten for Anthony Perkins; when appearing as Norman, however, Perkins got Hitchcock's approval to wear his own clothes in many of the scenes.

In conclusion, then, this careful costuming and research combines with the restricted locales and the black-and-white photography to enhance the film's low-rent, documentary verisimilitude.

And finally, before proceeding to the actual film, a word about Bernard Herrmann's brilliant music:

Herrmann scored dozens of films and TV shows, including the famous repeating four-note riff that introduces *The Twilight Zone*. He had written five scores for Hitchcock and would work with him again on *The Birds*, *Marnie*, and *Torn Curtain*, claiming that "When Hitchcock finishes a film, it's only 60% complete. I supply the other 40%" (quoted in Leitch, *Encyclopedia* 136).

To many, this assertion seems highly debatable; but even Hitchcock has been quoted as saying that "thirty-three percent of the effect of *Psycho* was due to the music" (Mogg 154). Indeed, Herrmann's contribution to *Psycho* can hardly be overstated — especially when you consider that Hitchcock originally wanted the dialogue scenes to be accompanied by music and the murder scenes to be silent. Herrmann scored the murders anyway, and after hearing the result, Hitchcock changed his mind. Indeed, as Krohn has noted, Herrmann's score wisely reverses Hitchcock's original intent; the crackling dialogue is largely unembellished, and the shrieking, slashing violin track that accompanies the murders is not only indelibly associated with *Psycho*, but also one of the most frequently imitated musical cues in film history. No wonder the characteristically stingy director nearly doubled Herrmann's salary on the picture.

Perhaps most brilliantly of all, Herrmann wrote what he called "black-and-white" music to match *Psycho*'s tone and photography. Composed entirely for strings, it has no brass, no woodwinds, no piano, and no percussion.

Indeed, Herrmann's pulsating, monochromatic assault on the nerves is almost the first thing that strikes us when we start to watch *Psycho*.

Almost.

Part 2.
Look at the Picture, Please:
A Detailed Analysis
of the Film

4

I Hate Having to Be with You in a Place Like This

Titles and Windows

The literature on Hitchcock and *Psycho* contains numerous analyses of the opening hotel room scene between Sam and Marion. It also includes several discussions of the brief sequence leading up to it — a series of pan-and-zoom shots across the rooftops of Phoenix, with the camera gradually zeroing in on the hotel. There have even been comments on the opening credits that precede the entire introductory scene. But no one has thought to analyze the Paramount logo that is actually the first thing we see in *Psycho*.

No one, that is, except Robert Kolker — whose essay on the picture's visual design goes into some detail on this generally unheralded feature.

At first, this may seem like comical over-analysis on Kolker's part; but even a glance at the studio's familiar stars-and-mountain logo shows that it is indeed laced with fine horizontal lines that cover the entire screen. Since the logo is normally shown with perfect clarity elsewhere, these lines appear to be deliberate. Kolker thinks Hitchcock may have wished to create the feel of a television screen; or more likely, that he wanted to start the graphic pattern of the film immediately. Specifically, the altered logo offers a contrast between horizontals and verticals (e.g., lines and mountain) — a contrast that is more fully articulated in the opening titles and in the body of the film itself.

Or perhaps Hitchcock was just "raking over" the studio that had refused to finance his picture.

In any case, when writers begin by dissecting a studio logo, you know you're in for a detailed analysis; indeed, the book you are holding willingly aligns itself with those whom Raymond Durgnat calls "connoisseurs who love *maximising* meaning in artistic texts.... If a text is rich enough, we tend to accept effects which any of the artists ... contributed, even unconsciously; nor do we fussily reject serendipity" (38).

In the case of *Psycho*'s opening moments, three of those contributing artists were designer Harold Adler, animator William Hurtz, and cameraman Paul Stoleroff; they turned Saul Bass's title designs into something that could actually be filmed. But it wasn't easy.

The moving bars in the credits were created in two ways. The vertical lines were done with cel animation, the horizontals with six-foot aluminum bars painted black and then manually pushed across a large surface, using pins for guidance.

As Stephen Rebello observes, the resulting graphics "simultaneously suggested prison bars, city buildings, and sound waves"; Bass himself said they evoked "clues coming together" (Rebello 140). Of all these, buildings seem to be the most likely corollary — since the final set of uneven vertical bars dissolves to the similarly shaped cityscape of Phoenix.

Others, including Kolker, have noted how these titles prefigure the contrasting verticals and horizontals that dominate the film: upright and prone figures in the first shot of Sam and Marion; telephone pole and car in the opening of the highway-cop scene; upright mansion and one-story motel on the Bates property.

Many writers have suggested that this contrast creates "tension"; but perhaps more tenable is the angle taken by François Truffaut, who said the contrast between "the vertical house and the horizontal motel is quite pleasing to the eye" (269). Tension? Not really. Opposition? Maybe. Contrast? Yes. Perhaps even *balance*: between high and low; active and passive; living and dead — all of which offset each other in the film itself.

Hitchcock's name is the first and last thing we see in the credits. Initially it's possessive, affirming that *Psycho* is his film artistically and financially; the second and final time, it's graphically split — as a "premonition of dismemberment and bifurcation," in Kolker's phrase (214).

As for the film's actual title, Donald Spoto points out that it could stand for "psychopath" or "psychoanalysis" — though whether the film psychoanalyzes Hitchcock, Norman Bates, or the viewer is a matter of some debate. Spoto chooses the latter, noting that the film takes us through a process of psychic analysis by looking inside at the beginning (through a window) and pulling something out at the end (Marion's car) — thus offering a "restoration of sanity, the basic psychic image of drawing up the depths of the psyche into the light" (380).

After the credits, with their carefully wrought sliding bars, we move into a series of shots that was even more problematic.

Modeled on the famous one-shot opening of Orson Welles's *Touch of Evil* (1958), *Psycho*'s post-credit cityscape sequence was supposed to be one continuous shot, possibly covering four miles: From high above Phoenix, the camera was to work its way gradually down and forward, moving slowly toward the hotel building and then finally going right up to the window — all in a single take, without cuts. Hitchcock had initially boasted that it would be "the longest dolly shot ever attempted by helicopter" (Rebello 80). But as assistant director Hilton A. Green recalled, "That was several years before the real solid [camera] mounts were developed," and as filmed from inside a rattling helicopter, "it was just too shaky" (Leigh 24).

Instead, the initial sequence contains three dissolves and a cut — mostly aerial footage, spliced to a final close-up of a studio miniature of the hotel window. Script supervisor Marshall Schlom found the results unsatisfactory, pointing specifically to a "definite 'color' change between the shots, even though the movie is in black and white" (Rebello 130). Others — such as Bill Krohn — find that "the illusion works. The film seems to begin with a continuous shot where Hitchcock's camera asserts its power..." (234).

Indeed, the camera chooses and moves toward this building with a baffling mixture of randomness and deliberation; it's a conscious movement with a seemingly arbitrary choice of subject. And as Rothman and others have noted, the movement is not entirely smooth, but slightly jerky — hesitating — almost human. In this way, the camera links itself with others in the film who hesitate at key moments: Marion, Norman, Arbogast, Lila.

In fact, the camera takes on human qualities not only by its hesitation, but also in its voyeurism. As the film begins, it moves slowly up to an open window and peeks in. What does it see? A half-naked couple. And with it, we peek in, too. In fact, as Spoto points out in his Hitchcock biography, the camera slips "into a darkened room, finds an empty chair, moves over, and — just like the spectator in the movie theater — 'sits' in the chair" (423). The camera then looks up, and the movie itself begins. Moral: Watching movies is a voluntary — though perhaps unconscious — act of voyeurism. And this isn't the last time *Psycho* will invite us to play Peeping Tom.

But we're getting ahead of ourselves.

Note how *Psycho*'s first shot *descends* toward the hotel window, establishing a downward movement that is crucial to the film: The knife always slashes downward; Marion's blood swirls down the drain; Norman descends the steps in front of his house; Marion's car sinks into the swamp; Arbogast falls down the stairs; Mom is carried down to the cellar — after which Lila, Sam, and Norman follow her descent. Some viewers have even suggested that the many *sinks* in the film form a verbal-visual pun on this motif of *sinking*; perhaps a similar pun is found in the name of Marion's boss — *Lowery*. Certainly this descending movement is reflected in the overall structure of the film: As is fitting for a tragedy, *Psycho* begins outside, up high, on a bright sunny day — and winds up inside, downstairs, in a dark, dank basement.

Note also how this opening shot articulates the motifs of birds and vision. Not only does the camera deliberately *look* around — and we look with it — but it also gives us a "bird's-eye view." This phrase, of course, encapsulates both motifs in one. It's also the first of several times when Hitchcock uses cinematic technique, or *form* (namely, "bird's-eye view") to create a pun or an echo of the movie's *content*. Other instances include the "cuts" in the shower scene, reflecting the literal "cuts" in Marion's body; the slashing violin bows in the shower scene music, reprising Mother's slashing knife; and the various *crane* shots, doubling Marion's surname.

In addition, the camera is flying across the rooftops like a bird — and almost the first thing it shows us is a large, rotating sign on top of a building, bearing the logo of a bird with its wings spread wide. It enters at the upper right and moves left across the frame during the first pan; you may need to pause to see it clearly — and if you have a sharp enough picture, you'll see that this sign says "Valley Bank," an apparent oxymoron that perhaps reprises the movie's vertical-horizontal motif.

At the same time, of course, the film announces its bird-like location: Phoenix, Arizona — the first of several titles that are timed to cover the

Opening shot announcing Psycho's bird-like setting; note the sign at the upper left, featuring a bird with its wings spread wide. Perhaps the locale is a precursor to Mrs. Bates, who, like the famous fire-bird for which the city is named, also rises from her own ashes. (©Universal Pictures; courtesy Universal Pictures–Photofest)

unwanted cuts. And for those who tend to idealize this film, we have here our first minor flaw: the date given in the second of these — December the eleventh.

With the palpable and oft-mentioned heat in the opening scenes, *Psycho* clearly takes place in summer (Stefano's script confirms this); but Hitchcock had to date it in December because his second-unit crew had already filmed exteriors which — unintentionally — showed downtown Phoenix in full Christmas regalia. This second-unit footage was to be used for backgrounds in the early scenes, and indeed the various seasonal decorations can be clearly seen when Marion first starts to drive out of town later on in the film.

During the series of cuts in the cityscape scene, the panning camera begins on a more upscale part of town — with a bank, a classy hotel, and a new building going up — and then moves to a drabber-looking group of buildings on a seedier side of the city. Stefano's script puts it this way: "As we approach the downtown section, the character of the city begins to change. It is darker and shabby with age and industry.... The very geography seems to give us a climate of nefariousness, of back-doorness, dark and shadowy."

As for the actual hotel, the script emphasizes its "hole-and-corner" quality and its "shoddy character." Stefano even calls for a sign promoting the hotel as a good place for "Transients." The word evokes several key ideas: It's a perfect description for Sam and Marion's brief liaison; an ironic precursor to her violently foreshortened visit to a motel later on; and a general commentary on the brevity and fragility of human life that is made so painfully apparent by this film.

With its seedy, shabby, shoddy setting, *Psycho* — as opposed to Hitchcock's color movies that preceded it — takes place in a world much closer to the everyday life of the average 1960 moviegoer. In doing so, it exposes what Rebello calls "the grinning skull beneath the rhythms and routine of the ordinary — workaday jobs, make-do relationships, dreams deferred, backwater locales" (22).

As Hitchcock told Truffaut, he wanted to achieve a "visual impression of despair and solitude" in this opening scene (268).

And this is surely what we find once we get inside that window.

5

Let's All Talk About Marion, Shall We?

Marion and Sam

"Never before had actors in a mainstream American film played an erotic duet horizontally, let alone in the seminude," writes Stephen Rebello.

Indeed, one contemporary viewer of *Psycho* noted that Marion's bra and half-slip gave her as great a shock as the shower scene; up till then, a full slip was preferred — the kind Elizabeth Taylor famously wore in 1958's *Cat on a Hot Tin Roof*. In Rebello's words, Hitchcock and Stefano had designed the scene "to announce that *Psycho* was a *sixties* picture" (86); Hitchcock told Truffaut he deliberately went for a racier feel, fearing that a "straightforward kissing scene would be looked down at by the younger viewers" (268).

Yet perhaps for this very reason, Hitchcock — as Rebello tells us — was infuriated by "the lack of erotic heat" between costars Janet Leigh and John Gavin; he filmed the hotel room tryst repeatedly without getting the chemistry he wanted. Finally, Hitchcock called Leigh aside and urged her to "take matters in hand, as it were. Leigh blushed, acquiesced, and Hitchcock got a reasonable facsimile of the required response" (86–87).

The problem, it seems, stemmed from the fact that Leigh and Gavin had just met, and both felt awkward — especially Gavin, who didn't like having his shirt off. As John Russell Taylor explains, Stefano urged Gavin to "use that very embarrassment as part of the scene, to play it that way, recognizing that the character he was portraying would also feel embarrassed and vulnerable, particularly when having an argument while half undressed" (256).

To make matters even more awkward, Hitchcock and his crew were gathered closely around the bed, and Gavin was distracted by an odd odor, possibly sweat or Hitchcock's cigar. In the words of Patrick McGilligan, "[T]hat's the way the tryst opening of *Psycho* plays: audacious but awkward, provocative but cold, sexy with a whiff of BO" (592).

The script describes Sam as "a good-looking, sensual man with warm humorous eyes and a compelling smile." Gavin, whom Hitchcock privately nicknamed "the Stiff," doesn't manage to flesh this out; many viewers wish Hitchcock had snared one of the other actors under consideration for the role — Stuart Whitman, Cliff Robertson, Rod Taylor, Leslie Nielsen, Brian Keith, or Jack Lord.

Yet this very lack of passion — the awkwardness, constraint, and embarrassment — ultimately seem to work in favor of the "despair and solitude" Hitchcock wanted in the scene. The romance and sexuality have a curiously unsatisfying nature — a "blocked" quality, to use George Toles's phrase. And this makes Marion's desperation somehow more pathetic, more desperate, more tragic.

Leigh told Hollywood memoirist Charlotte Chandler that she felt Hitchcock had deliberately coached and coaxed *her* into more ardor — rather than Gavin — in order to show that Marion "wanted her lover more, very much more, than he wanted her" (263).

As Leigh theorized for Rebello, "real passion" from Sam would have "justified Marion's theft. But the lack of the complete abandon with Sam might have led some audience members to think, 'I wonder if he really loves her that much?' It made Marion even more sympathetic, which Hitch was very concerned about her being" (Rebello 87).

Sam rejects marriage because he doesn't have enough money; as Robin Wood observes, this annoys us "because it is the sort of boring, mundane consideration we expect the romantic hero of a film to sweep aside, and we are very much drawn to Marion's readiness to accept things as they are for the sake of the relationship." Indeed, it isn't just the relationship she wants; it's the respectability marriage would provide. Along these lines, we might make note of her mild reproof to Sam, "You make respectability sound ... disrespectful." She probably means "disrespectable" — but her use of this word may be a Freudian slip, suggesting Sam's *disrespectful* attitude toward her needs. After all, he insists that he won't have her living in the back room of a hardware store — yet he has no qualms about asking her to make love in a cheap hotel on her lunch hour.

Wood asserts that our sympathy for Marion in this scene is "the first step in our complicity in the theft of the $40,000" (143); and certainly our sympathy and complicity are considerably heightened by the excellent acting of Janet Leigh throughout her portion of the film. In Rebello's words, Leigh was "a member of the Peaches-and-Cream brigade with Debbie Reynolds, Doris Day, and June Allyson, who were counterpoints to sultry mantrap types Elizabeth Taylor and Marilyn Monroe" (60–61). Leigh later recalled that, rather than the brazen sex-symbol type, Hitchcock wanted "someone who could actually look like she came from Phoenix"—someone with "a vulnerability, a softness" (McGilligan 586). Someone ordinary, not too glamourous — someone the viewer could easily relate to.

As William Rothman puts it, "Janet Leigh is not Ingrid Bergman.... With her flat affect and stiffness, she lacks a certain spark we once took for granted in a Hitchcock heroine. Would Cary Grant look twice at her?" (253).

"Then, too," writes James Naremore, "she has aged just enough; her body has grown thinner, her face taken on a hard-edged, slightly mocking intelligence that is perfectly appropriate for a secretary who has been treated a bit roughly and has begun to long for security" (31).

Perhaps *Psycho* also plays on Leigh's much-publicized marriage to the fabulously handsome Tony Curtis; if the buxom Leigh could net a man like Curtis and become one of Hollywood's best-known wives and mothers, shouldn't Marion be able to elicit commitment from the much more modestly appealing Sam Loomis?

Before leaving the topic of marriage and sexuality, let's address some important observations made by Raymond Durgnat in his 2002 book-length study of *Psycho*. He points out that the opening hotel scene probably gave censors fits, not only because of Leigh's risqué garb, but also because of the so-called "foot rule" imposed by the era's strict Production Code — a body that legislated what you could and couldn't show in a mainstream movie:

> The ... rule was that, given two lovers embracing on or about a bed, each must keep one foot on the floor. Hitchcock breaks it right away, with Marion's upper body flat on the bed.... But then again, in this particular shot, Sam isn't actually touching her. And with the camera winding round rolling faces in close-up, who can say which of all four feet is where? [26]

In the midst of this ambiguity, Durgnat goes so far as to assert that perhaps they did not actually have intercourse: The fact that they are both half-dressed suggests to him that maybe they were only "heavy petting" (28). Perhaps Marion is still a virgin — as she is in Bloch's novel, which makes it abundantly clear that she and Sam are abstaining until marriage. If this is the case, her desire for marriage can be seen as a hunger not only for "respectability" but also for sexual consummation.

Stefano's script is likewise ambiguous. There is one exchange (not included in the film) in which Marion says, "I've lost my girlish laughter," and Sam responds, "The only girlish thing you have lost"—quite possibly a reference to her virginity. Yet later, when Marion insists that this will be their last illicit meeting, the script says she's surprised to find that Sam still wants her "even after the sexual bait has been pulled in."

Intercourse or no, Durgnat also points out that the scene's sexuality is communicated "not by *anatomies*" as it would be in a modern-day movie, but in typically low-key Hitchcock fashion: by "hands, eyes, embracings" (28). It was an era when the restraint required by the Production Code often left room for the viewer's imagination. (This same ambiguity can be found in the mid-film train tryst from the previous year's *North by Northwest*— where Eve Kendall and Roger Thornhill chat coyly in the dining car about his having no place to sleep, after which they kiss passionately in her bedroom; yet she winds up insisting that he "sleep on the floor.")

And the sexual ambiguity in *Psycho*'s opening scene nicely reflects the ambiguity of the couple's relationship at this point. They've broached the topic of marriage; indeed, Marion has virtually popped the question ("Oh, Sam, let's get married!"). Yet she has clearly indicated that she won't meet like this again, and he then asks if she wants to "cut this off" and find herself "somebody available." This comes across as a serious, almost shocking question, and for a moment their relationship teeters on the brink of dissolution. This sense of peril is undercut by the way they both smile after he asks it — and by the smug tone of his question, "How could you even think a thing like that?" At the end, he still wants to leave together, but she refuses. We can hardly tell where the two of them stand — and neither can they.

Yet perhaps they are not alone in this. Sam complains that his ex-wife is "living on the other side of the world somewhere" — at which point he flings up the Venetian blinds, revealing another building across the way, its windows similarly ajar. Is that "the other side of the world" over there? And are those people also facing crises like this one? Is the stalemate of Sam and Marion just one random instance in a world full of people in similar pain?

Despite all this, what's perhaps most intriguing about this scene is the way it carefully prefigures the rest of the film, particularly Marion's fate.

For instance, when the camera enters through the window, the first thing we see is the hotel bathroom, with its faintly gleaming fixtures. (We will note these again in the background in Marion's own bedroom at home, just a few scenes hence, as she contemplates stealing the money.)

The film's first line — "Never did eat your lunch, did you?" — firmly establishes its food motif. (At the same time, it may also be Sam's smug way of reflecting on his sexual prowess, as if to say, "I made you forget your lunch.") Marion's uneaten sandwich likewise prefigures the unfinished sandwich she later shares with Norman — who might be the "somebody available" that she threatens to "go out and find." Indeed, Durgnat has noted the similarity between Sam and Norman — both in low-paying jobs, both dark-haired, both somewhat stiff and uncomfortable, both "hamstrung" by women from their past (37).

Here also the film announces its concern with the domination of the past over the present. Not only does Sam make it clear that he feels shackled by alimony payments to his ex-wife, he also complains about having to pay off his dead father's debts. And when Marion invites Sam to her home for a respectable dinner with "my mother's picture on the mantel," it's clear that Sam's father is not the only parent whose shadow hovers over these liaisons. Nor are these the last parents in the film to cast a shadow on the lives of their offspring.

There are many premonitions of Marion's death as well. Indeed, keying on her assertion that "They also pay who meet in hotel rooms," Spoto observes, "Everything in the opening sequence is an omen of how she will 'pay' when she meets someone in another rented room later" (361).

Sam passes under the slashing, knife-like blades of the fan when he refers to his father's grave; at the end of the scene, the fan seems to cut at Marion's head when she declares, "I'm late."

Marion also makes the incomplete statement, "Hotels of this sort aren't interested in you when you check in, but when your time is up" — and then declares that "This is the last time" she and Sam can meet like this. In a later motel room, Marion's time really will be up — and thus her declaration is appallingly accurate: This will indeed be their last time together.

In a subtler but more fascinating vein, Marion's line "They also pay who meet in hotel rooms" is a fitting allusion to John Milton's famous declaration, "They also serve who only stand and wait." It's the final line from the seventeenth-century sonnet "On His Blindness," in which Milton patiently resigns himself to being blind. This reference is thus tied to the film's motif of eyes and seeing — or rather, *not* seeing. After all, it is Marion herself who in so many ways is blind to her fate — and whose story concludes with a lengthy shot of her dead, unseeing eye.

Ironically, "Milton" is also the first name of the movie's private detective, Arbogast (we don't hear it in the actual film, but it is in both the book and script); and this 20th-century Milton is a man whose blindness and *imp*atience lead him swiftly to his death.

The poet's resignation contrasts not only with Arbogast but also with the impatience that leads to Marion's theft. Marion's sister is right when she later tells Sam that "patience doesn't run in my family"; Marion isn't going to "stand and wait" for Sam to pay his debts.

All she needs is a little opportunity...

6

She Sat There While I Dumped It Out
Caroline and Cassidy

Upon returning to her job as a real estate secretary, Marion finds herself "surrounded by vulgar, undeserving types who have marriage, money, and sometimes both"—to use James Naremore's telling phraseology (5).

One of these "vulgar" types is the other secretary who works in the office with Marion. When Marion asks if there were any phone calls while she was out, Caroline replies, "Teddy called me. My mother called to see if Teddy called...."

In two short sentences, screenwriter Joseph Stefano deftly sketches a nauseatingly self-centered young lady; neither of her first two answers can possibly have any interest for Marion — except that Caroline may intend them as a catty reminder that she herself has a husband, and Marion doesn't. This possibility seems all the more likely in light of Caroline's later statement about the rich man who visits the office during this scene: Caroline insists that Cassidy was flirting with Marion (rather than her) only because "he must have noticed my wedding ring"; it serves as a dig at Marion's unwed status and also informs us that Caroline is the type of woman who refuses to admit that any other female might be more attractive than she is.

At the same time, Caroline's description of the calls confirms and extends the theme of parental domination that was initiated in the previous scene. Like Sam's and Marion's parents, Caroline's mother is still making her presence felt in the life of her adult child. This idea is developed even further when Caroline offers to ease Marion's headache with tranquilizers that her mother's doctor gave her on "the day of my wedding."

We can certainly understand why — as Caroline puts it — her husband was "furious" when he learned that his bride had drugged herself before consummation; like Sam's complaints about his father's debts, this betokens a

34

world so enslaved by the past — particularly parents — that life, liberty, and happiness seem virtually unattainable.

That probably goes double for the daughter of the rich man, Cassidy. Upon entering the real estate office with Marion's boss, Cassidy announces that he's buying an expensive house for "my baby's wedding present." As Robin Wood observes, Cassidy's daughter — whom he continues to think of as "his baby," even though she's 18 — would probably be better off without the $40,000 house, through which her father will undoubtedly continue to exert his authority in her married life.

Naremore adds: "All these references to 'family drama' help prepare us for Norman Bates and his mother, revealing once more the narrow line between sanity and madness" (33). In fact, Caroline seems just the kind of woman who would eventually turn into a snippy, controlling matriarch like Mrs. Bates.

In other words, all of these seemingly normal and ordinary characters are really only a step or two away from the devouring parental domination of the Bates homestead.

Along with these thematic issues, the scene continues to develop our sympathy for Marion — and for her impending theft. Combining some thoughts from Thomas Leitch and David Sterritt, we find an unsavory composite portrait of her victims. Marion's boss, Mr. Lowery, keeps a stash of whiskey hidden in his desk, and he has air-conditioned his own office — but not that of his secretaries. Cassidy, meanwhile, seems little more than an overgrown child who insists that he be the center of attention, proudly cheats on his income tax, and dominates and humiliates Lowery — first by revealing the secret of his hidden liquor, and then by brashly deciding what they will do together for the rest of the day.

Internet writer Tim Dirks wonders whether Cassidy, by paying in cash and bragging about his undeclared income, might be urging Lowery also to cheat on his taxes by not reporting this particular sale. In any case, he certainly seems to be urging Marion to take the money — insisting that he never carries more than he can "afford to lose." When he tells Lowery, "Now it's yours," he could just as easily be talking to Marion.

Dirks further notes that Marion in any case plans to use the money for the exact same thing as Cassidy's daughter — as a sort of dowry to finance her marriage. In an omitted line, the script draws out parallels between the two relationships when Cassidy calls his future son-in-law "penniless." Both potential grooms are, in other words, badly in need of the money Cassidy can supply.

As writer Leland Poague points out, Hitchcock's cameo in *Psycho* seems closely tied to the theme of money, so this might be a good time to discuss it. By now, it's common knowledge that Hitchcock appeared in most of his movies — a custom he started in the 1920s but took up in earnest after coming to America at the behest of producer David O. Selznick in 1939. Reliable listings of the cameos he made in his own films can be found in Mogg's *Alfred Hitchcock Story*, in Leitch's Hitchcock encyclopedia, and at the websites VideoUniversity.com, Filmsite.org, and Wikipedia.

A fascinating explanation of these cameos appears in the introduction to David Sterritt's excellent 1993 book *The Films of Alfred Hitchcock*: The cameos, Sterritt asserts, remind viewers that Hitchcock is always nearby, always dropping in to check up on the picture and the audience.

In *Psycho*, however, there's a little more to it.

Immediately after the dissolve from Marion and Sam's hotel room to the real estate office, Hitchcock can be seen standing on the sidewalk outside the window, wearing his customary dark suit and a not-so-customary white Stetson cowboy hat (this latter detail is apparently a knowing nod to the Arizona locale). Hitchcock actually glances at Marion as she goes by him, and shortly thereafter, Cassidy comes in wearing a similar Stetson — and then he ogles Marion too.

Poague observes that it might just as easily be Hitchcock coming in, adding that, "Cassidy gets the film going, as it were — he finances it, is its

Hitchcock's cameo — he wears a white Stetson hat and stands on the sidewalk outside Lowery's real estate office. Hitchcock specifically wanted to be in this scene because it also features his daughter, Pat, playing the secretary Caroline. (©Universal Pictures; courtesy Universal Pictures–Photofest)

producer. And so is Hitchcock." The similarities become harder to ignore if you recall Cassidy's fixation on his daughter—and the fact that Hitchcock's own daughter, Patricia, plays Caroline in this scene. In fact, according to Rebello's book, costumer Rita Riggs recalled that Hitchcock specifically wanted to appear in the scene with his daughter.

But according to Poague, the comparison between Hitchcock and Cassidy only goes so far: Unlike Cassidy, Hitchcock "knows the ethical risks involved" in large amounts of cash—and "shows us in *Psycho* how not to use money, how letting money use us condemns us to death" (347).

Money has often been called the "MacGuffin" in *Psycho*—that is, the device around which the plot revolves, but whose actual nature seems unclear, irrelevant, or both.

The term springs from Hitchcock's interviews with Truffaut, in which he recounted an anecdote about two men traveling on a train. One asks the other what he's got in his parcel, and the other replies that it's a MacGuffin. As Hitchcock told it, "The first one asks, 'What's a MacGuffin?' 'Well,' the other man says, 'it's an apparatus for trapping lions in the Scottish Highlands.' The first man says, 'But there are no lions in the Scottish Highlands,' and the other one answers, 'Well then, that's no MacGuffin!'" (138).

In other words, as Spoto puts it in *The Dark Side of Genius*, a MacGuffin "gets the story going" but is ultimately "neither relevant, important, nor, finally, any of one's business" (145). Elsewhere in Hitchcock, it's the aircraft specs in *The 39 Steps*, the uranium ore in *Notorious*, the secret formula in *Torn Curtain*, and perhaps quintessentially, the microfilm in *North by Northwest*.

But is it also the money in *Psycho*? Is the money in this film ultimately "neither important nor relevant"?

It's certainly true that the money is at last flung aside—literally by Norman, who tosses it casually into the trunk of Marion's car along with her body and belongings; and figuratively by the psychiatrist, who, upon being asked about the money at the film's conclusion, says dismissively, "These were crimes of passion, not profit."

Yet the money is perhaps not dismissed quite so easily from the minds of thoughtful viewers. Poague sees money as a key theme, serving to corrupt or poison virtually every relationship in the film. This of course includes Sam and his ex-wife (and probably his dead father as well); Cassidy and his daughter; Cassidy and Lowery; and Marion's relationship with just about everybody—Sam, Cassidy, Lowery, the highway cop, and the used-car dealer. Those later seeking Marion (Sam, Lila, Arbogast, the sheriff) are similarly waylaid by the issue of the money: Arbogast insists that money would enhance a single woman's prospects ("Someone always sees a girl with $40,000"), and the sheriff is convinced that the money can explain the disappearance of both Marion and Arbogast ("He took off after her and the money"). Even Mrs. Bates was affected by the greed of her lover, who "talked her into building this motel"—and thereby laid the groundwork for both of their deaths.

Also worth noting is Sterritt's eye-opening essay on the film: Steering clear of territory already covered, Sterritt focuses instead on what he calls *Psycho*'s "preoccupation with anal-compulsive behavior" (100). In particular, he suggests that the film makes an explicit connection between money and human excrement—an assertion that at first seems outlandish; but it's hard to disagree with Sterritt's evidence: Cassidy calls it his "private money" (an odd choice of adjective); everyone in the office feels that there's something obscene about seeing Cassidy's pile in public; Lowery objects that Cassidy's excess is "most irregular"(!); and later (in Marion's thoughts), Cassidy is heard to exclaim, "She sat there while I dumped it out!"

Still think the idea sounds farfetched? Consider this: Marion handles the money in a bathroom at the used car shop, and later she writes monetary figures on a slip of Bates Motel stationery (shall we call it "BM paper"?)—after which she flushes it down the commode. As we shall see in Chapter 9, screenwriter Stefano claimed that this shredded paper in the toilet was a deliberate attempt to get as close as possible to human bathroom mechanics without actually reproducing them: Torn-up paper is floating in the water! And what's that dark stuff on it?

Money.

To cap it off, when Lila later finds a scrap of this paper with "$40,000" on it, she gives it to Sam—who takes this item straight from the toilet and puts it in his wallet.

While your head is still reeling from these rather shocking implications, consider a few random—and somewhat more mundane—items from the real estate office scene:

Dubbing Cassidy an "oil lease" man must certainly be an overlooked remainder from Bloch's novel, which takes place in Texas; after all, there aren't many oil wells near Phoenix, Arizona.

Furthermore, there's great irony in Marion's final exchange with Cassidy. When she complains of her headache, Cassidy declares, "What you need is a weekend in Las Vegas—the playground of the world!"

She insists, "I'm going to spend this weekend in bed"—a prediction that proves painfully untrue. The only thing that will get in Marion's bed is the $40,000 (that's where it's lying in the next scene); Marion, instead, will actually spend the night in her car. In fact, she will never get into a bed again.

On a side note, the script has Cassidy respond to Marion's line by referring to bed as the "only playground that beats Las Vegas!" but Hollywood censors made Hitchcock take this out.

Another significant item in this scene is the massive photograph of a desert on the wall behind Marion's desk. The picture is indeed so large that it's sometimes the only thing visible in the background — yet it's badly out of place in a real estate office; Mr. Lowery can't possibly be selling this property! Since it's behind Marion's desk and often seen with her in the frame, it's clearly here to suggest the emptiness that will shortly prompt her theft. At the same time, it foreshadows the moral wasteland she's about to enter.

Similarly significant is Marion's line near the end of the scene. In response to Caroline's offer of aspirin, Marion says wistfully: "You can't buy off unhappiness with pills." This piece of dialogue is not in the script, yet it's a fitting way to end the scene. As a reply to Cassidy's assertion that he "buys off unhappiness," it leaves us unsure about Marion's true feelings.

Is she, as Raymond Durgnat suggests, setting herself up for a fall by self-consciously moralizing against Cassidy's attitude? Or is she already considering that pills don't "buy off unhappiness" quite as well as money? What exactly is her stance toward Cassidy's blatant materialism?

To use Durgnat's words: When Cassidy flashes his wad, "Caroline marvels, Lowery worries; but Marion's calm, polite cool shows class. You can study this scene forever, yet never know if, or when Marion decides to rob and run." Indeed, Durgnat insists that "uncertainty is Hitchcock's little game" throughout *Psycho* (42–43), and thus just as the previous scene concluded with uncertainty about Marion and Sam, so this one leaves Marion's intentions about the money unclear — perhaps even to herself.

One possible clue to Marion's attitude is the careful use of shadows and framing in this scene. As several writers have noted, near the end of the scene, Marion's shadow precedes her as she emerges from Lowery's inner office. Has her personality already begun to split into light and dark — with the darker half preceding?

And taking another cue from Durgnat, let's look carefully at her movement as she leaves work for the day. On the way out, her shadow follows her (perhaps there's hope yet — the "real" Marion is still in the lead); then we dissolve to Marion's bedroom, where her shadow once again precedes her into the frame (this darker half has now fully taken control?).

As she makes these moves, she leaves the office by exiting screen right

and re-enters screen left, giving the impression of one continuous movement — except that she leaves fully clothed and enters in her underwear. Does
this also suggest a change — as though her defenses have been stripped away?
Or is it too seamless to tell — particularly when her subsequent exit resumes
the same line of movement?

"Game of uncertainty" indeed.

7

Am I Acting As If There's Something Wrong?
Marion and Marion

Much has been made of Marion's prolonged solitude during the scenes in which she flees with the money; in her book on the making of *Psycho*, Leigh said she was "pretty much doing a pantomime in this highly charged film" (60), and Truffaut observed that she acts alone for nearly two reels.

In fact, from the time she leaves the real estate office until the time Norman Bates greets her on the motel porch, just over 17 minutes elapse — and she is not actually alone this entire time, but spends about five minutes of it interacting with a policeman and a used car dealer.

To help flesh out the character during these solitary scenes, Leigh had actually written out a complete background for Marion: "I knew where she went to school, what church she attended, what kind of a student, daughter, friend, and relative she was. I knew her likes, dislikes, color preferences, favorite foods, favorite book, favorite movie. I knew her secrets, her passions, her fantasies, her fears. I knew her intimately" (Leigh, *Psycho* 61).

Hitchcock, of course, gave Leigh plenty of help — starting with his veteran visual technique.

A fan of such early masterpieces as *The Cabinet of Dr. Caligari* (1920) and F. W. Murnau's *The Last Laugh* (1924), Hitchcock was a director whose work often suggests the benefits of starting out in silent films, as he did — of being forced, that is, to tell a story visually, instead of relying too heavily on dialogue to advance the action.

Psycho includes several miniature "silent films" — most notably, Norman's cleanup after the shower scene and Lila's climactic visit to the Bates house; but the two-minute scene in Marion's bedroom is a textbook example of how to tell a story through images alone — of what Raymond Durgnat calls "a soliloquy without words" (50).

41

First, Marion enters in bra and half-slip. Maybe she really is going to get in bed, as she told her boss and Mr. Cassidy. But wait — these aren't the same undergarments she was wearing earlier in the day! In fact, instead of white lingerie, she is now wearing black — a pretty clear visual clue about what's to come.

As if to confirm our suspicions, the camera tips down and moves forward to show us the money, so we can see that she did not take it to the bank as she was told; the camera then looks gently left, where an open suitcase full of hastily arranged clothing rests on the bed — and with mathematical precision, each and every viewer instantly infers that she's planning to run off with the cash. This kind of scene was undoubtedly what Hitchcock had in mind when he made his oft-cited assertion that he was playing the audience "like an organ" when he made *Psycho* (Truffaut 269).

Incidentally, eagle-eyed viewers might note in this shot one of the very few outright flubs in *Psycho*: As the camera approaches the money on the bed, a shadow — perhaps of some crew member or piece of equipment — moves quickly in and out of frame at the lower right. This error was clearly visible in early prints of the film, but removed on subsequent VHS and DVD releases. It does, however, appear on the remastered 2008 Legacy Edition.

In addition to the strictly visual information in this shot, the bedroom scene contains many other important nonverbal cues:

Marion's bathroom in the background — with the showerhead clearly visible.

A record player — the first link between Marion and Norman. (As we shall see near the end, he has a similar phonograph in his bedroom.)

A picture of Marion's parents — perhaps the one she was referring to in the opening scene with Sam. (In her book on the film, Leigh says she "composed a running conversation" in her mind for these scenes, including a "pang of guilt when she walked by the picture of her mother and father" [60]).

And most sadly, a baby photo that must surely be Marion. Sad, because it hints at a profound division between the person she once was and the person she is about to become. In token of this, as she is packing her suitcase, she stands flanked by the baby picture on her left and the bathroom on her right — a concise summation of her beginning and her end.

Spoto has observed that even the very layout of Marion's bedroom — door to the right, window to the left, bed in the foreground, bathroom in the far left corner — is extremely similar to the room she rents at the Bates Motel.

This scene also marks the first time we see Marion in a mirror — highlighting the split in her personality that was earlier indicated by her shadow. The many mirrors in the film were hung liberally about the various sets according to Hitchcock's explicit instructions; yet this is the last time Marion will look directly at herself in one — suggesting that the split will become both less acknowledged and more severe. And this split, of course, also links her with Norman.

At the same time, as Durgnat has written, "the business of *putting things together for a trip* invokes a familiar experience, strengthening audience involvement" (50). And indeed, if the film has thus far sought to engage our sympathy for Marion, it now begins insisting that we identify with her directly. As Spoto suggests, we hear what she thinks, see what she sees, feel what she feels.

This certainly seems to be the main purpose of everything that happens between her exit from the real estate office and her arrival at the Bates Motel: to get us to identify with Marion so completely, to invest our emotions in her so thoroughly, that when she is killed, we will somehow feel as though we too have been slain.

The first time we "see what she sees" is when she looks at the money lying on her bed; as Philip Skerry points out in his book on the shower scene, this is in fact the film's first genuine point-of-view shot — and four more p-o-v shots follow in the bedroom scene. Indeed, Skerry further observes that of the 151 shots used during Marion's car trip, 53 are from her point of view.

Among the most effective are those that occur shortly after this scene — as Cassidy and Lowery cross in front of Marion's car while she is leaving Phoenix.

This brief but unnerving sequence was altered considerably from the script, where Cassidy sees Marion first, lets out a "cheery exclamation," and elbows Lowery. Infinitely preferable is what's actually in the film, with Cassidy trudging blindly ahead while Lowery smiles and nods absently at Marion; she returns an automatic half-smile (also not in the script), and he then stops and gives Marion a puzzled frown — another brilliant example of "dialogue without words."

At the same time, it's another piece of "organ-playing" by Alfred Hitchcock. He has shown us exactly what Marion is seeing and all but forced us to share her thoughts: "He's wondering why I'm not home in bed!" Thus we also share her feelings — specifically, fear and panic.

Of course, this only gets worse when a policeman arrives on the scene.

Before discussing our reaction to the law, however, it's worth noting that Janet Leigh was never on location for the sequence with the highway patrolman. His outdoor scenes — pulling over, getting out, approaching Marion's car, etc.— were shot on location near Gorman, California, and then melded with separate footage of Leigh filmed in a mock-up car at the studio. Yet as

Christopher Nickens writes in Leigh's book, the sequence is so carefully lighted, photographed, and edited that most viewers would swear Janet Leigh was actually on location with the officer.

Now about our reaction to the police:

Hitchcock never tired of recounting his nerve-wracking childhood encounter with the law. According to the story quoted in Spoto's *Dark Side of Genius*: "When I was no more than six years of age, I did something that my father considered worthy of reprimand. He sent me to the local police station with a note. The officer on duty read it and locked me in a jail cell for five minutes, saying, 'This is what we do to naughty boys'" (9).

There is some disagreement about whether this little story is genuine — and there's also some skepticism about Hitchcock's frequent claim that he never learned to drive for fear of being pulled over by police; but there's little doubt that Hitchcock was pathologically afraid of cops. Biographies by both McGilligan and Spoto include anecdotes from friends who were with Hitchcock during brief encounters with police; almost unilaterally, Hitchcock is described as frozen with panic. In one, recalled by writer Czenzi Ormande, Hitchcock "seemed to be in a trance": "Fists were clenched, face was pale, his eyes stared straight ahead. Visibly this was a very frightened man" (McGilligan 448).

In putting his own fears onscreen during Marion's encounter with the highway patrolman, Hitchcock once again forces us through a familiar experience; everyone, it seems, is intimidated by the police. Indeed, movie star Jamie Lee Curtis, who began her career being chased by knife-wielders in such thrillers as *Halloween*, *Prom Night*, and *Terror Train* — and who starred with her mother, Janet Leigh, in *The Fog* and *Halloween H20* — claims that the close-up of the policeman's face is *Psycho*'s scariest moment.

Hitchcock, of course, does much to heighten this natural fear.

Stefano's first draft had the policeman flirting with Marion — but Hitchcock told his writer to omit this. He also trimmed quite a bit from the revised draft, in which the policeman responds at length — and with some compassion — to Marion's assertion, "You're taking up my time":

"I never 'take up' anyone's time," he says, "whether it's to give a warning, or a ticket, or help! Believe that, M'am. (A little softer) Now if you woke up on the wrong side of ... the car seat, that's one thing. But when you act as if I've just placed you under arrest...."

This is simply too warm, too soft, too *human* for the kind of reaction Hitchcock wanted to inspire.

In his 1982 book *The Elements of Cinema* — which is dedicated to Hitchcock — Stefan Sharff uses *Psycho*'s cop scene as a key example of how to film two people talking. Among other things, he notes that the exchange between Marion and the cop begins with a shot of her awakening and sitting up, so that her close-up is introduced gradually, as we watch her face approaching the camera. This is followed at once by an extreme close-up of the cop; his face is much larger than Marion's, and in contrast to hers, it appears instantaneously, with no time to prepare or process — thus giving us the same sense of shock and disorientation that Marion feels.

More generally, Sharff discusses the implicit dynamics of what he calls "separation" — where people talking are filmed separately in an A, B, A, B, sequence. One aspect of such a sequence, Sharff notes, is that certain images — for example, a menacing policeman — have greater emotional weight than others, and this is why the shots of the cop in this scene are much shorter than those of Marion (hers average five to 10 seconds, whereas the cop is generally shown for less than three seconds at a time).

In addition, Sharff writes, such a sequence is able to create

> an intimacy of contact — a sort of electrical current — between the participants as the images ... succeed each other on the screen.... The viewer is engaged in the dramatics not only as a mere observer of the plot, but as an actor playing the part, of A while B is on the screen, and B while A is on the screen. Once "playing" the part, the viewer tries to impose his interpretation, expecting or wanting the next shot to "conform" to it. For example, if A acts rudely in shot 1, the viewer anticipates that B will be upset in shot 2 [64].

Or if A is menacing in shot 1, the viewer anticipates that B will look nervous and flustered in shot 2 — especially if she has a massive wad of stolen cash in her purse on the seat beside her!

All of this increases our involvement with Marion; we share her fear and uneasiness — exacerbated by the cop's opaque sunglasses. Among other things, the glasses make it impossible for Marion (or us) to return his intimidating glare — or to tell exactly where he's looking. And this in turn puts the policeman into that disturbing group of people in the film who stare blankly — particularly Marion after her death, but also the eyeless corpse of Mother. There's something soulless about it, something almost supernaturally disconcerting.

"The man who questions Marion," writes James Naremore, "is more than just an ordinary cop. Hitchcock has invested his implacable countenance with the power of a symbol; as he looks in the car we feel a psychic menace, a terror that is somehow moral" (39).

In addition to menace, there is also much irony here.

To begin with, it's inherently ironic to fear the police, who are supposed to "serve and protect"; indeed, Marion may be terrified of this man — but if he had arrested her, she would have lived. In fact, she probably wouldn't even have been convicted, since Lila later insists that the victims "don't want to prosecute — they just want the money back."

Though the officer *looks* scary, his "voice and manner are calm, soft, neutral" (Naremore 40); and his words, as written on the page, seem perfectly civil, perhaps even kind. When Marion asks why he wants to see her license, he simply says, "Please." He seems genuinely worried that there might be "something wrong" — and likewise alarmed that she spent the night in her car.

Indeed, in one of the film's cruelest ironies, he suggests that she should have stayed in a motel — "just to be safe." Repeat viewers can reflect with some bitterness that in actuality, she would have been safer if she'd spent the second night in her car as well.

Yet despite the policeman's obvious concern, we still feel distraught; and perhaps the most unsettling issue is one that has received virtually no attention in the various writings on *Psycho*: After taking her license, comparing it to the plate on her car, and apparently deciding she can leave — the cop never says anything else to Marion. He never tells her, "You're free to go," or "I'll let you off this time"; he simply hands back the license and returns to his car. Is he really giving her permission to leave? How can we — or Marion — be sure that he isn't going back to his car to check something out or write up a warning? It's more of that "game of uncertainty" mentioned by Durgnat. The issue is so bothersome that Gus Van Sant's 1998 remake finds it necessary to resolve the tension by having the cop say, "Have a nice day," as he hands back her license.

In Hitchcock's version, this uneasy feeling does not go away once Marion pulls out — because it seems as though the cop is still following her, at least until he finally swings onto an exit ramp. And if this present menace is now pursuing her toward a greater menace, that is reflected in the careful shots of her rearview mirror. As Peter Conrad has observed, visually the mirror puts the policeman ahead of her, when in fact he is behind her — and thus, her future is her past.

This rearview mirror shot perfectly encapsulates the film's fixation with the past: Marion is moving forward, but looking backward; the mirror, in turn, is a little piece of "what's behind" that she is taking with her — and the police car it shows is moving forward, yet everything around the mirror is receding. If you look carefully at these brief shots, objects seem to be moving forward and backward at the same time. It's a disorienting but effective visualization of the conflicted split that seems to affect so many of *Psycho*'s characters — and of the way so much of the story moves toward the past even as it seems to be moving forward.

Writers such as William Rothman and Tim Dirks have suggested that the road sign Marion sees ("Right Lane for Gorman") is an in-joke suggesting "Gore-man" / "Norman"; but this pun seems unlikely — because the cop, not Marion, takes that exit lane.

Yet as he pulls off, the palpable relief we feel only sets us up for a greater shock when he reappears in the following scene. It's a setup Hitchcock will use again: After the dinner scene with Norman, our relief that Marion decides to return the money is followed by the shock of her murder; much later, when Lila hides from Norman as he enters the house, our relief that he didn't see her is followed by dismay over her decision to visit the basement.

One final irony here in the patrolman scene: Though Marion is frightened of the cop in this scene and the next, it's apparent that he never really has any intention of pursuing or arresting her. Indeed, no authority figure will come after Marion until it is too late.

* * *

The sequence at the used car dealership, with its crackerjack performance by John Anderson as California Charlie, features several little-known but fascinating details.

For one thing, it was Leigh's only location shoot in the film — though even here, the brief scene in the rest room was filmed separately in the studio.

Also, as Stephen Rebello points out in his commentary on the 2008 DVD, Alfred Hitchcock's own car makes a cameo during this sequence — two cameos, actually. A large black Cadillac coupe, it passes the dealership twice, both times in the same direction (screen right to left) — once as the cop is pulling up on the opposite side of the street, and once as he is getting back into his car to move across into the used car lot.

Another intriguing but unheralded aspect of this scene is the quietly appealing residential neighborhood clearly visible behind California Charlie's lot: trees, pedestrians, a few parked cars, pleasant-looking homes — just the kind of respectable place Marion would like to settle into with Sam. Carefully fenced off and hardly even noticeable, that area is simply not part of *Psycho*'s world, and Marion will never reach it. Indeed, when she leaves the dealership, she drives directly away from it.

It might also be worth noting that the direction she heads in — toward a lot across the street — contains nothing but a small, bare space surrounded by a chain-link fence, evoking the sense of imprisonment, hopelessness, and emptiness that characterizes Marion's past and future.

In any case, Marion drives off hurriedly — because the cop has now pulled into the lot. As she accelerates, there is a loud "Hey!" and Marion slams on the brakes. This is another moment geared to rattle both her and the viewer. Of course, it's just the mechanic with her suitcase and coat from the car she has traded in. But as the script stipulates, she "sees the Patrolman, then the Mechanic. Her face goes white. She doesn't know which man called her."

Once the stuff is in the car, she pulls away, leaving the three men staring after her. More than one writer has suggested that the three men (mechanic, salesman, and cop) represent, respectively, the id, ego, and superego. While it's not always wise to read Sigmund Freud into scenes at will, the shot is so carefully composed — and the three men fit Freud's categories so well — that this possibility is hard to ignore. In any case, their puzzled staring is yet another piece of ambiguity, leaving us uncertain just how suspicious they are, and wondering whether the cop might get back in his car and pursue her further.

Another noteworthy item in the scene is Charlie's address: 4270 — the first number in the film that adds up to 13. It would have been easy to fit in a "13" earlier — say, as the number on Marion and Sam's hotel room in the first scene, or on her original license plate; but perhaps Hitchcock didn't wish to make her bad luck official until she had actually spent some of Cassidy's cash. After all, the numbers on her new license plate — 418 — do indeed amount to an omen.

Along these lines, Raymond Durgnat has pointed out how the used car lot scene very gradually reveals that Marion has crossed the state line from Arizona into California. First, eagle-eyed viewers might have noted "California Highway Patrol" on the policeman's car — but it's pretty tough to see; next, "Bakersfield" appears on two different signs during her brief time on the road between the cop scene and the dealer — not a very obvious clue, but enough for those who are paying attention and are aware there *is* a Bakersfield, California; then, more clearly, there is the name of the car dealer (California Charlie) — noted first above his garage and then in his dialogue; next, we see several California plates on cars in the lot; and finally, Charlie clinches it by noting that Marion's Arizona license plate is "out of state."

Of course, this is worth discussing only as a reflection of Marion's mental state. By the end of the scene, having actually spent some of the stolen money, she really has crossed the line — but it's hard to tell exactly when it happened.

As Durgnat further notes, all the things that worry us here — the dealer's suspicions, the loss of the money, the cop knowing what her new car looks like — are not important. "The cop and the dealer make no difference to the plot at all," he writes. They are here solely to heighten our nervous identification with Marion, and to "describe Marion's state of mind ... to convey the enormity of Marion's distraction," of her "deteriorating morale," her "mental lapse" (68–73).

And this will be the focus in the rest of her car trip, which is filmed as a descent into darkness and dissolution. Indeed, a strong indication of the control Hitchcock liked to have over every element of his film can be found in his memo to the sound department concerning Marion's two nighttime car trips — though in the finished film much of this is hard to hear beneath the music:

> Exaggerate passing car noises when headlights show in her eyes. Make sure that the passing car noises are fairly loud, so that we get the contrast of the silence when she is found by the roadside in the morning.... Just before the rain starts there should be a rumble of thunder, not too violent, but enough to herald the coming rain. Once the rain starts, there should be a progression of falling rain sound and a slow range of the sound of passing trucks.... Naturally, wind-shield wipers should be heard all through from the moment she turns them on.... The rain sounds must be very strong, so that when the rain stops, we should be strongly aware of the silence and odd dripping noises that follow [quoted in Rebello 137].

Or as Hitchcock put it somewhat more briefly — and more visually — in his very early notes: "The long traffic-laden route along Route 99 — the roadside sights — the coming of the darkness. Mary's thoughts about Monday morning and the discovery of her flight with the money. The rain starts" (quoted in Rebello 36).

Most of these car scenes were filmed using a mock-up car with highway footage rear-projected behind; but as script supervisor Marshall Schlom told Rebello, toward the very end of the rain scene Hitchcock and his crew simply draped black velvet over the entire stage behind the car. Passing headlights behind Marion were then rendered using a three-foot-wide wheel with lights mounted on it; this could be manually pulled away from the mock-up car and also rotated so that the lights would appear to move past the rear of the car and disappear to screen right; the lights had baffles on them and would shut off once they were no longer visible to the camera.

According to biographer John Russell Taylor, Stefano and Hitchcock had originally considered an actual filmed scene occurring Monday morning at the Lowery office back in Phoenix, outlining various reactions to Marion's theft. Deciding, however, that this would be a "fatal distraction," they "instead wrote the scenes as though they would be shown, then they were done as voices over while Marion drives, as her imaginings, so that this tells us more about her too" (257).

Hitchcock himself assisted Leigh in these scenes by sitting outside the studio car and coaching her during the shoot.

"'Oh-oh,' he'd say, 'there's your boss. He's watching you with a funny look'" (Rebello 90). Indeed, in her own book Leigh says Hitchcock "knew the dialogue of the voices he planned to superimpose, so he read the various characters' parts aloud to me.... That way I could let my face reflect my thoughts as I imagined these conversations" (60).

The first of these imagined conversations occurs much earlier. As Marion is leaving Phoenix, just before seeing her boss on the street, she imagines Sam's reaction to her unexpected arrival: "Of course I'm glad to see you, I always am. What is it, Marion?" Though not in the script, this is absolutely crucial, because it never actually occurs — nor can it, since Marion dies before reaching Sam. This sends us a clear signal that none of these conversations are real — that is, they don't reflect something actually occurring elsewhere, but are entirely products of Marion's imagination. This is further confirmed by Detective Arbogast's later statement that the Cassidy family "wants to forgive" Marion for her theft; once again, this reality contradicts the imaginary voice Marion hears in her own mind, with Cassidy wanting to take the money "out of her fine soft flesh."

And because these imagined dialogues are solely Marion's creation, they are among the most revealing and provocative scenes in the film. To put it simply, they show us the profound fragmentation of Marion's psyche.

In the first exchange with Sam, Marion is present but we do not hear her voice, even though she has clearly spoken to Sam. After this, she disappears from the imagined dialogue entirely. Indeed, not only has she herself been eclipsed by her own guilt and fear, but Sam's voice also is never again heard in these inner dialogues; possibly she can no longer bear to think about how this will all pan out. The script has her murmuring "Sam — Sam" as she falls asleep on the first night — but significantly, this was cut, as though she were losing sight of her goal. As Durgnat points out, when Marion forgets her suitcase at the car lot, "You don't have to be a Freudian to wonder if forgetting them means she's beginning to forget what she wanted the money for..." (68).

Indeed, given the amount of time Marion spends alone on the road — at least 20 hours of driving, not including the roadside nap — it's astounding that she didn't spend more time thinking about Sam, or about her own actions and their inevitable outcome. To persist in a course of action that she knew was wrong for well over 24 hours must have required her to distance herself from herself, to forcefully set aside her conscience — a marked splitting of the personality that links her pretty clearly to Norman.

Indeed, *Psycho* tends to foreground similarities between Marion and Norman — starting with their names, which are almost anagrams, as Donald Spoto has noted. This is the more noteworthy because the woman's name is usually spelled with two A's (as with Robin Hood's Maid Marian). Spelled with an O, Marion is also a man's name (it was John Wayne's real first name). Thus, in addition to the visual similarity, Marion's Christian name suggests mixed gender — which also points to Norman.

Furthermore, Marion and Norman share a determination to conceal a crime — in some cases by flushing away the evidence — together with a concomitant fear of being watched. And they are linked in the shower sequence, which begins with Norman's eye and ends with Marion's.

But most important, they are linked by their ability to supply disembodied voices — to create dialogue for someone else. In particular, both can reproduce someone else's personality with astonishing authenticity. The conversations Marion generates in her head — especially for Cassidy — sound so uncannily realistic that we're all but certain this must be what actually occurred. And of course, Norman can do the same thing; his conversations with Mother are so lifelike that we're convinced she's really there even after we know the truth.

Furthermore, the script says Marion is "repulsed" by Cassidy's imagined comments about taking the missing money out of "her fine soft flesh" — but in the finished film she smirks with an almost demonic pleasure, as though she is gladly wishing this punishment on herself. Several writers have aptly noted that Marion's virtual death-wish will come painfully true. Robert Kolker claims that Marion's creepy smirk, seen while voices run in her head, is "all but a foreshadowing of Norman-Mother's own lunatic smiles" — especially in the final scene (228).

In Lesley Brill's words, "If we intensify and extend Marion's actions and fantasies, we arrive at the full lunacy of Norman, who supplies not only his mother's voice but her person as well" (236).

Yet perhaps the most unsettling thing about these parallels is that we as viewers have linked ourselves with Marion — and thus, through her, we are linked to Norman. In other words: Marion's disintegration "establishes a bridge between the presumably normal world of the audience's perceptions and judgments and the *grand guignol* of the Bates Motel and Norman's California Gothic house" (Leitch 215). "With her, we lose all power of rational control, and discover how easily a 'normal' person can lapse into a condition usually associated with neurosis" (Wood 145).

And our closeness to her, our heightened concern, is certainly reflected in the way Hitchcock's camera keeps drawing closer and closer to her face during the repeated cuts as the rain begins pouring down during her drive. In this regard, a fine concluding overview of Marion's rain-drenched drive is provided by James Naremore, who calls the sequence "pure cinema" and praises the "expertise with which images and sounds have been manipulated":

> A tremendous anxiety is generated by the gradually accelerated tempi of the music and editing, by the steady movement of the camera in toward Marion, by the obsessive voices, by the growing darkness, the flashing lights, the sudden deluge, the hypnotic rhythm of the windshield wipers. All this takes us closer to the realm of pure nightmare, and prepares us to enter the world of Norman Bates [44].

To some degree, the sequence shows us that we already have entered Norman's realm; we entered it the moment we became complicit in Marion's crime.

And we won't get out of it any time soon.

8

Dirty Night

Marion and Norman

"The wipers clear the window, as if a curtain had been parted to reveal a whole new arena for the film." "Then, as if from some primal sea-world of chaos, the motel rises up out of darkness and water."

Thus James Naremore (44) and Donald Spoto (365) describe our arrival at the Bates Motel and Overnight Bog. In addition to the ordinary office and cabins, our first real taste of Norman's world is the massive house that looms behind them in the distance — built from the ground up under the supervision of art directors Joseph Hurley and Robert Clatworthy. As Rebello points out, Clatworthy had already shown his ability to recreate seedy motel settings and cramped interiors on Orson Welles's *Touch of Evil* (1958); he later did the marvelous Bates-like mansion in the unjustly neglected Charles Bronson cult movie *From Noon Till Three* (1976).

At $15,000, the Bates home was the most expensive set built for *Psycho*— though Hurley and Clatworthy saved a little money by reusing the tower from the house in *Harvey* (1950). Hitchcock biographer Patrick McGilligan fittingly describes the Bates home as "a blend of Charles Addams and Edward Hopper" (589); Tim Burton and his *Batman* art director Anton Furst called *Psycho*'s motel and house the best "special effect" ever created for a movie.

In appearance, the actual Bates home seems somewhat bird-like — poised much the way a hawk or an eagle squats in a tree, scanning the ground below for prey. As the house sits up there on its barren hill scowling down at the motel, one suspects that every move is under surveillance.

Part of the house's unnerving effect undoubtedly comes from the moonlit clouds we often see rolling along behind it. This was the brainchild of the film's pictorial consultant, Saul Bass, to whom Hitchcock said, "We've really got to do something to make the house look forbidding." Bass said he tried various effects before lighting on an answer that was "really wonderful and so dumb and simple.... I matted-in a time-lapse, moonlit, cloudy skyscape. The

Hitchcock chatting with an unidentified crew member in front of the infamous Bates mansion. Psycho's most expensive set, the $15,000 exterior was built from the ground up on the Universal lot; extensively refurbished over the years, it still stands, part of the "studio tour" at Universal's theme park in Los Angeles. (©Universal Pictures; courtesy Universal Pictures–Photofest)

rate of movement was not much above normal because I didn't want the eye to go right *to* it. So when you see the shot, what you look at is the house, but the clouds behind it are moving in a very eerie and abnormal way" (Rebello 130–31).

Of course, when Marion first pulls up, it's raining and you can't see the moon or its light — something that caused trouble for assistant director Hilton A. Green. In the DVD featurette "The Making of *Psycho*," Green recounts his chagrin when he arranged the filming of Marion's rain-soaked arrival —

complete with overhead sprinklers to provide the artificial drenching — only to find that there was a full moon that night. Noting Hitchcock's irritation that his assistant hadn't bothered to check the weather report beforehand, Green and crew quickly rigged up poles with blocks on top that could be manually held up in front of the moon during filming. "We followed that moon all night," Green recalled.

Though the creepy-looking house establishes a Gothic mood that the film has not yet even toyed with, there is no way our first impression of Norman Bates himself can possibly prepare us for what is to come.

Indeed, one of *Psycho*'s triumphs is the casting of Anthony Perkins, which occurred before the script was penned, and even before writer Joseph Stefano was hired. Because Perkins would forever after be permanently associated with Bates-like madmen and weirdos, it's difficult for modern audiences to understand that the character of a psychopathic, matricidal, Peeping Tom transvestite was then the polar opposite of Perkins's established screen persona.

The awkward, homespun lead in such movies as *Friendly Persuasion* (1956) and *Fear Strikes Out* (1957), Perkins was, in Rebello's words, "a bobby-soxer's dreamboat-with-a-brain ... a late-fifties fan magazine cover boy ... whom teen fans would mob if he dared step from his powder-blue T-bird." In 1958, he had even scored a modest top-40 hit with the song "Moonlight Swim" (59–60).

In Rebello's book, Perkins described Norman this way: "He would not plot malice against anyone. He has no evil or negative intentions." Shy and clumsy but also friendly and helpful, Norman is indeed so likable that, Rebello adds, he became "a national folk antihero" (88–89).

If that sounds like an odd description for one of cinema's most famous serial killers, consider this personal anecdote: I'll never forget sitting through *Psycho III* in a Manhattan movie house in 1986. During the scene in which Norman finally climbs into bed with an attractive woman, one young male viewer called out cheerily, "Go for it, Norman!"

That viewers could still feel this way years after knowing the truth about Bates is ample testament to Perkins's nuanced, sympathetic portrait.

Nevertheless, even at first there are some hints of a deeper darkness in the character — starting with his name, which original author Robert Bloch said he chose for several reasons:

> The first name was a combination of two words, "nor man," a pun which contains the secret of the story: my killer is neither woman nor man. Bates? I thought of his mother's sexual domination in childhood and youth: a domination young Master Norman could not escape except through masturbation. To say nothing of how Norman "baits" his trap and in another sense "baits" his pursuers [*Once* 229].

In addition, more than one writer has observed that Perkins's Norman sometimes resembles Marion (when he looks feminine), sometimes Sam (dark and handsome), and sometimes Mother's corpse (thin and angular). Nicholas Haeffner adds that this odd blend is possible because Perkins himself was "a very complex, and inwardly conflicted, bisexual actor" (112). Indeed, Perkins's bisexuality was "an open secret in Hollywood, and Perkins as Norman Bates couldn't help but draw on that subtext" (McGilligan 582).

In examining Norman's persona, it might be well to note Janet Leigh's assertion that Hitchcock didn't spend nearly as much time working with Perkins as he did with her. For example Perkins, unlike Leigh, was never invited to Hitchcock's home for discussions about the film. Leigh later wondered whether Hitchcock wanted to create "a kind of distance, a not-quite-worldly quality to how Tony played Norman" (Rebello 88).

Appropriately, our first view of Norman is in his guise as Mother, passing in a dress and wig across the upstairs window while Marion stares up at the house. Once she honks, Norman appears almost instantly from the front door and comes down with an umbrella — presumably to shelter his new guest from car to office. In any case, he doesn't open the umbrella for himself, but arrives with it closed.

Endless speculation is possible on this tiny detail: Is he allowing the rain to fall on him as some kind of punishment for playing Mother? Or to cleanse himself after doing so? Spoto suggests that it's an early emblem of his "derangement," adding that the umbrella might also be considered "in strictly Freudian terms as a phallic symbol, since Norman never opens it" (366–68) — and thus, presumably, it betokens his impotence, his emasculation. Any or all of these explanations are feasible — but one thing seems certain: The unopened umbrella allows Norman to get a brief shower, and thus provides an early key link between his character and Marion's.

Another such link is provided in the shot that occurs when Marion and Norman come into the motel office — a shot analyzed extensively in William Rothman's *Murderous Gaze*: First, we see the empty office with an empty mirror on the wall. Then we see Marion's reflection come into the mirror, and then Marion herself comes into the frame at the left. Next, Norman enters the room; he should come into the mirror first, as Marion did — but we can't see his reflection clearly because it's behind hers in the mirror. When his reflection does emerge from hers, there is a fleeting moment in which Marion appears to have two heads — male and female. The real Norman then enters the frame and passes between Marion and the camera, briefly obliterating our sight of her.

There's a lot of information in this very brief shot: Using the reflections,

Norman and Marion, briefly united in the mirror on the wall in the Bates Motel office. Is this two-headed, male-female figure a possible reference to Norman-Mom? (©Universal Pictures; courtesy Universal Pictures–Photofest)

Hitchcock shows us that Marion is still split, and that her "second self" continues to precede the real one; but since the same thing happens to Norman, the shot hints that he too is split, and serves as yet another link between the two characters. It also encapsulates the structure of *Psycho*'s storyline: Marion comes first; Norman then emerges from Marion in the same way that his story emerges from hers; and Norman then blocks Marion and consumes the entire screen — just as his story subsumes and succeeds hers. And of course, the brief "two-headed" male-female shot foreshadows Norman's personality as well.

There's a great deal of irony in this first meeting between Norman and Marion, starting when Norman insists, "There's no sense dwelling on our losses." It's the good old American spirit of constant forward progress — but *Psycho*, of course, proves the futility of trying to escape the past and "start over." Norman, in particular, literally does dwell on his losses: His entire life, especially the motel, is built upon them.

There's also Norman's hesitation over which cabin to put Marion in. He knows that if he puts her in Cabin 1, he'll be able to spy on her through the peephole. While he's hesitating, she's filling in the motel registry, and as she does, she lies out loud about her origin — "Los Angeles." At which point Norman chooses Cabin 1.

Is he more willing to spy on a worldly woman from L.A.? What would have happened if she'd told the truth? Did this little lie seal Marion's fate?

Speaking of which, another striking factor in this scene is how close Marion came to safety. In discussing the nearest diner, Marion asks, "Am I that close to Fairvale?" and Norman responds, "Fifteen miles"—at which point, most repeat viewers want to shout, "Get back in your car and drive the rest of the way—*now!*" The town's name itself, to paraphrase Philip Skerry, has an almost mythic quality—a place of Edenic rest and peace. As such, it's not the kind of location you can get to in *Psycho*. Thus, the moment Norman tells Marion how close she is, he instantly adds, "I'll get your bags"—and now her fate really is sealed.

Maybe it would have been best if she *had* forgotten her luggage at the used car lot.

During the brief ensuing scene in Cabin 1, we get a stronger sense of Norman's personality—particularly when he can't say "bathroom" in front of a beautiful woman. As Rothman observes, he also hesitates briefly on "mattress"—possibly out of sexual embarrassment (discussing bed with an attractive female), or possibly because it recalls the word "matricide" (the pronunciation is notably similar).

More broadly, Rothman also notes Norman's "habit of starting a sentence, pausing, and then starting it again, leaving it unclear whether the words he speaks are those he initially intended" (271).

And while he's showing her around the room, there's yet more irony in his description of the "stationery with 'Bates Motel' printed on it in case you want to make your friends back home feel envious." Sam and Lila later find a scrap of this paper in the toilet, so the stationery will indeed be seen by her "friends back home"; but no one is going to envy Marion for her experience at the Bates Motel.

Also intriguing is Norman's suggestion—after Marion has agreed to eat with him—that she should take off her wet shoes. In the script, it says "change your wet shoes"; but with them off (instead of changed), Marion will be more likely to stay. Perhaps this recalls Sam in the opening scene, where he is unable to leave with Marion because, in her words, "You have to put your shoes on."

After Norman exits to get dinner, Marion hides the money in a newspaper and places it on the bedside table; at precisely this moment—just as the word "OKAY" becomes clearly and ironically visible in the newspaper headline—we hear a loudly shouted, "No! I tell you no!" While this is a pretty clear indication that things are really *not* "okay," it also serves as our introduction to Mom, who is objecting to Norman's dinner plans. First-time viewers will not know this; they're much more likely to assume that this sudden disembodied voice is yet another accuser from Marion's subconscious. As in the mirror shot in the office, this important new player in the story seems to emerge right out of Marion's head.

Yet even if we assume that this is an imaginary voice in Marion's head, our wrong impression is actually closer to the truth; it's really only a single person talking to himself.

In one of Hitchcock's most brilliant decisions on this film, he actually hired three different people to handle Mother's dialogue — two females and one male. The females were Virginia Gregg and Jeanette Nolan. (The latter, married to John McIntire —*Psycho*'s Sheriff Chambers — also dubbed some screaming that was used in the final basement scene.)

The male playing Mom was a young actor named Paul Jasmin, a friend of Perkins who had developed a comic vocal impersonation of a crotchety old lady. Using this hilariously convincing voice, Jasmin would place prank calls to various Hollywood celebs like Rosalind Russell. "The woman's voice was really shrewish; that's the quality Hitchcock liked," Jasmin later recalled (Rebello 132).

After having all three of them read Mother's lines, Hitchcock and his sound men mixed them all together — so that Jasmin, upon seeing the film, could no longer tell which portions were his. "In postproduction," Jasmin told Rebello, "he spliced and blended a mixture of different voices — Virginia, Jeanette, and me — so that what Mother says literally changes from word to word and sentence to sentence. He did that to confuse the audience" (133).

During the course of the shoot, *Psycho*'s Mother is played variously by Anthony Perkins, a stuffed dummy, three different stunt doubles, and three different vocalists; with eight figures contributing to a single role, one can hardly blame *Psycho*'s original viewers for failing to figure out the truth.

A few of Mother's lines in this exchange bear further examination:

First, she assumes that dinner will be followed by a sexual liaison ("And then what? After supper? Music? Whispers?"). This serves as an uncomfortable reminder of Sam's similar assertion in the very first scene: "And after the steak — do we send Sister to the movies? Turn Mama's picture to the wall?" Fittingly, Sam sensed that Mother's hovering presence would make intimacy difficult — and now we see how right he was.

Another notable aspect of these lines — one that hasn't been discussed in the written material on *Psycho*—is the curious doubling in Mom's dialogue, her habit of repeating words and phrases. It's apparent elsewhere in the film — for example, in her monologue at the very end: "Let them. Let them see what kind of a person I am.... They'll see. They'll see and they'll know and they'll say...."

It's also present in the mid-film scene when Mother argues with Norman about going downstairs to the fruit cellar: "You hid me there once and you won't do it again, not ever again! Now get out! I told you to get out, boy! ... Don't you touch me! Don't! ... Put me down! Put me down!"

But this odd doubling — symptomatic, probably, of two personalities — is most noticeable in the conversation Marion overhears through the motel room window. First Mom complains about "the cheap erotic fashion of young men with cheap erotic minds." Norman responds, "Mother, she's just a stranger," and Mom then echoes him mockingly, "'Mother, she's just a stranger.'" Later, she adds: "I refuse to speak of disgusting things because they disgust me! ... Go tell her she'll not be appeasing her ugly appetite with *my* food — or my son! Or do I have to tell her 'cause you don't have the guts? Huh, boy? You have the guts, boy?" And Norman answers, "Shut up! Shut up!"

It's worth noting here that Mom doubles not only her own phrases but also Norman's — and that he himself winds up saying something twice — all of which indicates the complexity with which these two personalities are woven together (especially when you consider that Norman is actually speaking both parts).

Similarly revealing is Mom's cruel question, "Do you have the guts, boy?" Durgnat suggests that this is actually a playground taunt supplied unconsciously from Norman's childhood memories; after all, it doesn't sound like something any mother would say. More interestingly, it would be all but impossible to determine just who really has the guts in this relationship. Mom seems to have more; but literally speaking, she has none — because she's been eviscerated and stuffed. Norman supplies what guts she has — in more ways than one.

But perhaps the most fascinating thing about this exchange is pointed out by William Rothman: Marion hears it because Norman opened the window in her room — and indeed, the windows in the house must be open as well. Did he, however subconsciously, want Marion to overhear this conversation? Did he, however subconsciously, wish to plant the idea of a liaison in Marion's thoughts?

If so, he seems to have failed; when he greets her on the porch, she insists, "I really don't have that much of an appetite." Her precise use of Mother's word *appetite* — which doubles for both hunger and lust — may really be a way of saying, "I really don't have that *kind* of an appetite."

At the same time, Marion and Norman's blocking on the porch precisely reverses their earlier exchange in the office. There, Norman stood at the right of the screen facing Marion at the left, and we could see her reflection in the mirror behind her; here, Marion is at the right, and Norman is at the left, while his reflection appears in the window behind him. This again links Marion and Norman, not only through positioning but also because they are both seen to have a "second self." Furthermore, the idea of a "split personality" becomes even clearer if you look carefully at Norman's reflection in this scene — his "double," as it were. While the face of the "real" Norman, seen from his right, bears a small and slightly awkward smile, the left side of Norman's face, as reflected in the windowpane, is grim and tight-lipped.

And of course, the reversal of positions between Marion and Norman prefigures the narrative's forthcoming switch from her story to his.

Rothman also suggests that the lamp between them represents Mother, asserting that Mother is often associated with a lamp in the movie — not only here but also during the shower scene, where her first appearance is doubled by a head-shaped lamp on her left; and perhaps most significantly, in the final basement scene, where a wildly swinging bulb seems to give life to her desiccated features.

And speaking of Mother, the porch scene also contains what may be the film's most famous double entendre: Norman's insistence that Mother "isn't quite herself today." Of course she isn't herself; she doesn't exist; she's actually Norman!

This kind of sick joke is undoubtedly one of the things that led to Hitchcock's famous statement, "*Psycho* is a film made with quite a sense of amusement on my part. To me it's a *fun* picture" (quoted in Wood 142). Needless to say, it can be equally amusing for those who've seen it before and know the ironic truth behind many of its seemingly straight-faced lines.

But having made a meal and carried it down, why does Norman hesitate at the door to Marion's cabin? And why does he finally decide against bringing the food into her motel room to eat? The script tells us that "bringing down the tray of food, in defiance of his mother's orders, is about the limit of his defiance for one day" — the implication being, of course, that a bedroom is much too intimate a setting for a man and woman alone together.

But let's not overlook the distinct possibility that Norman doesn't want to eat in Cabin 1 because other young women have died there — and he had to clean it up.

Of course, as Internet writer Tim Dirks points out, Norman's decision here also allows him to lure Marion into his parlor — reminding many viewers of Mary Howitt's famous poem, "The Spider and the Fly," in which a female fly is lured to her death in the spider's parlor. This connection might seem a bit tenuous if it weren't for *Psycho*'s final line, in which Mother says of herself, "She wouldn't even harm a fly." Furthermore, there's a moment in

Psycho III when Norman says to his new motel manager, "Step into the parlor" — and the manager responds sardonically, "Said the spider to the fly."

Perhaps this very subtle omen is similar to the subconscious mood-setting that Durgnat sees in Hitchcock's emphasis on the stuffed birds in Norman's parlor. They're not the least bit necessary to the plot — but "it's important that they're macabre and have *some* threat. For thus they 'plant' the killing," which would otherwise seem "gratuitous, arbitrary, contrived, out of key" (97).

Of course, the two most prominent birds here are the owl and the crow. As Spoto points out, the stuffed owl is a killer who has been killed and thus reminds us of Norman — both victim and victimizer.

Or look at it this way: When Marion enters the room for the first time, we are shown the owl and then the crow — first a killer, and then the creature that feeds on corpses.

Or how about this: The owl, a killer, is often shown in the frame with Norman; the crow, associated with death and corpses, is generally shown in the frame with Marion. So does that make her first name a pun on "carrion"?

Or this: Directly underneath the owl is a classical painting of a woman trying to shield her naked body. As Rothman notes, this figure's pose — left hand crossed upward across breast to shoulder, right hand slanted downward across torso and groin — is precisely adopted by Marion during the second half of her conversation with Norman; she assumes it on her line, "No, not like me," though the figure really is like her. That is, it serves as a precursor to the naked and defenseless posture she'll adopt in a few short minutes; the nude figure's position under the ominous-looking owl reinforces her forthcoming role as victim.

Now that Hitchcock has set a mood and provided — as usual — plenty of ironic foreshadowing, the scene proceeds through a conversation that is the longest in the film and arguably the most important. Its focus, of course, is traps — specifically, Norman's assertion that everyone is clamped in a "private trap" and can "never budge an inch." This is true for many characters in the film: Sam is trapped by his father's debts; Marion is trapped in a dead-end job and a stalled relationship; Norman is trapped in a similar dead-end job and a literally dead relationship; and Mom, as Norman later says, is "confined" (indeed, she can't even move or speak without his help).

Of course, these confinements are reflected visually throughout the film: Arbogast's phone booth; a fruit cellar; Sam's "tiny back room which isn't big enough for both of us" (to borrow a phrase from his later letter); a cramped restroom at a car dealership; and a lethally confining shower stall. Concerning these two cramped bathrooms in which we see Marion, Philip Skerry suggests that *Psycho* subverts the classic American westward trek by having her travel not to freedom in the wide-open West, but rather to smaller and smaller places (motel room, bathroom, shower stall, car trunk) — eventually reaching confinement and death.

As Thomas Leitch asserts, this discussion of traps becomes, essentially, a debate about fate and free will. When Norman insists that he was born in his trap, Marion responds, "Sometimes we deliberately step into those traps" — implicitly rejecting Norman's assertion that traps are predetermined from birth. She seems to think we have a choice in the matter; he thinks we don't.

In the world of *Psycho*, Norman is right. And Marion's own odyssey proves it. By trying to escape from her previous trap, she stepped into a worse one; now when she decides to step back out "before it's too late" (to use her phrase) — well, it already is too late.

Incidentally, Marion's odd assertion that she is "looking for a private island" would seem clearer and more natural if a scripted line from Sam had not been excised from the opening hotel scene: "You know what I'd like? A clear, empty sky ... and a plane. And us in it ... and somewhere a private island for sale, where we can run around without our ... shoes on."

Hmmm. Private island. Private traps. Cassidy's odd-sounding "private money." A "Private" sign on Mr. Lowery's office door. And of course the upcoming "private detective." *Psycho*, in many ways, is a film about privacy — specifically, the penetration of privacy: peering through peepholes and windows, luring us into bedrooms and bathrooms, unearthing past secrets and hidden motivations. It recalls *Rear Window*'s line about voyeurism: "That's a secret, private world out there." And as in *Rear Window*, once you have stepped into that world, it's very difficult to get back out.

Durgnat suggests that one function of the parlor dialogue between Marion and Norman is to help us relate to Norman, whose life seems characterized by very common concerns: dreary monotonous work, a time-killing hobby, too much patience with his unhappy lot, mild resentment toward parents. And to top it all off, Norman seems very much aware of these things, perhaps more able to articulate the nature of his own trap — and his own role in it — than most of the other characters in *Psycho*. How could we ever suspect that a violent killer was lurking inside such a thoughtful, ordinary, normal human being?

Well, we could if we had seen the film already — or if we were unusually sensitive to some of the additional clues and omens with which the parlor scene is liberally laden:

Besides the ominous birds discussed above, Norman stumbles badly on the word "falsity," which has led other writers to all kinds of speculation about how this word suggests "fallacy" or even "phallus"—somewhat ridiculous, as neither of these words has the same 'A' sound we find in "falsity."

Folks, the answer is found in the script, where the word first comes out as "falsie"—old-fashioned slang for a fake breast (cf. *Catcher in the Rye*, "She had on those damn falsies that point all over the place").

Of course, there is the sexual embarrassment here that flummoxed Norman earlier on "bathroom" and "mattress." But even his awkward awareness of this word suggests a mother-obsessed man-boy who has done far too much thinking about breasts. And could it be that Norman is unusually sensitive to the issue of fake breasts, since he himself often dresses as a woman?

But of course, the real red-alert in this scene is Norman's almost casual insistence that "a boy's best friend is his mother." The script has Norman deliver this "with gallows humor"—but it's better in the film, where Norman plays it straight, and the awkward laughter is left to the audience. Even more potentially awkward is the line "A son is a poor substitute for a lover," which hints only vaguely at the incest theme that was much more prominent before censors got hold of the script.

At the time *Psycho* was made, films were not rated R or PG–13 as they are now; rather, they were evaluated using the Production Code, a set of moral guidelines that had been created by the Motion Picture Producers and Distributors of America in 1930 and strictly enforced since 1934. Using this code, a film would be either accepted or rejected by the MPPDA. If a film was denied the Code office's seal of approval, very few theaters would agree to show it. In other words, there were only two ratings when *Psycho* was made: "yes" and "no"—and the latter spelled box-office doom, unless the offending material were removed.

As Rebello describes it, when the Code office got hold of Joseph Stefano's script, there was great concern about the strong hints of an incestuous relationship between Norman and Mother. In Stefano's first-draft script, for example, Mother calls Norman "ever the sweetheart," Norman tells Marion that a son is a poor substitute for "a real lover," and the psychiatrist says their relationship is "more that of two adolescent lovers." In her final speech at the police station, Mother recalls Norman, "Always peeping ... and reading those ... obscene books and disgusting me with his love" (quoted in Rebello 77–78).

All of this is made alarmingly clear in *Psycho IV*, a made-for-cable movie about Norman's childhood, with the Oedipus theme played up heavily (though there is no actual sex between mother and son). Hitchcock fans may find it heavy-handed, but it is worth noting that *IV* was the only sequel written by Stefano; and Stefano told Philip J. Skerry that *IV* contained "all the scenes that were in my head when I wrote *Psycho*: the mother teasing him on the bed and then getting furious at him because he gets an erection. I used to talk to Hitchcock about these things, about how seductive she was with him and how he thought he had a right to be her only lover..." (88).

In fleshing out these aspects of Norman's personality, Anthony Perkins may have been drawing partly on his own life — which bore some uncanny similarities to that of Norman Bates: Perkins's father, actor Osgood Perkins, died when Anthony was only five. Sickly and noticeably disturbed by his father's death, the boy was raised by his mother — just like Norman, who says his mother "had to raise me all by herself after my father died." Perkins later described his mother as "strong-willed" and "dominant"; his biographer, Charles Winecoff, uses the terms "manipulative" and "iron grip" to describe her parenting techniques (29). In a 1983 interview, Perkins admitted that he had been "abnormally close" to his mother when very young — and that he felt a concomitant "Oedipal" jealousy toward his father (Winecoff 19).

Less noticeable than the Oedipal theme in this scene — but no less telling — is Norman's complaint about mental institutions: "Have you ever seen the inside of one of those places? The laughing and the tears and the cruel eyes studying you?" There seems little doubt that Norman has actually spent some time in one — particularly in light of the psychiatrist's later assertion that even as a child Norman was "already dangerously disturbed — had been ever since his father died." Skerry suggests he suffered from Oedipal guilt — wishing that his father were dead and then suddenly getting his wish. (In another Oedipal tale, this may also account for Hamlet's neurosis in the wake of his father's death.)

It's a fascinating moment when Marion suggests that Mom be put away. As Rothman points out, it's the first time Marion has been active in the conversation; up till now, she has been an almost entirely passive listener. Apparently, Norman doesn't like her new assertiveness much, and for the first time he seems capable of genuine menace, leaning forward and glaring intently while baldly insulting his guest and customer: "What do you know about caring?"

Personally, I can never watch this scene without remembering a friend of mine who sat through the movie with me for his first viewing in the late 1970s. At the end of this exchange, he turned to me and said worriedly, "I *already* wouldn't stay there"; so perhaps Norman's boyish charm lasts only as long as he — or Mom — doesn't feel threatened.

Indeed, it's quite possible that Marion is killed not because of Mom's sexual jealousy, but because Marion threatens Mom's very existence by suggesting that she be locked up. As Lesley Brill puts it, Marion's recommendation about the institution "may also evoke in 'Mother' an anxiety about her post-mortem survival quite as powerful as any sexual envy" (229).

Another beautifully evocative line in this scene occurs when Norman admits his conflicted feelings toward Mom: "I don't hate her — I hate what she's become." As Rothman points out, since Mother is now dead, this line implies a hatred of death — and a certain self-hatred as well, since Mother has now "become" Norman. Like many moments in the film, it's almost Shakespearean in its depth and emotional resonance.

The scene concludes with Marion's decision to return to Phoenix with the money — so we might well ask what facet of this conversation caused her to make such a remarkable determination.

On the surface, she seems to have gained a clearer understanding of traps — namely, that they aren't so easy to get out of. In particular, she has realized that the stolen money is just a different kind of trap — probably much more confining and permanent than the one she was already in.

This explanation is supported by a scripted line that was omitted from the finished film; at mid-scene, as Norman describes his trap, he says, "It's too late for me." This helps us understand Marion's later declaration that she is going to step back out of her trap "before it's too late for me too."

Thus, she foresees herself getting into a trap that is just as hopeless as Norman's. Perhaps she even sees herself getting into a trap that is very *similar* to Norman's. After all, Marion is seeking to get married, settle down, start a family, and live a normal American life. But Norman has shown her that this is no guarantee of happiness; he tells the tale of a woman who did indeed find marriage and family — after which she lost her husband and then a second lover as well ("she found out he was married," says Sheriff Chambers later); all of this resulted in a fractured family whose existence is at least as pathetic and stultifying as Marion's own life in hotel rooms and offices. Through Norman, perhaps, she has come to understand the world of *Psycho*, in which neither money nor marriage can make you happy or set you free.

Naremore suggests that Norman's discussion of his own "confinement" has given Marion a sense of perspective — that is, her life in Phoenix may also be a trap, but at least it's not as bad as Norman's. Durgnat goes so far as to suggest that Norman's submission to his own limitations has inspired her to tough it out, to stick to her moral convictions: He hasn't taken the easy route of putting his mother in an institution, so she won't take the easy route of stealing a dowry for her own marriage.

In any case, when Marion concludes this scene with a heartfelt "Thank you" — and a cleaner conscience — it's clear that she is grateful to Norman for more than just food.

Rothman has pointed out the careful composition that occurs as Marion leaves. First, we see her in profile facing right — the first profile shot of her in the scene. Once she leaves the frame, we are left briefly with nothing but the stuffed owl and a classical painting; Norman then rises, and is seen in profile facing right — virtually replacing Marion in the frame. It's Hitchcock's way of preparing us to transfer our sympathies to Norman — a transfer that is effected almost subconsciously in the following shot, which gives us Norman's point of view as Marion exits the office. This is the first time in the film that we've been alone with Norman, seeing something strictly through his eyes. But it won't be the last.

It's interesting as well to note the subtle change in Norman's personality after Marion's back is turned. He seems wiser, slyer, more worldly and cynical. He pops a piece of candy coolly into his mouth (significantly, we see the carrion-eating crow behind him as he begins to chew); then he glances skeptically at the registration book, sees that the name she first used is not the one she just gave him, deftly douses the light, and listens thoughtfully before peeping into Marion's room.

Rothman claims that this mood shift actually begins earlier in the scene, when Marion insists that she must go to bed; and there does indeed seem to be a slight change in Norman's tone — a bit of condescension, perhaps a bit of skepticism, a bit of irritation. Together with his earlier menacing coldness ("What do you know about caring?"), it seems apparent that Norman contains a variety of personalities, even if we disregard his maternal alter ego.

* * *

Viewers and writers often wonder whether a discussion of Norman's peephole scene belongs more suitably with the parlor sequence or the ensuing shower scene. On the one hand, it makes a very logical prelude to the murder; yet on the other, as we saw above, the transition to the peeping scene is uninterrupted — virtually continuous from the dinner scene with Marion. By contrast, there is a very clear emotional break after the peeping scene — between Norman's return to the house and Marion's scribbling at the desk in her room.

Yet the difficulty of isolating the peeping scene is noteworthy. Like so much else in this part of *Psycho*, it serves as an effective link between the two halves of the film — between Marion and Norman. In the first place, the scene in some ways reenacts the earlier scene of Marion secretly eavesdropping on the conversation between Norman and Mom.

More significantly, it's our first opportunity to observe Norman alone, and thus to begin identifying with him. Yet like our identification with Marion, the connection we feel with Norman is troubling: As Norman watches Marion undress, we watch too, and thus we share his guilt — just as we shared some guilt for hoping Marion would succeed in her theft. This new guilt, however, is considerably more problematic. After all, we didn't actually *do* what Marion did (stealing money); but now we are indeed physically engaged in the same act as Norman: watching.

The scene works on us in other ways as well:

After Marion has put on her bathrobe, we see her glance toward the cabin door and walk in that direction, as if to make sure the door is closed and locked. Of course, we know this is the wrong direction to worry about, and this increases our separation from her, as well as our complicity with Norman.

Worse, Hitchcock accentuates the culpability of viewers — or at least of those viewers who are male — by cutting away just as Marion is about to remove her brassiere. In Rothman's words, "This shot withholds Norman's view from us, allowing us to recognize our wish for it" (289). The script takes this farther, insisting that "we see his eye run up and down the unseen figure of Mary"—though this is not especially apparent in the finished film.

Durgnat agrees that the cutaway will frustrate males, but adds that female viewers could be pleased by the respect Hitchcock shows for Marion's modesty. Meanwhile, as Naremore observes, Marion's "breasts are especially desirable to a psychopath with an unnatural love for his mother" (31).

After he is finished peeping, Norman carefully replaces the painting; so this might be a good time to discuss the subject of that particular art work. It has proven difficult to track down the artist or title of the picture itself; but most writers agree with Spoto, who identifies it as one of many classical renderings of the story of Susanna and the elders (others were done by Rembrandt, Tintoretto, and Van Dyck). Found in Daniel 13 in the Old Testament Apocrypha, the tale describes two men spying on a beautiful wife while she bathes — after which they burst in on her and attempt to blackmail her into having sex with them.

In addition to pointing a Biblical finger at the sin of Norman's voyeurism, the story posits a connection between lust and forced sex, subtly paving the way for Norman-Mom to "burst in" on Marion and commit the rape-like murder. Since it also concerns a woman bathing, the painting is yet another instance of Hitchcock's careful attention to detail in his *mise-en-scène*.

Curiously, Norman's final emotion after this act of voyeurism appears to be anger. Initially, this may seem to be Mom's jealous anger kicking in — a reaction to her son's attraction to another woman. (As the psychiatrist later says, "He wanted her. That set off the jealous mother, and Mother killed the girl.") But it's really only Norman who's mad. In the script, he looks up at the house and then turns back "resentfully. In his face we see anger and anguish. And then resolve." He "squares his shoulders" and "strides manfully" up the path to the house, where he pauses as if to ascend the stairs.

Clearly, he is ready to face down Mother for having cut him off from the world of romance and sexuality. Yet he can't bring himself to do it, and in dejection he slumps off sadly to the ground-floor kitchen instead of going up the stairs to Mom's room. He has proven his own assertion that there is no escape from one's "private trap."

Yet if this is all part of Norman's struggle to free himself, Durgnat suggests that this admittedly perverse voyeurism nonetheless puts Norman a little bit closer to a *normal* love life than his habit of stuffing birds and kowtowing to a corpse. Strange, twisted, backwards world, this world of *Psycho*— where voyeurism seems like a step toward normal.

But you have to admit, Norman's invasion of Marion's privacy — however perverse and objectionable — is infinitely preferable to Mom's.

9

Blood! Blood!
Marion and Mom

As Donald Spoto says in *The Dark Side of Genius, Psycho*'s shower scene "has evoked more study, elicited more comment, and generated more shot-for-shot analysis from a technical viewpoint than any other in the history of cinema" (419). Indeed, the word "most" seems to dominate the commentary on this sequence:

> James Naremore says Hitchcock's shower scene "may be the most horrifying *coup de theatre* ever filmed" (54).
>
> Jean-Pierre Dufreigne: "undoubtedly the most famous murder sequence in all film history" (35).
>
> Robin Wood: "probably the most horrific incident in any fiction film" (146).
>
> Paul Condon and Jim Sangster: "one of cinema's most infamous sequences" (245).
>
> Philip J. Skerry: "*the* most analyzed, discussed and alluded to scene in film history" (285).
>
> David Sterritt: "the most celebrated montage of Hitchcock's career" (108).
>
> Dennis R. Perry: "*the* cinematic thunderbolt of the twentieth century" (204).
>
> Richard J. Anobile: "the most terrifying murder sequence ever shot on American celluloid" (6).
>
> Steven Jay Schneider: "the most significant scene in film history" (v).

Several of these accolades (and more) are listed in what may be the single most substantial tribute to the scene: Skerry's *The Shower Scene in Hitchcock's* Psycho (2005)—409 pages devoted entirely to Marion's murder and its place in the annals of cinema.

In addition to these encomiums, the shower scene topped the list of "Best Movie Deaths" in a 2004 critics' poll by Britain's *Total Film* magazine;

and it was voted the No. 1 horror scene of all time in a 2005 Sony Ericsson poll of 1,200 viewers. The scene also ranked No. 2 in *Entertainment Weekly's* 1999 list of "The 100 Greatest Movie Moments." *Psycho* itself, of course, sits at the top of the American Film Institute's list of the 100 best American thrillers.

And to top it all off, a quick run of "psycho shower scene" at Google.com nets nearly a quarter of a million entries.

It's intimidating to approach such a scene in a single chapter, so I've divided the commentary into three sections: first, some background on how the scene was filmed; second, a detailed analysis of the scene itself; and third, a discussion of its effect on viewers.

* * *

Two of the best-known "facts" about the shower scene are that it required 78 shots, and that it took a week to film.

Both of these details are misleading.

As Bill Krohn notes in his meticulously researched *Hitchcock at Work,* the "week" was actually seven different shooting days spread out from December to March—and some of them did not constitute full eight-hour workdays. Though Leigh said the scene claimed one-third of her total shooting time, Krohn shows that even she was there for only five of the seven days, and that much of the work was done without her, using doubles.

Nevertheless, that's a lengthy shoot for a relatively brief scene—and the time was indeed necessitated by the multiple shots Hitchcock laid out in advance. Most sources—including Stephen Rebello—cite 78 camera set-ups for the scene, though the director told Truffaut there were 70. These well-known and substantial figures may reflect what happened during the shoot, but Skerry's careful breakdown shows that the final cut of the four-minute scene—beginning with Marion at the desk in her room and ending with the Bates home seen through the window—contains either 60 or 61 shots. (There's a mid-scene moment where it's tough to tell whether there is a cut.)

Because these shots are filmed from a wide variety of perspectives—looking up, looking down, looking at the killer, looking at the victim, looking at the shower head, looking at the drain—and because cameras in that era were so unwieldy, Hitchcock's crew built a separate shower unit with four detachable walls and an overhead scaffold for high-angle shots; the entire unit could also be attached to the larger bathroom set when necessary. Yet despite all this maneuvering, assistant director Hilton A. Green told Rebello that the scene was not especially difficult because it had been laid out so thoroughly beforehand.

Some of this advance work involved 48 storyboards by pictorial consultant Saul Bass, who later insisted that he himself— and not Alfred Hitchcock — had actually directed this scene.

His claim has been contradicted by Hitchcock, Leigh, Green, costumer Rita Riggs, writer Joseph Stefano, script supervisor Marshall Schlom, and makeup man Jack Barron. Green told Skerry, "I saw Saul years later ... and I said, face-to-face, 'Saul, how can you possibly say you directed that?' And he was very embarrassed" (153). When Leigh was asked whether Bass directed her in the scene, she replied, "Absolutely not! I have emphatically said this in any interview I've ever given. I've said it to his face in front of other people" (Leigh 67).

But the real nail in the coffin is a look at Bass's actual storyboards (available as an extra on the 1999 and 2008 DVD versions). They are markedly different from the finished scene; in particular, they lack many of the extreme close-ups that make the scene so confusing and claustrophobic.

And in spite of Bass's claim that he had "a sort of purist notion of making a horrible murder with no blood" (Rebello 102), his storyboards also show considerable gore on Marion's hands and body. Hitchcock, however, was careful to show blood only in the tub. In his interview with Skerry, Stefano points out that blood is seen in the water but not on Marion — because Hitchcock specifically did not want to show blood on her body.

In this regard, it's worth mentioning that Hitchcock decided against using a fake torso that could squirt blood when stabbed — though he claimed that he did have the crew design one to see how it would work.

There's a good deal of argument, in fact, over whether one ever sees the knife actually enter Marion's flesh. In his interview with Skerry, Green vehemently denied that such footage was shot; but many viewers have noted the knife-tip entering Marion's belly, just below her navel, in a brief but clear torso shot. If you advance slowly through this brief segment using *pause* or *slow* on your DVD player, you can clearly see the knife go *into* the flesh during in a fleeting mid-scene moment — though no blood comes out. Since the torso is slightly shifting and moving as the knife-tip enters, one wonders whether this shot was filmed with the mock-up torso mentioned above; it's hard to imagine how it could have been achieved with either Leigh or a stand-in.

Similarly, *Psycho*'s viewers have long debated just how much nudity the scene contains — specifically, whether Marion's breasts are ever fully visible. A careful look reveals two or three shots in which they appear either very briefly or out of focus. But in general the views are so fast and so vague that even Production Code censors in 1960 could hardly tell what they had seen.

This shot refutes the many claims that *Psycho*'s shower scene never shows the knife penetrating flesh. It's brief but definite, and if you watch it on "slow" mode, you can actually see the knife go in. Significantly, it enters near the navel, symbol of one's attachment to Mother. (©Universal Pictures; courtesy Universal Pictures–Photofest)

As Rebello relates, when the Code office previewed *Psycho*, "Three censors saw nudity; two did not." Requested to remove the offending footage, Hitchcock instead simply repacked the scene and sent it back with no changes. "Now the three board members who *had* seen nudity the previous day did *not* and the two who did not now *did*" (146). This argument continued for more than a week, until Hitchcock offered a trade: He would re-shoot and tone down the opening hotel room tryst (which also bothered censors), if they'd let him keep the shower scene intact; but he insisted that someone from the Code office be present during the re-shoot. This never happened, and both scenes went out uncut.

Almost.

The censors did force Hitchcock to excise an overhead shot after Marion's fall; it showed her body from the back, draped over the edge of the tub, with her buttocks clearly exposed.

Psycho's assistant editor, Terry Williams, told Skerry that all the outtakes from the shower scene were blithely — and tragically — thrown away by an irritated shop steward who didn't want to sort and label the pieces. A still of this omitted image is reproduced in Skerry's book — and Gus Van Sant included the shot, complete with slash marks on Marion's back, in his 1998 remake.

Stefano repeatedly expressed his personal grief over the loss of this shot, which he called "heart-breaking." As he told Skerry, "All I could think was, 'All that youth, all that beauty. All down the drain.' It made me think of all the girls I ever liked and how easy it is for men to kill women" (71).

The body in that shot wasn't Leigh's, of course; virtually no major star in that era would have appeared fully and visibly nude in a film. Rather, Leigh in that frame is doubled by a 23-year-old dancer and model named Marli Renfro; she was hired because, as Hitchcock put it, "I want someone whose job it is to be naked on the set" (Rebello 104). Renfro was used mostly for testing how various shots would look — and as a body double when Norman wraps up Marion's corpse later on. Leigh always insisted that no shot of Renfro appears in the finished scene except the early blurred view of Marion behind the translucent curtain. Krohn's book, however, indicates that well over four hours of shooting took place using Renfro alone, without Leigh present on the set. Renfro, for example, must certainly be the one who appears in the aforementioned shots that show Marion's breasts, however briefly. Furthermore, in the 2008 DVD commentary, *Psycho* expert Stephen Rebello indicates that stand-in Ann Dore was used in the overhead shots of Marion fending off Mom's knife. He also tells us that Hitchcock himself was the one who held the knife in many of the shots throughout the shower scene.

Speaking of stand-ins, Anthony Perkins was in New York preparing a Broadway stage show when the shower scene was filmed. Mother in this scene was played by veteran doubler Margo Epper, and by the above-mentioned Dore, whose face was blackened so as not to be seen clearly — though her "burning eyes, dimly visible in some prints, add a horrible touch when she tears open the curtain" (Krohn 230).

In any case, the unusual presence of a naked female was one reason why the shower shoot took place on a "closed set."

The other reason was Janet Leigh, who spent several days nearly nude and found the ordeal so difficult that she claimed she never took another shower. (In interviews, Leigh was always quick to point out that she did use the bathtub — and that she kept a shower in her home for guests.)

Indeed, one of the scene's greatest challenges was finding a way to make Leigh look nude without requiring the star to expose her breasts or privates.

As Leigh recounts in her book on the film, she and costumer Rita Riggs pored over strip-tease catalogues and magazines, seeking something that would cover up only the essentials: "There was an impressive display of pinwheels, feathers, sequins, toy propellers, balloons, etc., but nothing suitable for our needs. Rita solved the puzzle. Nude-colored moleskin! Over the vital parts! Perfect!" (66).

This was a felt-like material, adhesive on the inside, that could be sculpted and trimmed as required for each individual shot — but it had a tendency to peel off in the steam and water; and it had to be carefully removed between takes because it would make the flesh raw if left on too long.

All this took time, and according to Riggs, Hitchcock sometimes grew exasperated — especially when the moleskin peeled off before the take was done (this would require an instant cut to preserve Leigh's modesty, followed by careful reapplication and a retake).

Nevertheless, Leigh insists that Hitchcock was considerate toward her throughout the ordeal. In particular, she vehemently denied that the director asked her to do this scene completely nude; she also refuted the rather silly rumor that he used cold water to help her act shocked. On the contrary, Leigh insisted that Hitchcock "was adamant about the water temperature being very comfortable" (72), in which case one wonders whether an unusually large water heater was needed for these scenes (there is no specific record of this in the many writings on the film's production).

Beyond the problem of keeping Leigh both covered and warm, the shower scene required solutions to several other difficulties. One involved the head-on shots of the showerhead, which necessitated using a longer lens and blocking off the inner holes of the showerhead to keep the camera from getting soaked.

Another set of problems was presented by the various sounds in the scene — especially important given the fact that between the parlor sequence and the hardware store scene lie 17 minutes of film with only one line of dialogue.

According to Rebello, Hitchcock initially stipulated no music whatsoever during the murder — or during any of the motel sequence with Marion and Norman; as we saw in Chapter 3, composer Bernard Herrmann changed Hitchcock's mind with a shrieking violin cue — arguably the most recognizable piece of music in movie history.

Incidentally, Hitchcock took the one line of dialogue ("Mother! Oh God, Mother! Blood! Blood!") and instructed the sound man to remove all the bass from this line — making Norman sound pathetically childlike.

And let's not forget the sound of the stabbing. Script supervisor Marshall Schlom told Rebello that he sent the prop man off to the store for various melons, and that Hitchcock then sat with his eyes closed while a knife was plunged into each one. In a now fairly well known story, Hitchcock chose a lowly casaba for the most famous knifing in the annals of cinema.

On the other hand, Danny Greene — an uncredited sound editor on the film — told Skerry in no uncertain terms that he used beef. That story is not well known — yet it seems credible not only because of Greene's job title but also because he claims to have done the stabbing himself. Here is Greene's account:

We had changed the stabbing sounds three times, but they still didn't work.... I was going to go to the closest market, buy a big roast beef and stab it in front of a microphone.... The prop guy said, "Here, you might as well take the same knife we used in the scene...." So, I got this giant chunk of meat, a big roast with gristle on the side. I stabbed it about 50 times, in the gristle and in the meat part. It was just a vicious sound of slicing meat.... And the new stab sounds were a hit! Hitchcock leaned back in his chair and said, "Ah, yes — very nice." ... Melons were never used in any way to create sound effects for *Psycho* [Skerry 232–33].

Greene adds that his wife later used the meat for dinner — curiously reminiscent of the famous *Alfred Hitchcock Presents* episode "Lamb to the Slaughter" (1958), in which a wife bludgeons her husband to death with a frozen piece of meat and later feeds it to policemen investigating the crime.

Greene also points out that the sound of the shower was carefully adjusted throughout the scene, depending on the angle of the camera in relation to the water.

In any case, whether the victim was melon or meat, the sound is clearly tied to the ongoing motif of food in the film — as is the fake blood used in the scene: It was actually chocolate syrup, squirted handily from a new plastic squeeze bottle that had just hit supermarkets.

But of all the difficulties faced and solved by Hitchcock and his crew in this scene, perhaps the most notable involved the prolonged reverse tracking shot of Marion lying dead on the bathroom floor.

In particular, Janet Leigh found it all but impossible to remain completely still during this lengthy sequence. Not only was she draped awkwardly over the tub, but she also found the trickling water "maddening"—and the moleskin kept peeling off her breasts. The camera couldn't see this — but Leigh often joked about how many extra technicians seemed to be loitering around for this shot, and the take kept getting stopped and re-started in order to preserve her modesty.

They shot it more than 20 times. As Leigh recalled in her book, on what may have been the 25th or 26th take, she could once again feel "the damn moleskin pulling away from my left breast. I knew the lens would not pick it up — that part was below the top of the tub. But I also knew the guys in the balcony would get an eyeful. By that time, I was sore ... my body ached — and I didn't want to shoot this thing again.... The hell with it, I said to myself; let 'em look!" (73).

After nailing the shot, Hitchcock found that the initial close-up of Marion's eye wasn't the right size. Using an optical printer, he enlarged the shot to match the drain that is superimposed over her eye.

Also, cameras in that era didn't have auto-focus, so the focus had to be adjusted by hand while the shot was being filmed. This was especially difficult due to the shot's length. At approximately 65 seconds, it's the longest single shot in the scene.

But calling it a single shot is inaccurate; it actually blends together five separate pieces of film.

Approximately 30 seconds into the shot, there is a brief cut to the showerhead, necessitated because the supposedly dead woman moved — though there is some disagreement about whether it was a gulp or a blink (Leigh claimed the latter). Amazingly, despite the repeated takes, no one noticed this until a rough cut was being screened, at which point it was called to Hitchcock's attention by his wife, Alma — whose own film career had included work as a continuity checker.

After a cut back to Marion, the camera continues tracking farther back and then pans right to look out through the door — after which it moves across the bedroom for a close-up of the stolen money. But Hitchcock and his crew couldn't get the camera through the too-small doorway. So shooting stopped when the camera reached the door; the camera was then moved into the other room, re-set on the door, and re-started. Eagle-eyed viewers will note the subtle cut, including a very slight change in hue, which occurs just as the door panel fills the frame.

After tracking across the bedroom to the money, the camera again pans right and looks out the window at the Bates house — but the shot of the house, with Norman coming out the front door, was filmed separately and then projected on a screen outside the window; thus, the timing on this forward track and pan had to be perfectly synchronized with the existing footage of Norman.

Despite all the care and effort expended on this shot, it does contain one obvious mistake: A person's pupil dilates upon death — but the close-up on Marion's dead eye shows that hers is still contracted. After *Psycho's* release, Hitchcock received several letters from ophthalmologists pointing out this error; Rebello believes this is why, in the later *Frenzy*, Hitchcock deliberately included a close-up of murder victim Brenda Blaney, complete with her pupils fully dilated.

In his careful analysis, Philip J. Skerry divides the shower scene into "three acts": first, from Marion's work in her bankbook up to the moment Mother pulls back the curtain; second, the actual attack; and third, "the Descent of Marion" — from Mother's exit to the shot out the window (301). This seems more useful than Durgnat's six parts — or for that matter, the seven segments found in the script; and so let's use it now as we turn from how the scene was filmed to what it means and what it does.

Act I

The opening shot of Marion at her desk echoes the preceding shot of Norman, reminding us that it's unwise to isolate this scene from the rest of the story. Indeed, both the introduction and the conclusion to the shower scene are firmly linked to Norman. The entire sequence is so seamlessly welded to *Psycho*'s overall narrative that it's hard to say exactly where "the shower scene" begins and ends.

In Skerry's view, Act I begins with Marion seated at her desk. She is facing right — just like Norman in the previous shot of the Bates kitchen. Both she and Norman are framed by vertical lines, suggesting the traps from which they seek to free themselves — Norman by defying his mother and Marion by defying conventional morality.

At the same time, her calculations show that she plans to pay back, from her own bank account, the $700 she spent on the car — and thus she is also struggling to free herself from this latest trap of crime and chaos. But since she tears up the paperwork and flushes it down the toilet — wishing to leave no trace of her crime — Internet writer Tim Dirks suggests she may have changed her mind once again; or at least she's keeping her options open. But this seems unlikely. Her joy and relief are much too apparent in the following moments under the shower — a scene in which she seems to be purging herself of guilt and sin.

As Rothman puts it, in this private place of washing and refreshment, "she can imagine herself once again a virgin, unsullied by any man ... completely undefiled by the world..." (294). Indeed, the strong emotion is much more apparent in the film than in the script, which claims, "There is still a small worry in her eyes, but generally she looks somewhat relieved." The clarity of Marion's relief is due to strong work by Leigh, who repeatedly asserted that she played the scene as a "cleansing," "a baptism," a "kind of rebirth," "a taking away of the torment." She also insisted that this is precisely the way Hitchcock told her to play it — "so that the moment of intrusion is even more shocking and tragic" (Rebello 109).

Act II

The stabbing of Marion is preceded by a 12- or 13-second shot in which a figure enters the bathroom and approaches the shower, unseen by Marion and obscured even for us through the translucent curtain. Skerry observes that this tense moment differs markedly from standard "approach-of-the-killer" scenes in such films as *Scream, The Silence of the Lambs,* and even Hitchcock's own *Dial M for Murder.* It differs because first-time viewers do *not* know who this figure is; indeed, they cannot even know that the figure is a killer.

Thanks to the scene's fame, it is now all but impossible to experience Marion's death as it must have felt to novice viewers back in 1960. But one thing seems certain: Rather than a murderous female, first-timers would have been much more likely to assume that the trespasser was Norman — about to step up his discomfiting invasion of Marion's privacy.

Stefano confirms this in his interview with Skerry: "Sometimes, when I'm talking to a group of people, I ask, 'What did you think was going to happen to her when she got in the motel and had that nice talk with the guy and then he peeked at her?' And everyone thought, 'He's going to rape her'" (79).

Yet there's still a surprise even for *Psycho* veterans when the curtain pulls back and Mother raises her knife: Mom is right-handed — but the earlier scenes show that Norman is a leftie!

Philip J. Skerry noticed this, and amazingly, he seems to have been the first and only writer to do so. In the various notes on the film's production, there is no indication whether this was Perkins's decision or Hitchcock's. But it's one of those fascinating details that set *Psycho* apart from your average thriller. Perkins himself was left-handed, and according to Charles Winecoff's biography, early attempts at getting him to write with his right hand resulted in a persistent stuttering problem in his youth.

And as long as we're talking about surprises: One might well wonder just how clear a look Marion gets at her killer in this scene. Since the sequence ends with a close-up of her eye, one wants to know what, exactly, was the last thing she saw. Is her initial shriek of horror merely a reaction to the knife? Or is she also screaming because she has recognized, even in the wig and dress, the awkward young man who so recently treated her to a friendly meal?

Certainly, as Skerry points out, Norman-Mother is revealed with a self-conscious, highly theatrical gesture: "She makes her appearance as if she is a character in a play or on a movie screen back when movie theaters had curtains that parted" — as many of them still did in 1960. This effect is heightened when Mother pauses briefly before stabbing, as though she demands that we acknowledge her presence and her power — a gesture that is even more apparent when she enters and raises her knife in the final basement scene.

Also, this dramatic view of Mother is presented to the audience first, before Marion turns; in this way, we viewers "are the first recipients of the revenge of mother" (Skerry 316).

Thus begins the most famous murder in movie history — and though the likable Marion Crane is its victim, the scene does indeed feel like an assault on the viewer.

In the first place, Durgnat points out that the initial knife-slash descends past Marion's face and disappears below the frame, followed by a clear stabbing sound. Striking somewhere on Marion's torso, this first wound is almost certainly fatal. The scene is thus instantly removed from the realm of suspense — which requires at least some hope for the victim; instead, the mood becomes one of horrified shock, coupled with dread and despair.

More significantly, the script makes it clear that Hitchcock intended to attack his audience. As indicated when Mom "removes" the curtain, Hitchcock seeks to destroy the "safety barrier" that has always separated characters and viewers: "The flint of the blade shatters the screen to an almost total, silver blankness," says Stefano's script. And then: "An impression of a knife slashing, as if tearing at the very screen, ripping the film."

As Skerry makes clear in his meticulous, shot-by-shot breakdown of Act II, the actual stabbing takes 40 seconds and is depicted in 34 shots (maybe 35). The sequence is tough to digest, in part because of the rapid cutting — familiar to modern viewers through commercials and movie trailers, but virtually unheard-of in popular movies 50 years ago.

Even more disorienting are the rapid changes in what we see:

Some shots are from a high angle; some are from below. Some are brightly lit; some are dark. Some are medium shots, some extreme close-ups. In most, the camera is stationary; in some, it is moving slightly. Most of the shots are clearly focused; some are blurry. Most are at regular speed; some are in slow-motion.

And the length of each shot varies widely, refusing to give us a predictable rhythm; at the center of Act II, the cuts come so fast that they're virtually impossible to count at regular speed.

We also see a bewildering array of subjects: killer, victim, knife, tub, curtain, rod, hands, feet, head, back, belly, mouth. Not only that, but the diagonal composition of the shower spray and stabbing knife keeps getting reversed — sometimes upper right to lower left, sometimes upper left to lower right. And Durgnat makes note of the contrast between the knife's vertical movement and the lateral, side-to-side motions of Marion's head and arms.

As one young viewer phrased it in an unpublished essay, watching the scene is like looking through a kaleidoscope — except that we aren't controlling the movement.

In the words of Bill Krohn, the rapid cutting is a metaphor for the attack;

"the shift to a montage style 'rips' the film into pieces and deprives us of the mastery we have exercised over events through the intermediary of the camera" (230).

Skerry adds that the varied angles achieve the effect of "fragmenting the body of Marion, of 'cutting it up'; in this way, the form of the film reflects — even creates — the content" (323).

Confirming that the hurried cuts represented "a very new idea stylistically," Saul Bass said the scene delivers "an impressionistic, rather than a linear, view of the murder" (Rebello 105). According to James Stephens Hurley III, "With its disorienting barrage of staccato editing, the shower murder looks, on a formal level, more like a sudden swerve into experimental or avantgarde film practice — 'cubism,' or even action painting brought to cinematic life — than anything to be found in a classical Hollywood movie..." (quoted in Skerry 286).

Exacerbating our disorientation is something that becomes painfully apparent if you watch the scene in *slow* mode on a DVD: the extraordinary claustrophobia of the scene — how Hitchcock puts us right in the middle, directly underneath the shower, closed in between Marion and Mom, no more able to escape from the attack than its terrified victim.

Writing of the composition and framing in the scene, Skerry says Hitchcock creates for us "a purely abstract space of terror" (320).

This, he posits, is achieved in several ways — initially in Act I, which uses the blank bathroom tiles and dull gray curtain "to disengage the viewer from a realistic sense of space and place, and of time." Throughout the scene, Hitchcock is "relentlessly and methodically enclosing the viewers in smaller and smaller spaces, cutting them off from the outside world ... and subjecting them to claustrophobic stress" (312).

Skerry also invokes anthropologist Edward T. Hall's maxim about "intimate space" — namely, that anything closer than 18 inches can easily feel intrusive or invasive; though *Psycho* has avoided such invasive close-ups until now, nearly every shot in Act II violates this space.

Similarly, the scene often flouts the well-established "180-degree rule," which stipulates that persons or objects in a series of shots should always maintain the same left-right orientation. That is, consistency and perspective for viewers are maintained by imagining a line through the center of the visual field (perpendicular to the camera) and then keeping the camera on the same side of that line, lest the viewer's field of vision be suddenly reversed.

In other words, if the camera shows a character standing in the right half of the frame and pointing a gun toward the left, you cannot suddenly move the camera to his opposite side and show his gun pointing toward the right.

It confuses and disorients viewers. Yet this is exactly what the camera does in Act I — reversing Marion just before Mother enters the room. And Hitchcock continues to violate the rule during Act II — so much so that one can hardly tell where the imaginary line lies. The "line" in fact is more like a single point between the two figures — and the camera rotates around it (and above it and below it) with a freedom and speed unprecedented in American film.

It's worth noting too that Hitchcock strove to keep these unusual filming methods a secret. As Stefano told Skerry, Hitchcock stoutly insisted that the script should not reveal exactly what the murder would look like — just in case the text got leaked. Stefano certainly appears to have complied; the script's relatively brief and straightforward description gives no idea how dizzying and dazzling Marion's death would look on film.

Yet the scene's elusive, fragmentary nature was not used solely to disorient viewers; the very era in which *Psycho* appeared made an indirect presentation absolutely crucial. To put it bluntly, neither the Production Code nor the mid-century audience — weaned on Doris Day and *Leave It to Beaver*— could possibly tolerate the clear, graphic knifing of a naked woman. So the quick cuts prevent us from getting an exact view of what we aren't supposed to see.

Similarly, the cuts also help conceal Mother's identity. In Rebello's words, "the sequence was a masterstroke. Hitchcock simultaneously succeeded in titillating and shocking the viewer while concealing the nudity of the victim and the true identity of the attacker" (117).

Indeed, Naremore writes that the fleeting nature of the shots prevents "an alienating nausea" in viewers; and David Sterritt goes so far as to state that the scene's refusal to depict graphic violence or nudity presents "a paradoxical suggestion of squeamishness and a bizarre sort of tact in the midst of horrific violence" (108).

Thus, the scene never clearly shows us Marion's naked body, or the knife plunging in, or blood squirting out. Significantly, it never even shows blood on Marion's body — all of which betokens a respect for victims and viewers which contemporary cinema no longer finds necessary.

In the featurette "The Making of *Psycho*" — available on both the 1999 and 2008 DVD releases — Leigh insists that the film has endured

> because of the restrictions that were put on us.... It's fairly uncomplicated to take a picture of a lethal weapon apparently slashing an obviously naked body with blood gushing in full view, which is tolerated today; but far more complex to present the *illusion* of that happening.... [Hitchcock] allowed the audience to create what they thought they saw. And when the audience becomes a part of the creative process, they're not going to forget that.

In considering the indirect presentation of unseemly material, we might also note the number of writers who interpret the scene in terms of sexual assault. Gene D. Phillips, for example, claims that the murder takes on "the nature of a symbolic rape, giving the dripping knife and the gushing shower nozzle a definite phallic significance" (164). Tying a vicious murder to rape might seem unlikely were it not for the fact that rape is often regarded as an act of violence, not sexuality.

Naremore broadens the idea somewhat, calling the scene a remarkable fusing of rape and revenge. This suggests that the rape is Norman's, and the revenge is Mom's. Or is Norman himself simply striking out against his mother, as represented by any and all females?

In any case, reading the scene as a rape can seem reductionistic. In Skerry's words, "We must remember that the knife may indeed be a symbol of the phallus, but that it is *not* a phallus" (322). Durgnat agrees, insisting that the crude equation of long weapons with phalluses ignores several important factors: "No knives desire a woman or give pleasure to the person in whom they're stuck, or start a new life. To that extent, the shower scene is *anti*-sexual." Durgnat goes so far as to assert that the scene evokes not so much lust and vice in the viewer as "*tenderness* towards the maternal body, first object of love to both sexes" (112).

Indeed, the whole sequence becomes much richer if we think of it this way. What may be the most remarkable insight about this scene comes from Bill Krohn, who notes that the only shot of knife-penetration occurs next to Marion's navel — and thus Norman is "striking at Marion's womb and at the scar which symbolizes separation from the mother" (230). There remains some question, however, about whether Norman is attacking the *loss* of this connection — or whether he is actually trying to sever it.

Skerry extends this idea in a fascinating manner: In attacking the womb of a young woman, Mom is attacking the very notion of family — the thing that makes it possible. In so doing, she prevents Marion from ever marrying and thus helps "kill off" the traditional cinematic happy ending (e.g., *Rear Window, North by Northwest*) in which star-crossed lovers like Sam and Marion finally overcome all the obstacles to their union.

Act III

Once the deed is done, Mother exits in a hurry, showing us, as Danny Peary points out, the depth of Norman's dementia: He's afraid Norman might catch him in the act!

Now that it's too late, Hitchcock seems content to reestablish the barrier between film and audience. The dying Marion reaches out to us — but gets only the curtain.

Spoto suggests that Marion is here fulfilling Norman's phrase about how we humans "scratch and claw, but only at the air, only at each other; and for all of it, we never budge an inch." That is indeed precisely what happens in the shower scene: Mom and Marion swipe at the air and at each other; and as the sequence ends, they are both more firmly fixed in their traps than ever — especially Marion, for whom escape has become literally impossible.

In token of that, as Durgnat observes, Marion bringing down the curtain suggests the actual moment she dies. Immediately afterward, the curtain hooks swing "like crazy bells" (117), bells that toll both her death and ours — for the camera puts us on the floor with her.

This last point is from Skerry, who also notes the prevailing downward movement in Act III — as well as the more leisurely pace of montage that serves to release tension after the brutal killing. Specifically, rather than 34 shots in 40 seconds (Act II), the final act features 11 shots in two minutes — including one that's more than a minute long.

This long shot — from Marion's dead eye to the Bates house seen out the window — effectively serves to continue transferring the narrative from Marion to Norman. Indeed, invoking the first name of Mrs. Bates, which isn't actually revealed until the film's climax, Skerry calls Act III "The Descent of Marion: The Ascent of Norman/Norma" (301).

But we shall deal with this narrative transfer in more detail in the ensuing chapter. For now, let's examine the brilliant symmetries in this final act:

In the track away from Marion's eye, the clockwise camera movement mirrors and reverses the "spiralling counterclockwise movement of the bloody water going down the drain" (Krohn 230).

In a similar reversal, we might recall Marion's earlier statement to the highway cop, explaining why she pulled off the road: "I couldn't keep my eyes open." Now she can.

Furthermore, if we see the peephole scene as the beginning of the shower sequence, then this final shot means the sequence is bracketed by close-ups of an eye.

Others look at it this way: Both the showerhead and the drain resemble eyes (the showerhead is shaped like an iris — a dark spot in the middle with lines radiating outward — and the drain is shown in conjunction with Marion's dead eye). Since the showerhead appears when Marion enters the tub, and the drain appears after she has died, the sequence begins with an "eye" that is the water's *source* and ends with an "eye" that is the water's *goal.*

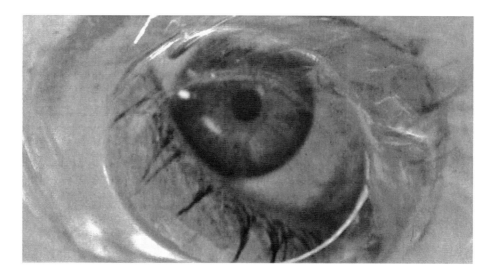

After the murder, the shower-drain shot dissolves into a close-up of Marion's eye, establishing a visual link between these images. Since the sequence also begins with a similar image, a head-on look at the showerhead, Hitchcock has bracketed his most famous scene with, at first, the water's source and, at the end, its destination. (©Universal Pictures; courtesy Universal Pictures–Photofest)

Let's conclude with Durgnat's assertion that as the camera looks out the window at the Bates mansion, it both reverses and echoes the film's initial entry into the Phoenix hotel room; thus Hitchcock begins Marion's storyline by looking into a hotel window — and concludes her narrative by looking back out of one.

* * *

Despite our lengthy examination of this relatively brief sequence, we have not yet done justice to its most vital aspect — namely, its stunning effect on viewers, especially those who first saw it in 1960.

We have already considered two major reasons for this: First, the rapid cuts and changes in subject combine to unsettle and disorient the audience; and second, the violent murder surprises first-time viewers who are just starting to experience relief over Marion's decision to return the money.

Note also how this differs from other horror films, where the murders often feel like "punishment" for bad behavior — usually teenagers having sex. In *Psycho*, the murder occurs *after* the character decides to do the right thing — and thus her death seems not merely shocking but downright senseless, meaningless, unnecessary.

In addition to the cuts and the relief, however, there are many other reasons for the scene's overwhelming impact.

To viewers in the 21st century, perhaps the oddest of these is the shocking shot of something that had never before been seen in an American film — something that, in the words of John Russell Taylor, would have "knocked the underpinnings out from under 90 per cent of an American audience" (254). That little something was: a toilet.

This was Stefano's idea. "I thought if I could begin to unhinge audiences by showing a toilet flushing, ... they'd be so out of it by the time of the shower murder, it would be an absolute killer" (Rebello 47).

In part, having Marion write in her bankbook serves to take an internal process from the novel — Marion's decision to return the money — and recreate it in strictly visual, nonverbal terms. More important, the need to then dispose of the figures allowed *Psycho* to come as close as possible to actual, physical bathroom procedures — by having torn paper thrown into the toilet and flushed down. (Note how the ghastly gurgle and gulp get emphasized when Herrmann's music cuts out just before the flush.)

Stefano told Skerry that he really had to fight the censors to include this scene. For modern viewers who wonder why the relatively bloodless *Psycho* caused such panic in its initial audiences, this little anecdote about the "shock" of seeing a toilet provides a great clue to American culture in that era. When average folks can't admit publicly that they use the bathroom several times a day, they're bound to feel stunned by a film that flirts with nudity, incest, and transvestitism.

Another reason for the scene's unnerving effect is its location in the shower and tub — a setting that combines "instability, vulnerability, and confinement," to use Neil Sinyard's telling phrase (113).

Naremore points out that this sense of helplessness only gets worse on repeated viewings — that it destroys any peace or pleasure we may at first have felt during Marion's shower; instead, knowing what's to come, we can only note "how soft, how incredibly vulnerable she is," with her "fragile arms" and her "long throat raised to catch the shower spray" (55).

On the other hand, the shower-bath setting is perhaps Hitchcock's greatest achievement in his oft-mentioned principle of bringing murder into an unexpected place — of having it occur not in a dark alley but in a place familiar and safe. After all, the shower is certainly a comfortable spot — private, warm, tranquil, secure, and clean; or at least it must have seemed that way until the arrival of *Psycho* — a film that left countless viewers unable to shower for months or years afterward.

In one oft-recounted story, Hitchcock received a letter from an angry father whose daughter had refused to take a bath since seeing *Diabolique* — with its deliriously scary bathtub scene; and now that she'd seen *Psycho*, she wouldn't take a shower either. Hitchcock's reply: Send her to the dry cleaners.

Less well known is the droll response of original *Psycho* author Robert Bloch to this phenomenon. As he writes in his delicious 1993 memoir *Once Around the Bloch*, "From time to time people come to me and volunteer the information that after seeing the film they were unable to take a shower. I can only tell them that they're lucky I didn't kill off my victim on a toilet seat" (232).

Andrew Sarris sums up this aspect of *Psycho*'s effect very nicely:

> You cannot commit a murder in a haunted house or dark alley, and make a meaningful statement to the audience. The spectators simply withdraw from these bizarre settings.... However, when murder is committed in a gleamingly sanitary motel bathroom during a cleansing shower, the incursion of evil into our well-laundered existence becomes intolerable. We may laugh nervously or snort disgustedly, but we shall never be quite so complacent again [*American* 57–58].

In addition to tubs and toilets, one can hardly ignore the effect of Herrmann's gut-wrenching music. Skerry posits that Herrmann's shrieking violins match both Marion's scream and the *screak* of the curtain-rings against the metal rod. As the attack begins, we are assaulted by three extremely uncomfortable sounds.

Nor can we overlook the element of guilt. Cult-movie expert Danny Peary sees guilt as key to the whole experience of *Psycho* — especially in the shower scene. In 1960, kids who had sneaked in against parents' wishes, and young men with arms around their dates, watched in guilty fascination as Marion disrobed and showered. Peary claims the death of Marion feels like punishment for this forbidden pleasure; he likens the killer's arrival to a mother bursting in on an adolescent boy perusing adult magazines.

Similarly, Philip J. Skerry, working with ideas from Cyndy Hendershot and Georges Bataille, discusses the relationship between "taboo and transgression" — namely, that when something is labeled "taboo," it instantly becomes more desirable. Citing American taboos against nudity and murder, Skerry posits an attraction-repulsion phenomenon in the shower scene, and suggests that this is why we keep returning to the scene. We want to see it, but we don't want to see it. In essence, that's probably why horror films in general have always been successful.

Perhaps more than all these factors, however, *Psycho* and its shower scene shocked viewers simply because this was not what folks had come to expect from Alfred Hitchcock. In a post–*Psycho* world, it is easy to forget that even before 1960, Hitchcock was already *the* most famous film director, and he didn't make this type of film. His previous hit — 1959's *North by Northwest* — was a splashy, colorful, larger-than-life spy adventure, complete with chases, microfilm, a femme fatale, and a smooth, sophisticated villain. Fans who came to *Psycho* expecting another film like this were in for a surprise.

As Stefano pointed out, neither Leigh nor Perkins — nor the screenwriter himself — had any prior association with a film like *Psycho*; and neither did the director: "There was no precedent for *Psycho* in Hitchcock's body of work" (Rebello 42). Indeed, we might call *Psycho* a "slasher movie"; Hitchcock of course had never made one of these. What's more, the genre itself barely even existed before *Psycho* came along.

Many of these comments, of course, describe the film as a whole, rather than the shower scene per se; but they are relevant in this context — because only at the shower scene does *Psycho* finally declare, in no uncertain terms, that it is indeed a horror film — a gothic film, a slasher film. Up to that moment, it's really a crime thriller, filled with the standard cinematic fare from decades of melodramas — illicit love, girls gone bad, stolen money, police pursuit.

A friend of mine who knew of *Psycho* but had never seen it was channel-surfing one night and came upon the film just after it had started. Having missed the opening titles, she told me she watched for more than half an hour before figuring out that she was seeing the most infamous horror movie ever made.

It seems likely most first-time viewers in 1960 had the same experience.

And if no one expected such a film from Hitchcock, viewers were equally unprepared to see the main character die less than half way through the film — especially one played by a major star like Leigh, who had already made 34 features, including *Angels in the Outfield* (1951), *Houdini, The Naked Spur* (both 1953), and *Touch of Evil* (1958). Indeed, this very shock effect is apparently what drew Hitchcock to *Psycho* in the first place. As he told Truffaut, "The thing that appealed to me and made me decide to do the picture was the suddenness of the murder in the shower, coming, as it were, out of the blue" (268–69).

Hitchcock exacerbates this effect by insisting that we identify with Marion throughout the preceding scenes. As we observed earlier, almost from the very first scene, we see what she sees, hear what she hears, feel what she feels. She looks out the car window, sees her Mr. Lowery, and thinks, "Oh no — it's my boss!"; at the same time, we look out the window and think, "Oh no — it's her boss!" In the following scene we, along with Marion, see the highway cop and think, "Uh-oh — the police!" We share her profound unease at the used car lot and, much later, her profound relief on deciding to return the money. In a sense, we *become* Marion Crane; and when she dies, a part of us dies with her.

As Stefano told interviewer Steve Biodrowski, "Audiences would be sucked into a character who did something wrong but was really a good person — they would feel as if they, not Marion, had stolen the $40,000. When she dies, the audience would become the victim!"

This profound victimization, the bewildering loss, also sets *Psycho* apart from modern horror films, many of which feature faceless characters dying in various grisly ways long before we've had a chance to know them — or to understand what it really means to lose a living, breathing soul to an untimely death. These films deal with dying the way pornography deals with sex — treating it as a purely physical phenomenon, a matter merely of flesh and fluid, with very little deeper significance. Such an approach is dishonest, suggesting there is nothing worse about death than the physical sensation ("I don't care if I die — I just don't want to die *that* way!"). In *Psycho*, on the other hand, we feel emotionally, even spiritually *wrecked*— as though the very soul of the film has been blotted out. We feel the *reality* of death — the way we might feel, for example, if a close friend or loved one suddenly passed away.

Several writers have commented on this crucial aspect of the scene.

William Rothman: "At this juncture we are completely bewildered. We are at a loss to know how this film could possibly go on, to know how the remaining half of its running time could be filled.... We believe we know who did it and why, and there is nothing further we wish to know.... Nothing we have viewed makes us wish to be drawn back into this world" (313).

James Naremore: The scene leaves us "unable to continue watching *Psycho* as if it were an ordinary movie" (59).

Robin Wood: "The murder ... constitutes an alienation effect so shattering that (at a first viewing of the film) we scarcely recover from it. Never — not even in *Vertigo*—has identification been broken off so brutally.... So engrossed are we in Marion, so secure in her potential salvation, that we can scarcely believe it is happening; when it is over, ... we are left shocked, with nothing to cling to, the apparent center of the film entirely dissolved" (146).

Durgnat insists that "Marion's body-identity is shattered by a man whose body-identity is shattered already," and thus the scene becomes "a *double* abolition of the human subject" (119) — that is, an assault of the very nature of classical narrative.

In this way, according to Skerry, *Psycho* with its shower scene "marks a boundary between two different worlds of cinema": on the one hand, studio films with big-name stars, linear narratives, happy endings, and carefully cen-

sored content — and on the other hand, "the cinema of sensation" (239), experimental works and independent films, stories of alienated outsiders in sordid
settings, films with more cynical and pessimistic themes. We might almost
say that with *Psycho*, Hitchcock helped kill off the very type of movie for
which he himself he was most famous.

Skerry's conclusion: "Hitchcock's shower scene is an attack — on the Production Code, on the studio system, on the star system, on the American family, on the American dream — and finally on the audience itself" (226).

10

He Had to Erase the Crime
Norman and Us

"After the surprise slaughter, the 1960 spectator needed a few good minutes to cool off," writes Raymond Durgnat.

Hitchcock provides this with nine wordless minutes of Norman tidying up after Mom; yet this scene hardly qualifies as *relaxing*.

In the first place, as Durgnat observes, if Hitchcock had really wanted to let viewers distance themselves from the recent horror, he would have chosen the "routine move" of "Meanwhile, back at Lowery's office..." (127). He's going to release some of the tension — but not too much!

Second, we'll admit that the movements and motives here — in contrast to the previous scene — bear at least some resemblance to our own daily lives (tidying, wiping, stowing, straightening); and more than one writer sees the scene as playing out Hitchcock's statements about his own personal bathroom etiquette: "When I leave the bathroom, everything is so clean you'd never know anyone had been in there" (Spoto, *Dark* 423).

Nevertheless, in spite of the apparent normality (or perhaps because of it), the scene ultimately gives us what Durgnat calls "the quintessence of Hitchcock's poetic vision"—a scene in which extreme horror "saturates a familiar, mediocre, everyday activity" (129). Indeed, as Harold Schechter has observed, the film as a whole is remarkably adept at using the most innocuously familiar people and places — a motel bathroom, a timid clerk, a little old lady — to fashion incarnations of the deepest shock and horror.

To initiate the familiar "everyday activity" in this scene, Norman closes the motel room window and then the door. At precisely this moment, Marion's newspaper appears at the bottom of the frame, and one word on it is clearly visible: NEW — a subtle way of letting us know that we are now watching a very different story from the one about Marion. Indeed, this scene effectively finalizes the transfer of our interest from Marion to Norman.

Skerry puts it this way:

Given Aristotle's notion of audience identification, "the killing of Marion creates for the viewer what Ortega y Gassett calls 'existential shipwreck': 'Instinctively, as do the shipwrecked he will look round for something to which to cling....' The piece of driftwood — or life preserver — that we cling to is thus the seemingly innocent, naïve, charming, boyish and attractive character of Norman" (224–25).

To put it more simply, there is now no one but Norman for us to care about or identify with. Yet Norman isn't really "innocent" or "naïve" — and we already know this. Indeed, Durgnat says that in this scene "the spectator goes from bad to worse"; that is, compared to our dubious empathy with Marion, this new identification with Norman is "far more guilty, hopeless and morally disturbing" (127–28).

In the 2008 DVD commentary, Stephen Rebello recalls that when he saw the film in 1960, women sitting behind him kept commenting aloud on "what a good boy" Norman is in this scene — and many of us may share a similar admiration for Norman's willingness to clean up after Mom and protect her from discovery. Yet at the same time, we acknowledge that it is not good for Marion's killer to remain undetected and unpunished.

We may admire the fact that Norman, once fascinated by Marion's body, shows absolutely no lascivious interest in it during this scene — and the camera shares his indifference, consistently refusing to show us the bloody body. However, the blood that we don't see on Marion is shown instead on Norman's hands.

We may even admire Norman's calmness in cleaning up the mess, but as Rothman points out, his logical and methodical approach strongly suggests that he has done this before — perhaps twice, to account for the two missing girls mentioned at the film's conclusion. And even if those girls didn't die in this room, Norman must certainly have known that "Mother" killed them. If so, then despite his insistence to the contrary, he knew all along that his mother really was "a maniac, a raving thing" — and that Marion was in mortal danger the minute she arrived at the motel.

Equally problematic is the subtle transformation of Norman that Durgnat observes during this sequence: He starts out horrified, nauseated, almost unstrung; he soon becomes brisk and efficient; and finally, standing beside the bog, he appears downright sardonic, even amused — much closer to the sort of hardened criminal that we might have trouble identifying with. Yet by now it is too late for us; we have already grabbed a piece of driftwood that is, apparently, rotten.

Perhaps the real problem here lies not with Norman but with us. As Naremore puts it, "If we feel somehow implicated in Norman's desire to smother the crime, it is because, even in the midst of our horror, we are relieved to see the gore disposed of, the immaculate bathroom restored" (61).

As this comment suggests, there's more going on here than simple concern about Norman. We viewers seem to have some deep-seated compulsion that manifests itself uncomfortably in scenes like this — the same sort of compulsion that led us to hope Marion would get away with her theft, even though intellectually we knew it was wrong. Perhaps it's a certain fastidiousness, a desire for things to be smooth and unruffled, for the maintenance and restoration of order and tranquility — a desire so deep and so strong that it often trumps our reason and our innate sense of right and wrong. If so, then David Sterritt's essay is right on the money; *Psycho* really is a film about "anal-compulsive behavior"— about the desire to flush away filth and dirt, which is essentially what Norman does in this scene.

Nowhere is this more apparent than at the end of this sequence, when Norman sinks Marion's car into the bog. During one of my many screenings of the film for teenagers, at the point when the car suddenly stops sinking in this scene — when it halts with its white top standing out boldly against the black water — there was a stunned silence in the classroom, during which one student was heard to say firmly, "Oh, man — that would *suck!*"

Funny, yes — but this is precisely the reaction we all have. And maybe that really isn't so funny. Because it means we are hoping that the crime will remain concealed — hoping, by extension, that the killer will get away with it and go on to kill again someday.

This is *Psycho*'s take on the famous "Hitchcockian transfer of guilt" that was first pointed out by Eric Rohmer and Claude Chabrol in their landmark study *Hitchcock: The First Forty-Four Films.* As Rohmer and Chabrol see it, moral culpability in Hitchcock films is often transferred to a relatively good character from a bad one (as in, for example, *Strangers on a Train* and *Frenzy*). In the case of *Psycho*, however, guilt is transferred not between characters, but rather *from the film to the viewer. Psycho* works not merely because it makes us nervous or fearful; *Psycho* makes us *guilty*. In a sense, it reveals some deep inherent guilt — because something within us instinctively identifies with criminals and killers. In this way, *Psycho* is disturbing on a far deeper level than your average horror film.

A few other observations on this fascinating sequence:

First: Watch closely when Norman goes into the motel office for his mop and bucket. As he turns out the inside light, a sharp slanted shadow appears on the closed door, making the framework look alarmingly like a guillotine. Is this Hitchcock's way of suggesting who the killer really is?

Also, as Norman is driving toward the swamp, the camera fixes on the back of Marion's recently purchased car, giving us our first clear view of its license plate: NFB 418.

It's more than a little tempting to suppose that "NFB" gives us Norman's initials, and that the car's disappearance into the bog prefigures Norman's absorption by his mother.

The numbers add up to 13 — the second time this has happened in the film (the first was the address of the used car dealership), but this time around, it suggests more than bad luck: Thirteen may well be the age at which Norman killed his mother and her lover.

Regarding the "F" in "NFB," Leland Poague speculates that it stands for "Ford," and that Norman's family is somehow associated with this man whose automobiles transformed American culture; but this seems a bit tough to swallow. After all, how many people do you know with the middle name "Ford"? But it does enable Poague to point out that, except for Sam's Dodge pickup, every car in *Psycho* is a Ford: both of Marion's vehicles, the highway patrol car, Arbogast's Mercury — technically a Ford product (the script specifies "a white Ford sedan"), even the battered jalopy that Lila later passes behind the motel, which appears to be an ancient Model A. It makes one wonder about the fact that Ford co-sponsored *Alfred Hitchcock Presents*.

But regarding Norman's moniker, many viewers prefer Tim Dirks's suggestion that "F" stands for "Francis" — a much more common male middle name that also happens to extend *Psycho*'s avian motif, since the best-known bearer of this name was a saint closely associated with birds.

As for the bog itself: Rebello relates that the final swamp sequence was filmed using a man-made lake at Universal-Revue studios, "one of many such large backlot waterways maintained by the studio for films and TV shows." To help "dramatize the bland topography" of the area, and to create a moodier *mise-en-scène* for the disappearing car, art director Robert Clatworthy painted an 8'-by-20' canvas of reeds and shrubbery for a backdrop to this scene.

The sinking auto, however, required more effort. As assistant director Hilton A. Green told Rebello:

> We built a hydraulic device into the ground very much like an automatic garage door opener. We pushed the car in and the car clamped on as it hit. The device turned and pivoted a little bit, then pulled the car down steadily at a certain tempo, then stopped cold — all mechanically done. You could only do it once, or else you'd have to clean up the whole car and set it up for reshooting the following day. It was done in one take, but it was another scene that took an awful lot of preparation [Rebello 125–26].

Stefano's original script contains an extension of the cleanup scene, with Norman hosing down the tire marks from Marion's car, then going up to the house and finding a bloodstained dress and shoes outside Mother's bedroom door. From an extremely high angle, we then see Norman descending the stairs with this unsightly bundle — and after that, a long shot of the house with smoke coming out the chimney, as Norman disposes of yet more evidence.

Durgnat points out that the extremely high angle over the landing would have been the first of three such shots in the film, and would have helped mask the oddness of the other two — which, occurring when Arbogast dies and when Mom is carried to the cellar, are necessary to conceal Mom's identity.

This dress-and-chimney sequence was filmed, but cut during editing; also omitted was a scripted moment near the bog when Norman is unsettled by an airplane buzzing overhead. This could easily have been linked to other elements in the film: the opening aerial view of Phoenix; a scripted reference to a bothersome fly in the initial hotel room scene; and of course, the film's final line ("She wouldn't even harm a fly"). All of this suggests that Hitchcock was working out a sort of "fly-on-the-wall" motif in the film, a sense that someone is always watching — often from above.

More generally, the cleanup scene as a whole has a dual function that complements our identification with Norman:

On the one hand, the scene reminds us that it really isn't so easy to eliminate a human being — especially as Norman must collect up, one at a time, the disparate remains of Marion's existence. After all, how many other horror films spend nearly ten minutes showing us a killer disposing of the body?

On the other hand, removing all that remains of Marion seems far too easy; note how quickly and completely the physical evidence of her life is packed up and sealed away. More to the point, as Durgnat observes, Marion is given an alarmingly thorough, four-fold burial: in a curtain, in a trunk, in a car, in a swamp. And Durgnat adds that this annihilation is underlined when the car sinks into a black swamp, and the black swamp then fades into a black screen — "a sort of 'doubled finality'" (138).

Yet emotionally at least, Marion is not so easily forgotten — as the next scene makes painfully clear.

11

If You Still Haven't Come to Your Senses

Sam and Arbogast

When *Psycho* fades in on the letter Sam is writing in the back room of his store, it's almost as though the film were starting all over again — like we're back at square one. Indeed, several elements in this scene distinctly recall that opening scene in the Phoenix hotel room. Not only is this the first time we've seen Sam since then, but other links are provided by the long tracking shot across the hardware store — echoing the slow series of pan-and-zoom shots to the first scene's window; by the discussion of lunch for Sam's clerk — recalling the movie's opening line ("Never did eat your lunch, did you?"); and especially by Sam's letter, which references much of what he and Marion talked about on that sultry afternoon.

Yet if the film has indeed "re-started," we must recognize that the main players will be different — and we are about to meet two new ones.

One of them is Marion's sister, Lila. She is played by Vera Miles, who had already worked with Hitchcock on *The Wrong Man* (1956) and on "Revenge," a 1955 episode of *Alfred Hitchcock Presents*—one of only 20 teleplays that Hitchcock directed. But to Hitchcock fans, Miles is perhaps best known as the woman who almost starred in *Vertigo*.

Hitchcock was so impressed by Miles in "Revenge" that he used it as the series premiere, bumping the originally scheduled episode, "Breakdown," starring Joseph Cotten. After *The Wrong Man*, Hitchcock signed Miles to a five-year contract, hoping he had found another Grace Kelly or Ingrid Bergman; he even hired legendary costumer Edith Head to oversee Miles's public appearance.

Miles was slated for the female lead in *Vertigo*; but when filming was delayed, she had to bow out due to pregnancy. She was philosophical about losing her role in what many regard as the greatest movie ever made: "Hitchcock got his picture," she said. "I got a son." But Hitchcock, in Rebello's words, "fumed like a rebuffed suitor." After all, he'd already lost two other major stars — Kelly and Bergman — who had put their personal lives before their careers.

All this is worth noting because it may well explain why the radiant Miles — who lit up the screen in such films as *The Searchers* and *Autumn Leaves* (both 1956) — could look so unbearably plain in *Psycho*. As Rebello describes it, she was still under contract to Hitchcock, and "in what could only be regarded as a comeuppance, Hitchcock tossed his would-be ice goddess a drab, underdeveloped part," dressing her in a thick coat throughout, "like a dowdy old-maid schoolteacher." Worse, Miles had just had her head shaved for a role in *5 Branded Women* and had to wear a frumpy-looking wig for *Psycho* (Rebello 64–73).

In fairness, Hitchcock may have toned down Miles's looks "to ward off any distracting hints of romance between Sam and Lila" (McGilligan 588); and Durgnat further defends the "drabbing down" of Miles by observing that nearly everything in the second half of the film is plainer, quieter, more low key: "It's as if, with Marion's death, all joy, all sensual shine, has gone from this world.... (Gavin, too, is drabbed down — no more beefcake)" (147).

Even the music is low key. Years ago, back when two-sided vinyl records were a music staple, I bought a rare Italian import of the *Psycho* soundtrack. Side 1 featured everything up to and including the shower murder — and it didn't take me long to notice how strident and piercing Side 1 was compared to the much quieter and more subdued Side 2. Flipping the record was like putting on an entirely different album.

The second half of the film works much the same way. Hitchcock told Truffaut, "As the film unfolds, there is less violence because the harrowing memory of [the] initial killing carries over to the suspense passages that come later" (277). Hitchcock told interviewers Ian Cameron and V. F. Perkins that as the film goes on, "there's less and less violence because it has been transferred to the minds of the audience" (quoted in Sarris, *Interviews* 244).

Naremore explains: "The murder of Marion Crane has generated such anxiety in the audience that the suspense mechanics of the plot can do their job without much further help from Hitchcock [or Herrmann!]. As he told Peter Bogdanovich, 'The audience goes through the paroxysms in the [rest of] the film without consciousness of Vera Miles or John Gavin. They're just characters that *lead* the audience through the final part of the picture'" (60).

Indeed, it's not entirely accurate to suggest, as we did in Chapter 10, that the second half of *Psycho* belongs to Norman. Rather, Sam and Lila — together

with the other new character, Detective Arbogast — also demand identification, functioning as projections of our fear and curiosity. This is made
abundantly clear when Arbogast first arrives at Sam's hardware store.

Entering via the front door, he is shown in an uncomfortable close-up;
except for the shots of Marion's mouth and eye in the shower scene, it's certainly the largest close-up in the film. His approaching face completely fills
the frame just as Sam asks Lila, "What 'thing' could we be in together?" The
answer is obvious: We are all in *Psycho* together — and Arbogast will soon be
the chief representative for Sam, Lila, and the audience.

Yet despite these new developments, what's most impressive about this
scene are its compelling ironies — ironies such as Lila's line about wanting
to find Marion "before she gets in this too deeply." Having been killed
and buried in a bog, Marion is already "in too deep" — in more than one
sense.

Or how about Arbogast's assertion that Marion is "not back there with
the nuts and bolts"; since Marion did go temporarily crazy and flee Phoenix,
this line puns on the alternate meanings of "nuts" and "bolts." (Cf. the gag
in 1999's *Runaway Bride*, where the flight of the reluctant young lady — who
also works in a hardware store — is described by this tabloid headline: "Hardware Honey Goes Nuts and Bolts!")

Indeed, the opening portion of this scene may be the most richly ironic
60 seconds in the film — starting with Sam's letter to Marion. This appears
only briefly, and it's often missed nowadays by viewers watching on a small
screen; so here it is in its entirety:

> Dearest right-as-always Marion:
>
> I'm sitting in this tiny back room which isn't big enough for both of us, and sud-
> denly it *looks* big enough for both of us.
> So what if we're poor and cramped and miserable, at least we'll be happy!
> If you haven't come to your senses and still

At this point, Sam turns the paper over and the camera pulls away; but
we have already seen enough to understand that another layer of anguish has
been added to the horrific murder: Sam would have wed Marion even without the stolen money. If he'd been willing to make this commitment in the
first scene — or if she had simply waited about ten days — she would still be
alive; and she'd be well on the way to fulfilling her desperate dreams of marriage and respectability.

On a narrower level, the letter reminds us of several other uncomfortable truths: that Marion is *not* "right-as-always" — either now or when she
committed larceny; that at this moment, stuffed in a trunk, she is indeed

"cramped and miserable"; that she will never again "come to her senses." Even the final word we see — "still" — suggests her lifelessness; and the fact that Sam doesn't finish his sentence may betoken Marion's foreshortened life — the failure of goals that Sam's letter never manages to articulate.

Lesley Brill extends some of these ideas: "In one of the grimmer clusters of ironic jokes in *Psycho*, Marion's dreams of domestic fulfillment half come true, but only after she dies." For example, Norman carries Marion's body over a motel room threshold, precisely as a groom would do with his bride. And not only does Sam manfully accede to marriage, but later — particularly during exchanges with the sheriff and his wife — Sam and Lila will play out "the sort of domestic scenes that Marion hoped to buy with Cassidy's money" (228): living room evenings with a middle-aged couple; Sunday church; family dinner invitations; even posing as husband and wife to check into a cheap motel. This last instance recalls the opening scene, when Sam claimed married couples sometimes did this deliberately; and the invitation to dine at the sheriff's home is exactly the type of respectable scenario Marion once envisioned with Sam.

Yet there is more irony to come. As the camera leaves Sam's letter and tracks backward through the store, we hear a middle-aged female customer speculating about a can of "Spot Insect Killer": "They do not tell you whether or not it's painless; and I say insect or man, death should always be painless."

In case we aren't thinking what a contrast this makes with the brutal slaying we watched a mere 12 minutes earlier, we can clearly see a display of large knives mounted on the wall behind this woman. On the floor to the right are several bags labeled "Peat Moss," which comes from swamps and thus recalls the bog where Marion's painfully hacked-up body now lies.

And in case this all seems a matter of mere chance, it's worth noting that the script specifically stipulates "a display of various size carving knives" in this scene. In fact, during the hardware store scene later that night, Stefano's first draft called for a shower nozzle to fall to the floor. (Eagle-eyed viewers will note that in this later store scene, a display of shower nozzles is visible on Lila's left as a breeze kicks up just when Sam departs to look for Arbogast.)

But this is not just a matter of a few knives lying about; Naremore observes that Sam's store "looks like a torture chamber," crammed with scythes, axes, saws, weed killer, insecticides, and a sign saying "tools sharpened." "Murder and mayhem," Naremore concludes, "are being contrasted with small town niceness, as if the grotesque horrors were related to the bland surface" (62).

Nowhere is this more apparent than in the "insect lady," who in the

A finicky hardware store customer worrying about whether "Spot Insect Remover" hurts the bugs when it kills them; but the viewer recalls that some deaths are not especially "painless." (©Universal Pictures; courtesy Universal Pictures–Photofest)

script is heard to add, "All I can do is hope if it isn't painless, it's quick!" The script says that she gives a "delicious bite" to the word "quick"—and that she "nods happily" and exits the store.

In the finished film, this is all condensed to a prim and precise "Thank you" as she pays for her purchase—which is almost worse: It didn't take her more than a moment to overcome her scruples about killing! Durgnat goes so far as to say that "the insect lady as a serial killer is a 'normal' version of Mrs. Bates..." (154). After all, it's Mrs. Bates who concludes the film by claiming ironically that "she wouldn't even harm a fly."

All of this, from Sam's letter to the female customer, is accomplished in about 90 seconds; and such notable economy—including the excision of the bug lady's dialogue—reflects Hitchcock's determination to keep the second half of *Psycho* moving steadily toward its resolution. This hardware store scene, for example, runs less than four minutes, vigorously condensed from nearly 11 pages in the script—not to mention three omitted pages of additional dialogue between Sam and Lila after Arbogast leaves.

While much of this deleted material seems extraneous, some of it is quite revealing.

First, excised dialogue between Sam and Lila makes it clear that Cassidy himself was the one who hired a private detective instead of going to the police; this lets us know that when Marion imagined his reaction ("I'll take it out of her fine soft flesh"), she was indeed being cruel to herself— and per-haps unfair to him as well.

On the other hand, in the omitted dialogue, Lila tells us that Cassidy "talked so loud and so fast, and I ... I should've called the police"— to which Sam responds, "He must have had a darn good reason for wanting to keep them out of it... All that cash...." If Cassidy was really angry, but specifically didn't want the cops involved, then perhaps the $40,000 was "dirty money." After all, Cassidy did suggest it was undeclared income.

An equally small but intriguing point is made when Sam, having learned of the theft, indicates his respect for Marion's probity: "I can't believe it. Can you?" In the film, Lila doesn't answer; she merely glances downward — an efficient way of conveying her doubt, which is much more obvious in the script:

SAM: I don't believe it. Do you?
LILA: Yes ... I just ... did. The moment they told me....
SAM: You might have doubted for say five minutes or so, Sister.

Stefano was upset by this omission; along with some later omitted mate-rial on Marion's early years with her sister (see Chapter 13), it's one of the few moments when we see that Sam actually feels a sense of loss and love for Mar-ion. "Any time I tried to get across a few seconds of silent memory for a lost life, it got cut," Stefano complained to Rebello (145).

And finally, there's a telling moment between Sam and Lila just before Arbogast enters:

SAM: Is Mary ... in trouble?
LILA: Yes.
SAM: Well why didn't she come to me ... call me...?
LILA: Not that kind ... You men and your egos.

So much for Durgnat's suggestion that Marion and Sam weren't sleep-ing together.

Yet Lila's final reflection is appropriate; the famous "male ego" has already caused a lot of trouble in the film: Sam's refusal to wed until he can provide for a wife; Cassidy flaunting his $40,000; Norman's defiance of his mother's wishes.

And the male ego will cause even more trouble in the following scene.

12

People Just Come and Go
Arbogast and Norman

In pursuing the truth about Marion, Arbogast now "becomes virtually our agent, the instrument of our curiosity" (Naremore 62). This is certainly aided by the "ordinariness" of this particular private detective. As Durgnat observes, he is not a genius like Sherlock Holmes, or a moral warrior like Raymond Chandler's Marlowe; he's just a regular fellow doing his job. Arbogast has a strong "everyman" quality that invites us to identify with him, just as we identified earlier with Marion—and Norman.

Durgnat is also helpful in pointing out something that is easy to miss even after repeated viewings: Arbogast really is a pretty good detective. "He knows every trick in the thousands of books about salesmanship. He elicits sympathy from his 'prospect' (or suspect), acts weary but hopeful, switches deftly between disarming reassurance and light threat, shoots the sudden direct question." He is, Durgnat concludes, the first "cunningly deferential" detective in the movies—a precursor, perhaps, to TV's Columbo (158).

More specifically: Arbogast catches Norman in his inconsistencies (Norman can't know that Marion "didn't make any phone calls" because he wasn't with her all night long); he pitches two very plausible theories (that Norman is serving as Marion's accomplice—or that she somehow fooled him); most strikingly, he even manages to discover that Marion stayed in Cabin 1—and he is later able to pass this information on to Lila.

Unless Norman wrote her cabin number in the registration book (there is no indication of this in the film), the only way Arbogast could have deduced this is by observing Norman's hesitation with his armload of sheets at the door of Cabin 1. That's some pretty observant sleuthing; among other things, it must have suggested to Arbogast that Marion was still at the motel—probably hiding out in Cabin 1.

Yet at the same time, Arbogast's knowledge is limited, and most of his guesses are wrong. Durgnat points out that in many mystery stories, the detective knows more than we do (at least until the end) — whereas in *Psycho*, we know more than Arbogast. Yet even *our* superior knowledge is limited! "Like everyone else in the film," Durgnat writes, "Arbogast swerves between being half-right (inspiring hope — but also fear of running into the unpredictable Mrs. Bates) and half-wrong (generating frustration/despair). As a form of suspense, it's more intricate by far than 'hope against fear,' for this hope *brings* fear..." (158).

And this indeed is part of the exquisite intricacy and complexity of the dialogue between Arbogast and Norman in the motel office. The fact is that while we identify with Arbogast and want him to find the truth, we also identify with Norman and hope he can conceal it.

Yes, says Durgnat, Norman is deceitful in this scene — but "in a vulnerable way." As he fumbles and stutters before Arbogast's inquiries, viewers recognize their own experiences; after all, who hasn't squirmed in a similar fashion while trying to dodge uncomfortable questions? "The dramatic dialog," Durgnat writes, "becomes a conflict inside our own psyches" — a conflict between wanting to see justice done and hoping Norman can get off the hook (156–57).

Certainly our concern for Norman reflects our knowledge that he is still valiantly trying to protect his mother; and his apparent likability — his *ordinariness* — is further stressed by the bag of "Kandy Korn" from which he's eating when Arbogast pulls up. (This was Perkins's idea; the script has him darning one of his own socks.)

More important, the tension of our alliance with both men is heightened by the editing in this scene — by what Krohn calls its "jazzy rhythm" (224), stemming partly from the fact that two cameras were running continuously throughout the scene. Indeed, the editing in this sequence is almost as skillful as that in the shower scene — particularly because it calls so little attention to itself, despite the many cuts. George Tomasini reportedly spent three or four days editing this relatively brief scene — in part because the vocal tracks on the various takes didn't match up with one another.

Durgnat has observed that the scene contains very few "two-shots" of both men. Certainly the separated shots of Arbogast and Norman heighten both tension and clarity in the dialogue — yet the repeated shifts are prevented from being monotonous or formulaic by slight but constant shifts in angle, closeness, lighting, and background, as well as the fact that the cuts don't always occur precisely when the speaker changes.

And let's not forget the acting — so effective that after the first take, when Hitchcock had run his actors all the way through it, the technicians on the set burst into applause. After this initial shoot, Perkins told Hitchcock that he and Martin Balsam had worked up a somewhat more improvisational version — one in which the two actors sometimes spoke over each other — and asked if they could try it this way. As Stephen Rebello observes in the 2008 DVD commentary, this rendition was greeted with even louder applause — and after seeing it, Hitchcock tore up the storyboards for the scene and threw them away.

"So much for Hitchcock being dictatorial and thinking that actors were cattle ...," Rebello remarks.

As it appears in the actual film, the scene's overlapping dialogue has a sizzling electricity, a realism, a feeling of being virtually unrehearsed; and indeed, the scene in its final version shows subtle and continuous alterations to the dialogue as originally written — perhaps more so than anywhere else in the film.

The script, for instance, provides this line when Norman refers to his mother late in the scene: "She's ... ill. Confined to her room. It's practically living alone." Here's what Perkins actually says in the film: "She's — she's an invalid — an invalid. Uh, it's, uh, *practically* like living alone."

As another example, here is what Stefano wrote when Norman finally admits that Marion was at the motel:

> NORMAN: She was sitting back there, no she was standing up, with some sandwich still in her hand, and she said she had to drive a long a long way.
> ARBOGAST: Back where?
> NORMAN: What do you mean?
> ARBOGAST: You said she was sitting "back there," or standing rather....

Compare this to the finished film:

> NORMAN: Uh, she was, she was sitting back there — no, no, she was standing back there — with a sandwich in her hand, and she said, uh, she had to go to sleep early because she had, uh, a long drive, uh, ahead of her.
> ARBOGAST: Back where?
> NORMAN: Back where, uh, she came from.
> ARBOGAST: No, you said before that she was sitting back, standing back there....

This long exchange is worth quoting partly because it shows an almost improvisational approach to the script in this scene, but also because it reveals one of *Psycho*'s saddest ironies — one that has gotten virtually no attention in the many writings on the film. Apparently added on the spot, Norman's declaration that Marion was going "back where she came from" is the story's one and only fleeting opportunity for someone from the outside world to learn that Marion had changed her mind about the theft.

If Arbogast had been more attentive, he might have been able to relate this information to Lila later on the phone; this would certainly have given solace to Marion's sister and boyfriend, letting them know the theft was only an aberration in Marion's life, that she hadn't really lost her mind — that she somehow returned to sanity before her death.

Yet this priceless fact is simply ignored, flung to the wind, blotted out — like Marion's other possessions, like her hopes and dreams ... like her life itself.

* * *

Before we get to the second murder, let's look at a few points about the scenes leading up to it.

First, Arbogast's phone call to Lila moves the plot forward in a swift and efficient little vignette, giving Sam and Lila all the information they need to finish the investigation. Furthermore, Durgnat points out that Arbogast asks to talk to Lila, not Sam — instinctively recognizing that she is the stronger, more active, less patient of the two. We also see, as the murder approaches, that Arbogast is becoming softer, more human, more likable — telling Lila she'll be "happy to know" that he no longer suspects Sam of being involved with Marion's theft.

In addition, Arbogast's return to the Bates Motel gives rise to two questions contemporary viewers frequently ask when watching the film:

Among other things, they want to know why Arbogast slides across the front seat to get out the passenger side of the car (he did it on his first visit, too). The likely answer: Cars of yesteryear were a lot bigger than today's, and front seats were generally one complete piece, not separated as they are now by a gear shift or storage compartment; so it could legitimately take more time and energy to exit the driver's side and walk all the way around the car.

More important, eagle-eyed modern-day viewers want to know how Norman-Mom knew that Arbogast had returned; in other words, how did Norman manage to get into his dress and be ready for the murder before Arbogast got to the house?

The answer is simple: Immediately after the phone call, there is a dissolve to the motel, and we see Norman standing on the porch holding bed sheets. If you watch carefully, you can see him looking off toward the highway, where he must certainly be spotting Arbogast's approaching car. He then moves more quickly along the porch, away from the office, and makes a left between the two sets of cabins. The motel, you see, is shaped like an L, but there's a space between the two sections; later in the film, Lila moves toward the house by walking through what the script calls "the small alley at the end of this L of cabins"; that must be what Norman does here, to head up to the house in preparation for Arbogast's return.

Originally, Hitchcock wanted Norman to turn right and head straight to the house after seeing Arbogast's car; writer Stefano insisted that Norman walk *away* from the house, lest viewers get suspicious and connect him to the murders.

And finally, there's a small continuity error as Arbogast leaves the office and decides to go up to the Bates mansion. When he first looks up at the house, the sky behind it is clear, dark, blank; then, when we see him walking up the steps a second or so later, the sky is replete with light, fleecy clouds. It's a careless error, yes — but it's the only serious continuity error this writer has noticed in well over 100 viewings. Few other films could stand up under such repeated scrutiny.

As for the second killing, Rebello's research tells us that Hitchcock regarded the murder of Arbogast as even more crucial than the shower scene — and indeed, it required similarly complex preparation.

The interiors of the Bates home were filmed on the famous Phantom Stage built for the 1925 silent version of *The Phantom of the Opera*, starring Lon Chaney. Built to accommodate five tiers of opera house seats along with underground catacombs, it was the perfect choice for a home requiring three stories and high camera angles. According to Rebello, Hitchcock especially relished the fact that the Bates staircase was built on the same spot where the chandelier fell in Chaney's *Phantom*.

In Bloch's original novel, Arbogast's death takes place on the house's front porch; Hitchcock moves it to a vertiginous staircase — where the crew ran into some problems in filming both the ascent and descent of the victim.

After extensive rehearsals, Hitchcock was ready to film Arbogast's stairway ascent — and then he came down with a flu bug that had already hit Vera Miles and others on the crew. So assistant director Hilton A. Green handled the shoot while talking on the phone to Hitchcock at home. But when Green and script supervisor Marshall Schlom later showed their rough cut to Hitchcock, he rejected it at once.

As the director told François Truffaut that the sequence they'd filmed featured "a shot of [Arbogast's] hand on the rail, and of feet seen in profile, going up through the bars of the balustrade.... As that sequence was cut, it wasn't an innocent person but a sinister man who was going up those stairs" (273). In other words, the sequence as filmed created an aura of menace around the victim, not the killer.

For this reason, Hitchcock determined to shoot the ascent from the top of the staircase, with the camera moving backward as Arbogast comes up the steps.

This shot — along with the descent after the stabbing — required a complicated "metal bipod run by pulleys that would lift a cinematographer and a relatively lightweight camera to the upper reaches of the soundstage on over-head tracks built to run parallel to the stairs" (Rebello 123). But this system also required the camera operator to run the camera and manipulate the focus at the same time. Green told Rebello that two camera operators as well as an assistant cameraman were eventually required, since the camera also pans right during this extremely complicated shot.

Focus in the ascent was particularly crucial, since the viewer's attention is fixed on Arbogast's face as he climbs. His subsequent backward fall during the murder, however, was another matter.

Leigh's book on *Psycho* seems to indicate that Arbogast's descent was done live, with some sort of chair contraption to hold Martin Balsam and move him backward down the stairs. In that account, Green is quoted as saying, "I think Marty Balsam did suffer some minor back problems from the shot" (85).

He may have suffered back problems, but it wasn't from moving backwards down the stairs. As recounted in Rebello, in Krohn's *Hitchcock at Work*, and by Hitchcock himself in the Truffaut interviews, the scene involved rear projection.

In other words: First, they rolled the film while moving the camera forward down the empty stairs; the resulting footage was then projected onto a screen behind Balsam as he sat on an out-of-sight chair, waving his arms and pretending to fall backward.

Most modern viewers find this process shot unconvincing. As Durgnat observes, "Arbogast loses his footing so early that he'd have slithered down half the stairs flat on his back" (173). Younger viewers often laugh at this scene because "it looks so fake."

Nevertheless, the second murder works. In the words of William Rothman, "The murder of Arbogast is, if anything, even more terrifying than the shower-murder sequence" (315). Internet writer Tim Dirks calls it "one of the most horrific murder scenes in film history." Even hardened modern-day teens sometimes jump or shout when Mom appears in this sequence. During a classroom showing I oversaw in the 1980s, one young lady shrieked so loudly that I had to rewind the scene and show it again; the entire class had turned to look at the screamer and completely missed the murder!

So why does the scene work so well, in spite of its artificiality?

For some viewers, the deliberate artifice gives the scene "the clarity and strangeness of events in a dream" (Naremore 15). Indeed, on the 2008 DVD commentary, Rebello indicates that Hitchcock didn't want this scene to be "realistic"; he deliberately used rear projection because "he loved the idea of free floating," and he wanted the sequence to be "stylized and bizarre."

But much of the scene's effectiveness also seems due to the very high camera angle used when Mother comes out of her room; we are looking directly down from a height of 20 or 25 feet, giving us a sensation of hanging in midair. Then, in the tracking shot *down* the stairs, we feel as though we are leaning forward at a precarious angle — and thus about to topple right down the steps along with Arbogast. This sensation of leaning a bit too far forward is heightened by the fact that the camera is actually moving forward — as though we were already beginning to fall.

These queasy sensations would have been considerably greater if Hitchcock had decided to use an idea proposed by art director Robert Clatworthy: He wanted to put the camera inside a large medicine ball with a hole cut in it for the lens — and then run the camera as the ball rolled over and over down the stairs, with Mom and her knife in hot pursuit. One imagines a kaleidoscopic whirlwind of half-blurred images rushing repeatedly past the lens — like the dizzying shower scene, but without cuts.

In any case, the scene as conceived and shot certainly conveys a loss of equilibrium. Naremore calls this Hitchcock's "greatest fear, expressed in virtually every film he has made" (64) — though Neil P. Hurley claims that Hitchcock's greatest fears are acrophobia and claustrophobia.

It may be tough to pin down what Hitchcock was most afraid of, but there's no doubt that many viewers share the fear of enclosed spaces or of heights — and no doubt that the shower scene plays on one of these, while Arbogast's death plays on the other.

In addition to utilizing our fear of heights, the overhead shot achieves several other important effects:

First, it helps conceal the true identity of Mom, since we cannot see her very well. (In fact, Mom in this scene was played by a somewhat diminutive female double named Mitzi — not by Anthony Perkins.)

Second, Hitchcock told Truffaut that the overhead shot was used to startle viewers by making a contrast between image sizes on the screen. More specifically, in a single cut Hitchcock takes us from figures of the smallest feasible size — seen from high overhead — to a massive close-up of Arbogast's face.

And Krohn observes that just as in the shower scene, the "cut" of Mom's slashing knife is represented by the "cut" to the close-up of Arbogast.

William Rothman asserts that the "static framing" in the overhead shot "does not allow us to anticipate the precise instant of the attack" (316); this, together with the sudden shriek of Bernard Herrmann's violin cue, is enough to jolt us out of our seats — even though we already suspected that Arbogast was about to buy the farm.

Indeed, there is quite a contrast between this murder and the first one — most notably the gradual approach of Arbogast's death, as contrasted with the unexpected suddenness of Marion's. These two deaths, in fact, can be seen to encapsulate the difference between surprise and suspense that Hitchcock was so fond of discussing. The shower scene is surprising; the staircase scene is suspenseful. Yet in another sense, the careful cuts, angles, and sound in the second murder somehow manage to create both surprise and suspense in the same scene — which may be why some find it even more harrowing than the first murder.

And as a final note on this scene, we might observe that the fade occurs as Mom's knife plunges up and down, underlining another way in which Arbogast had stumbled on the truth without knowing it — namely, when he told Norman that "sick old women" are "usually pretty sharp."

13

A Bad Day Coming

Sam and Lila

With Arbogast out of the picture, we are left to focus on Sam and Lila, and in the subsequent scenes these two characters — especially Lila — will become our means of penetrating the recesses of the Bates homestead. To move toward this, Hitchcock also begins forging fate-like links between Lila and Norman-Mom — links that will culminate in a basement confrontation between these two strong-willed characters.

The first of these occurs when Sam leaves the hardware store to search for Arbogast at the Bates Motel. We see a headshot of Lila watching him leave, which dissolves to a shot of Norman standing by the swamp; as Durgnat has pointed out, the protuberant rakes behind Lila are echoed by the tree branches sticking up behind Norman in the ensuing shot. (Watch also for the display of shower nozzles to Lila's left during this shot.)

Sam's brief and fruitless search for Arbogast is in fact both preceded and followed by very similar dissolves involving Lila: After Sam has finished shouting for Bates, we see *another* shot of Norman at the swamp, and this shot *again* dissolves back to Lila in the store — as though the two are somehow connected.

More significantly, when Sam returns, Lila then runs the length of the store — approaching the camera — and arrives in a headshot carefully backlit so that we cannot see her face. This again links her to Norman-Mom, for the only other similarly backlit shot occurs when Mom pulls back the shower curtain before stabbing Marion.

Other links between Lila and Norman-Mom: The sheriff concludes his scene by asking, "Who's that woman buried out in Greenlawn Cemetery?" — and the camera then shows us Lila, as though she were somehow the answer to this question; and this headshot of Lila again dissolves to Norman. Later, when Lila is exploring the Bates home, she sees herself in Mom's mirror. And Lila, like Mom, is a "fierce avenger" (Durgnat's phrase). Perhaps most powerfully, in the final basement scene, Lila's shriek of horror is instantly echoed by Norman's high-pitched scream ("I am Norma Bates!"); in the script, Lila's cry is "joined" to Norman's, making one continuous scream. We might also mention the film's final moments, when the sheriff asks Lila if she's warm enough — linking her to Mom, who will shortly request a blanket because s/he "feels a little chill."

As intimated earlier, these parallels serve partly to foster a sense of Lila's destiny as the one who will discover the truth about Mom. So why do the links continue through the final example above — that is, even after the truth has been revealed? Well, earlier in the film, Marion's temporary insanity linked her to Norman, suggesting that even ordinary people "go a little mad sometimes." In the same way, perhaps the possibility of becoming Mrs. Bates also exists in a woman like Lila — or in Marion's catty fellow secretary, Caroline. Or the bug lady at the hardware store, who, like Mom, is afraid of harming flies. Perhaps in any woman, for that matter.

Yet as we follow Lila to the home of the sheriff and his wife, we can see that this older couple is also linked with the world of the Bates Motel.

When François Truffaut admitted that he felt "a letdown" during the scene with the sheriff, Hitchcock responded, "The sheriff's intervention comes under the heading of ... 'Why don't they go to the police?' I've always replied, 'They don't go to the police because it's dull'" (269). Yet some viewers relish the sheriff scene — partly because it resonates so deeply with many ideas and issues in the film.

Consider, for example, the unusual way Hitchcock shoots the exchange in the sheriff's living room. We might well have expected a series of shot–reverse shots alternating between Sam and Lila on the one side, and Mr. and Mrs. Chambers on the other; instead, we get several alternating shots with the sheriff's wife in the frame *both* times — which comes perilously close to making her seem like two persons. In addition, the décor in the Chambers home — with its columns, old-fashioned lamps, and wood-framed pictures — bears marked similarity to that of the Bates home and motel. (Though this didn't make it into the finished film, the script calls for roses on the Chamberses' wallpaper — a clear link to the decor in Marion's cabin.) All of this seems to suggest that the sheriff's home — like the lives of Lila and Marion — is only a few steps away from the madness of the Bates family.

But it is also possible to see the sheriff and his wife as a *contrast* to Norman and his mother — specifically, as a healthier and more normal male-female partnership. Consider, for example, the way the man and woman work together in this scene. In most of *Psycho*'s other male-female pairs, the woman seems to take the lead: Marion feels she has to steal money in order to elicit a commitment from Sam; Lila's restless assertiveness contrasts with the passivity of Sam, who wants to "sit still and hang on" rather than pursuing Arbogast; and certainly Mom is overseeing and directing virtually everything in Norman's daily life.

By contrast, Durgnat suggests that Mr. and Mrs. Chambers show us the working out of a *normal* "unisex tendency" that has gone haywire in Norman's life (187). Rather than domination and passivity, we get an almost unconscious cooperation — so smooth and natural that it's easy to miss.

The sheriff directs most of the conversation, asks questions, proposes solutions, reveals the story behind the deaths at the Bates Motel; his wife, meanwhile, supplements his narrative with additional information (Mrs. Bates's burial attire, Norman finding the couple "dead together — in bed!"); yet she is hardly a passive partner, as she also both proposes and initiates the phone call to Norman.

Perhaps nowhere does their mutual understanding appear more clearly than when Sam insists he saw Norman's mother: Knowing that Mrs. Bates is dead and this is therefore impossible, Mrs. Chambers glances with concern at her husband; he responds with the briefest of sidelong glances — a mere flicker that says volumes about their relationship, their common thinking, and their mutual understanding.

Speaking of which, Durgnat has pointed out another exquisitely low-key aspect of this scene: Sam and Lila, as they lay out their story, begin to feel a growing shame and embarrassment — about exposing Marion's crime to the police, and about how flimsy their worries sound. This growing uneasiness works to engage our sympathy for the young pair; yet like the sheriff's sidelong glance at his wife, it's amazingly subtle, almost subconscious — part of the intangible emotional subtext of film that is so difficult to reproduce in print.

Much of this subtlety — and much of the pleasure to be found in this scene — is due to the fine performance by John McIntire, best known to viewers as a supporting player in countless Western films (*The Far Country*, *The Tin Star*, *Winchester '73* and many others).

In fact, in a curious way, McIntire's familiarity as a Western star reminds us that, however normal and healthy this husband and wife may seem, "going to the police" does not provide a solution in *Psycho*. When Sam at first proposes a visit to "our deputy sheriff around here," it conjures up a mental picture of the very Western roles associated with McIntire's movies: a rangy, tough-looking dude with dusty boots, a Stetson, two pistols, and perhaps a belt of bullets — and much of this is present in the character of Chambers as he appears in Bloch's original novel. In the film, however, this mental image is quickly squelched by the sight of a pudgy, balding man with disheveled hair, descending the stairs in his plaid bathrobe, accompanied by his chipper, similarly bathrobed wife.

For all their "normalcy," the Chamberses are no match for the world of dementia and hatred represented by the Bates home. With their homey aura of nightgowns, Sunday church, and dinner invitations, the Chamberses ultimately join that group of people whose polite world seems utterly incapable of facing, defeating, or even understanding the evil that flourishes in their midst.

This world of civility was neatly exemplified much earlier by Arbogast's touching gesture in the foyer of the Bates home. Even though he is intruding into a forbidden place — a place to which Norman specifically refused entry — he takes off his hat! Other "polite but useless" gestures in the film: the sheriff asking if Lila is warm enough in the final scenes; Mrs. Chambers's dinner invitation to Sam and Lila; the car dealer offering Marion a cup of coffee; the concerned highway cop saying "please," and urging Marion to take better care of herself.

Note how many of these civil but futile gestures are associated with the police. It is perhaps significant that in the climax of Bloch's original novel, the sheriff arrives at the motel just in time to revive Sam, so that he can go save Lila from Norman. Hitchcock's version simply omits this; he has no such confidence in the police. To this end, it's worth keeping a close eye on John McIntire during the final scene at the police station. As the psychiatrist expounds the complexities of Norman's twin personae, Sheriff Chambers looks distant, dazed, befuddled, ineffectual — clearly out of his depth amid these bizarre and unexpected new developments.

In spite of all these important ideas, the real triumph of the sheriff scene occurs as Chambers asserts that Mrs. Bates has been dead for ten years. Since we've already seen and heard Mrs. Bates several times, first-time viewers can't understand how this is possible; like Sam, they respond by insisting that she certainly must be there. And while their heads are still spinning, Chambers concludes with another disorienting line: "Well, if the woman up there is Mrs. Bates, who's that woman buried out in Greenlawn Cemetery?"

Durgnat points out that this piece of dialogue has "sarcasm" that is "a touch thoughtful": "He delivers the line with eyes enquiringly wide open and face half-turned to the camera, as if intimating direct address to the audience, and we're just as bewildered as Sam.... Here's a new dimension of gruesome confusions ... teetering on the edge of a ghost story ... like *Vertigo*" (182).

Certainly the line is designed to unhinge first-time viewers, to suggest that Mrs. Bates really is still alive, and that there must be some massive, as-yet-unfathomed mystery connected with the Bateses' distant past.

Coupled with the assertion of Mother's burial, the suggestion that she is alive tiptoes up to the truth (she's dead but still here!) without giving us quite enough information to figure it all out.

And immediately after Hitchcock has tantalized us with these conflicting suggestions, he moves to a strong affirmation of Mom's reality — the scene where Norman argues with her and then carries her down the stairs. After all, if we can see Mom and hear her talking at the same time, doesn't that mean she's really alive? Why, if you watch closely, you can even see Mom's foot moving as Norman takes her down the steps!

Is Hitchcock deliberately tricking us here?

In one sense, yes — particularly in the long dolly shot that opens this scene, which may well be the most impressive piece of camerawork in the film. As Norman begins ascending the staircase to Mom's room, the camera is at the base of the steps looking up; during the ensuing conversation between Norman and Mom, it begins to rise up along the stairs while moving slightly forward; it seems for a moment to be heading for Mom's room — but as it rises past the top of the stairs, it begins panning left and down, continuing to rise upward and pan downward until we are directly overhead, to the same lofty perch we had when Mom emerged from her room to murder Arbogast.

Hitchcock told Truffaut that he wanted to reach this high angle with a continuous shot because a cut would have made the audience "suspicious as to why the camera has suddenly jumped away.... Meanwhile, I had an argument take place between the son and his mother to distract the audience." Hitchcock, of course, doesn't want us to get a good look at Mom — but more important, he doesn't want us to *notice* that we aren't getting a good look at her. "It was rather exciting to use the camera to deceive the audience," he concluded to Truffaut (276).

Yet even as we are being tricked, this brief scene contains numerous hints of the truth.

The first of these is something that often elicits laughter when the film is screened for younger viewers: the exaggeratedly effeminate way Norman swings his rear end as he goes up the stairs. It certainly looks odd — but it also makes perfect sense, as Norman is about to assume his mother's feminine persona.

Other hints about the truth: In the overhead shot as Norman carries Mom down the steps, the stair railing neatly *splits* the screen, thus suggesting the truth about Norman's personality. (It's interesting to note that this scene was actually filmed directly after the final monologue at the police station.)

The swaying and the split screen are, of course, much too elusive to be picked up by first-time viewers, but two other factors could give careful observers some food for thought.

First, consider the marked thinness and frailty of Mom's body; carried so easily in Norman's arms, she scarcely seems capable of murdering two healthy adults. And regarding the suggestive movement of Mom's foot: We can clearly see was that it jiggled not because Mom is alive, but rather because it struck the banister; and yet Mom does not protest this. We'd expect something like, "Ow! Norman! Be careful!"—but Norman can't supply this dialogue because he hasn't seen the mild collision occur. In these ways, as Robert Kolker has observed, we are once again presented with a visual explanation about the true nature of Mother; indeed, it's right there in front of us, but we don't see it.

Another intriguing aspect of this scene is highlighted by Bill Krohn, who suggests that this stairway scene resonates with Hitchcock's personal life. In particular, the fact that the scene fades out in mid-sentence and mid-action suggests some "unfinished business" between Hitchcock and his mother (234). Hitchcock had in fact been unable to be at his mother's bedside when she died because he was in America—ironically, finishing *Shadow of a Doubt*, which ends with a fade on the mother (Mrs. Newton, played by Patricia Collinge). The staircase scene in *Psycho* thus suggests conflict—a question of whether Mother really doesn't need her son and can take care of herself; yet it also provides some closure, with the dutiful son carrying Mother downstairs, as if for burial. Note the appropriately tolling church bells that begin during the fade from Mom's descent. And Norman is, in a sense, taking her to her final resting place. After this trip to the crypt-like basement, she will not stir to trouble anybody any more.

* * *

Though the sheriff scene occupies nearly four minutes, all the other scenes we've examined in this chapter are quite brief: 70 seconds with Sam and Lila arguing at the hardware store; 38 seconds while Sam searches the Bates Motel; then another 46 seconds after he returns to the store. The relatively lengthy sheriff scene is followed by about two minutes of Norman and Mom in the house, and then 88 seconds at the Fairvale Church.

As we saw in Chapter 11, this brevity reflects Hitchcock's desire to keep the film moving toward its climax—and a concomitant willingness to cut material from Stefano's script, which features extended footage of Sam wandering about the Bates property and knocking on doors while he is looking for Norman. It also has a scene at the sheriff's front door, with Mrs. Chambers complaining at length about the difficulty she has in getting her husband out of bed.

Nowhere are these cuts more drastic, however, than in Sam and Lila's drive to the Bates Motel, where all but two of the 20 scripted lines are cut — reducing three pages of screenplay to a mere 14 seconds in the finished film.

During the drive, the script gives Lila a chance to provide much of the otherwise-unknown background on the Crane family. And as it turns out, Marion's risky theft for the sake of her financially strapped boyfriend was a typical act for this self-abnegating character.

As Lila tells Sam in the original script, she and Marion were orphans and "lived together all our lives." Marion "quit college and got a job" so that Lila could attend college — but Lila decided not to go. Talking with Sam in the car, she now wonders "if that hurt her, my not letting her sacrifice for me?"

Lila further relates that Marion never told Lila about her relationship with Sam; she suggests that perhaps Marion didn't want to reveal her relationship with Sam until "you were able to marry her.... She always tried to be proper." Nevertheless, Lila learned about their relationship when she found one of Sam's letters — which she now describes as "a nice letter."

That last line, hints at a growing fondness between Sam and Lila — something Hitchcock wanted to avoid, feeling that this would be an undue distraction from solving the mystery of Marion's disappearance.

As for the material on Marion's background, this seems to have become a sort of unstated subtext throughout the film. Leigh told writer Philip J. Skerry that she kept all this in mind while fleshing out Marion's character: "I figured that her parents were killed in an automobile accident and she had to forego college to support her younger sister...." Speaking of the sisters' life together in Phoenix, Leigh added that Lila "has grown up, but Marion still takes care of her, but her life is passing her by..." (28).

Yet none of this is stated in the finished film. Krohn suggests that instead of providing verbal background on Marion, Hitchcock "found ways during filming to evoke Marion's memory visually, by centering the film's last movement on Lila" (224). Indeed, Sam and Lila's visit to the motel often calls up memories of Marion: the act of signing in; the visit to Cabin 1; the bathroom where she died. Somewhat more subtly, the film's final scenes continue to reemphasize Sam's fatal obsession with money (which really precipitated Marion's theft). He insists, for instance, on paying for the room and getting a receipt for business expenses — and he later grills Norman mercilessly about the $40,000.

Yet there is one change from the script that's tough to see as a mere attempt to tighten up and keep things moving: When Sam and Lila are exploring Cabin 1, the script stipulates a pan away from their ongoing discussion and a zoom to one of the wallpaper rosebuds, where we can see Norman watching and overhearing what they say through his familiar peephole.

Of course, this is cut from the final film — as is a brief moment when Norman steps outside and checks the registration on Sam's car, no doubt confirming that he is a local man and not the long-distance traveler he claims to be.

If these scenes appeared in the film, they would certainly give a much tenser feel to Norman's ensuing conversation with Sam: The audience would know that Norman is on to him. It would explain Norman's suspicious, reticent, angry tone with Sam. And it would clarify the later moment when Norman asks Sam, "Where's that girl you came here with?"— rather than the much more natural "Where's your wife?" Clearly, Norman knows the two aren't really married.

Without the peephole shot, we're left to conclude that Norman somehow deduced this on his own — but this isn't really a logistical problem. On the contrary, it fits perfectly well with the gradual change we've seen in Norman's personality.

It started, of course, with Arbogast's visit — and it's not so much a *change* in Norman as it is a radical *eclipsing* of the shy, hesitant, helpful young man who greeted Marion on her arrival. Some evidence of this persona is still apparent when Arbogast first arrives; but by the end of that scene, Norman has all but completed his transformation to a shifty suspiciousness — a hard-nosed determination to protect home and mother.

When Sam briefly visits the motel shouting for Arbogast, we see two shots of Norman standing by the bog, where he has clearly interred Arbogast's body and car along with Marion's. (This scene, incidentally, makes some viewers wonder wistfully just how many cars are stacked up at the bottom of that bog — and whether Norman might eventually open a used car lot alongside his motel.)

But look closely at Norman during this second scene beside the bog; look closely at his hardened, bitter, silent scowl, and you will see that the friendly young man has simply disappeared. When Lila and Sam arrive the next day, they've been preceded by a visit from the sheriff, which no doubt made Norman even warier — and thus the script tells us that in greeting Sam and Lila, Norman "does not smile.... His usual grin and soft friendliness are gone," replaced by "containment and impassivity."

Note, then, that he immediately decides to put Sam and Lila in Cabin 10 (no hesitation about Cabin 1, as we saw with Marion and more briefly with

Arbogast); nor does he wish Sam and Lila to sign the registration book, a look at which precipitated Arbogast's curiosity and death. (However, Norman did apparently show the book to Chambers, according to the sheriff's comments during the brief scene outside the church.)

In his commentary on the 2008 DVD, Rebello reflects that Norman's suspiciousness is simply a projection from his own psyche. Since he himself is constantly covering up the truth and pretending to be someone he's not, he is naturally wary toward others who may not be what they appear to be.

But whatever the reason for Norman's unfriendliness toward Sam and Lila — whether it's from his own duplicity, from a radically altered personality, from an innate instinct about these two, or from factual discoveries made by checking and peeping — Norman's inimical demeanor certainly increases our uneasiness. For one thing, Norman's transformation makes it harder for us to identify with him. Furthermore, we can sense that now both Norman *and* his mother are hostile toward these guests — guests through whom we hope to learn the truth — and that he will now make considerably less effort to restrain her hostility toward such outsiders.

No doubt this uneasiness gives a tint of irony to Lila's line, "That old woman — she told Arbogast something. I want her to tell us the same thing." Surely she doesn't *really* want the same treatment Arbogast got! And when Lila insists that she "can handle a sick old woman," repeat viewers may chuckle as they recall that Mom isn't really sick.

Or old.

Or a woman.

14

I Can Handle a Sick Old Woman

Lila and Mom

Raymond Durgnat has pointed out how difficult it is to subdivide this final section of the movie. Certainly there is no marked break after the scene with Sam and Lila in Cabin 1; nevertheless, it seems clear that the film's climactic act has begun once Lila starts her ascent to the Bates mansion: It's like that initial pause on a rollercoaster, when you reach the top of the first hill and look down at the drop you are about to make.

Durgnat has also noted that Sam and Lila will succeed in learning the secrets of the Bates Motel because they come as a pair, while everyone else fails by arriving alone (Marion, Arbogast, Sam, the sheriff). Perhaps this pair is particularly suited to penetrating the mystery of Norman-Mom because it is a male-female duo; and indeed, to this end, the two will split: The man will deal with the man, the woman with the woman. And the pair will not reunite until the truth about Norman is discovered — until, indeed, the male and female halves of Norman's split personality are also together again in the same room.

This final voyage of discovery begins with Lila emerging behind the motel; Hitchcock initially resisted that shot, because it required building an additional set — namely, a back wall for the motel. Joseph Stefano fought for it, and according to John Russell Taylor, Hitchcock finally gave in to Stefano's insistence that "exact geography was important here" (255).

And a fine decision it was. The film is greatly enriched by the two brief but evocative shots of Lila passing the back of the motel, with its piled-up detritus: a discarded mop, heaps of broken crates, the bedsprings from an old mattress, and in particular, a broken-down automobile. Easily 25 years old, this wreck clearly hasn't been used for a decade or more — so the shot makes us wonder whether Norman even *has* a car (there's certainly no evidence of one in the film). It also deepens our sense of his stagnant, dead-end

119

existence, literalizing the notion that he is *going nowhere*. And this deadness, this inaction, is further stressed by the waterless lawn fountain — briefly visible to the right about halfway through Lila's ascent.

As we move toward the Bates mansion, Hitchcock alternates between

Hitchcock standing near the specially built set behind the Bates Motel; the broken-down jalopy in the background suggests the loneliness and stagnation of Norman's home life. (©Universal Pictures; courtesy Universal Pictures–Photofest)

reverse tracking shots of Lila walking up the hill and forward tracking shots from Lila's point of view. The point-of-view shots are slightly unsteady, as though Hitchcock were using a handheld camera—very unusual for him.

As Lila enters the house, there begins yet another in the long series of emotional assaults that *Psycho* makes on its viewers.

When we ask why this movie still works—why it's still effective even for a younger generation raised on films with much more gore, murder, and mayhem—we must certainly consider Hitchcock's mastery of cinematic technique: sound, editing, lighting, camerawork, etc. As we have seen, all of these play into both of the murders—particularly the shocking death of the main character less than halfway through the film.

But perhaps *Psycho*'s greatest strength is that it consistently inflicts on its viewers two of the most unpleasant feelings in the entire range of human experience: nervousness and guilt.

The nervousness stems from the fact that in nearly every scene, from beginning to end, the characters are doing things they shouldn't be doing—and we are generally hoping that they don't get caught. In the opening scene, for example, an unmarried couple is having an illicit lunchtime tryst that will keep the woman out of the office past three o'clock—a late and lengthy lunch! Once Marion has returned to work, her boss is also found to be concealing illicit activity: He's got a bottle of liquor in his desk.

After Marion steals the money, of course, we spend the next 20 minutes hoping she won't get caught. And after she's been killed, we share Norman's jitters during the cleanup—especially when it seems as though the car isn't going to sink all the way into the bog. Next comes Norman's interview with Arbogast, during which we share some of the distress experienced by the stammering young motel clerk. After that, Arbogast sneaks around motel and mansion, seemingly about to get caught and killed at any moment; then Sam and Lila, doing the same in Cabin 1; and now at last, Lila heading into the house.

In other words, there is scarcely a moment in *Psycho* when we aren't feeling fear and trepidation over some morally discomfiting activity. And it's not enough to say that we're simply afraid somebody might get killed. Such a simplistic reading does not account for the fear regarding Marion's theft, or the nervousness we feel with Norman. In particular, it can't explain what is probably the strongest moment of sheer panic in the film—the one that occurs later in Lila's search of the house, when she looks out the front window and sees Norman racing up the stairs toward her.

Even first-time viewers feel a surge of terror in this scene—yet as far as they know, Norman is *not* the murderer; he might even be able to prevent Mom from killing yet again.

No, it's not the fear of death or attack; it's the fear of being *found out*—of being discovered in the act of doing something wrong. Fittingly, then, our fear in such scenes is seamlessly welded to the guilt we feel over our complicity in the characters' transgressions. In Chapter 10 we examined the "transfer of guilt" that makes us accomplices with Norman as he covers up the crime. Now, as Lila is about to enter the Bates home, consider how much we *want* her to go in there, to explore the house, to find and see Mom; how in our hearts we're secretly saying, "Yes, yes; please go on in!"—despite the deep-seated dread we feel. The same bafflingly mixed feelings occur later when Lila hesitates on the basement stairs, considering whether to descend to the place where danger and death surely await. Certainly there is fear for Lila here—but there is also a strong desire for her to go on down and find out the truth.

And if we have wished both Arbogast and Lila into the house—if any part of us has *willed* them into peril—then we share their guilt over trespassing in someone else's home. More significantly, we share guilt for the fate they face.

There's little doubt that *Psycho*'s shattering effect is due not so much to the actual murders; after all, there are only two. Nor can it be due to the blood, of which we see little. Indeed, considering the number of times Marion is stabbed, the shower stall really ought to be a good deal bloodier than it is.

No, it isn't murder and gore that undo us in *Psycho*; rather, it's the fact that we have willingly spent 109 minutes tainted by nervousness and guilt—two emotions most of us avoid at all costs.

If the idea of guilt over Lila's trespass seems unlikely, consider a bit further how Lila does exactly what we want her to do—penetrating into the deepest recesses of the house and unveiling virtually all of its secrets, particularly those in Mom's bedroom. Consider, in fact, the way Hitchcock has been tantalizing us with Mom's room from the very first time we entered the house—right after Norman peeps on Marion. After heading back up to the house to confront his mother, Norman makes it to the bottom of the steps, then loses his nerve. A short time later, Arbogast makes it a good deal farther—all the way to the top of the stairs. But he doesn't get into the room either. This is soon followed by the vertiginous dolly shot during which Norman and Mom argue—right before he carries her out of the bedroom; on this third trip, we get awfully close to the room—the camera even seems to be heading in that direction—but we don't actually go in. Hitchcock has, in other words, carefully fueled our hunger, our desire to enter this room along with Lila.

And when we do, we are faced with some of the richest visual material in the film; indeed, in both Mother's bedroom and Norman's, we again witness Hitchcock's superb nonverbal technique. This time, however, it's not so much "soliloquy without words" (Durgnat's phrase), but rather what Durgnat again so aptly calls "back-story silently told by *possessions*" (204).

Regarding Mom's bedroom, the back-story reveals two principal things, both summed up in James Naremore's book:

First, virtually everything in the bedroom is "designed to express Mrs. Bates' repressive character; a meticulously ordered wash-basin [with an unused cake of soap!]; a rack of flowered dresses which button at the neck; a bronze moulding of a pair of hands ... with lace cuffs down to the wrists."

Second, Mom's "house and her possessions belong to a different age" (67). Indeed, set decorators Joseph Hurley and Robert Clatworthy seem to have taken a page right out of Bloch's original novel, where the room is described thus:

> It was a room such as ... had not existed for the past fifty years; a room that belonged in a world of gilt ormolu clocks, Dresden figurines, sachet-scented pincushions, turkey-red carpet, tasseled draperies, frescoed vanity tops and four-poster beds; a room of rockers, china cats, of hand-embroidered bedspreads and overstuffed chairs covered with antimacassars [144].

As adapted by Stefano's script:

"It is ornate, damask-and-mahogany, thick and warm and ripe, an olla podrida of mismated furnishings and bric-a-brac of the last century."

Indeed, everything in the room seems geared to demonstrate that Norman's whole world is dead, frozen, trapped in the past.

Over Mother's bed, for example, is a large portrait of a middle-aged woman in an old-fashioned dress; since Mom was the only occupant of this room for years, this figure is probably Norman's maternal grandmother. It seems as though this stern-looking matron must have presided regularly over the bedroom trysts of Norman's parents, including the act of love that gave him life.

Furthermore, as Lila looks at Mother's vanity, we can see to its left a half-finished square of embroidered needlework — complete with a hanging piece of thread — that seems to be waiting for Mother to return and finish it. But it's probably been waiting in that position for 10 years. In addition to preserving the past in the present, this could also be a hint of Mother as one of the Fates — a controlling goddess, weaving people's destinies as she sits up here in her home on the hill.

Perhaps most powerful is the brief shot of the massive fireplace — a shot that actually gives us the clear look at Mom we've been wanting all this time. Atop the mantle are two framed photos: a man on the left and a woman on the right. Surely these must be Norman's parents. Between them, mounted just over the hearth itself, is an oval-shaped bas-relief portrait of a boy (quite probably Cupid). Given its position, this figure seems to represent Norman, still virtually frozen in childhood. Below this, we can see the fireplace grate, unlit, with no wood, merely ashes — recalling what Norman told Marion much earlier: If he left his mother alone, "her fire would go out."

Cold, dark, and dead, this place; yet Stefano's script also insists that "there is in the room an unmistakably live quality, as if ... it has not been long vacated by some musty presence."

Nowhere is this presence more apparent than in the creepy indentation left by mother's corpse on the bed — a baffling mix of new and old, with a shriveled, aged, mummy-like shape clearly assuming a fetal position. Indeed, this cadaverous figure — together with the bronze hands, the dresses, and the pictures — evokes such a powerful sense of Mrs. Bates that, as William Rothman writes, in this place "we feel closer to Norman's mother than at any other moment in the film" (321).

As Naremore has written, given the uncomfortably intimate aura of the bedroom, Lila and Sam's invasion of the motel and house can begin to feel "like a sort of violation." This becomes especially apparent as Hitchcock cuts from Lila's exploration of the house to Sam's conversation with Norman in the motel office — where "the madman begins to look like a trapped insect" (66).

Indeed, now that Lila has become more active and assertive, Sam too grows aggressive, almost bullying Norman while clumsily trying to get at the truth about Marion. As Durgnat observes, if we were to view this scene alone, out of context, we might well conclude that Sam is the "heavy" and Norman is the persecuted "hero" (203).

Rothman points out that "we have little sense that Sam is really acting out of concern for Marion"; rather, "his cruelty seems primarily a matter of self-gratification" (320). This is especially clear in the earlier scene when he and Lila check in; there, Sam's demands to "sign in and get a receipt" exude an inexplicable hostility.

Because of this apparent malice, our sympathies are curiously divided in these interchanges between Sam and Norman — as they were in Arbogast's earlier interview with Bates in the exact same spot. We feel empathy for Norman under the pressing questions, yet we also hope the inquisitor can unearth the facts. Perhaps it's part of the moral taint of *Psycho* that we continue to empathize with the guilty party even as we hope this not-so-good-guy will lead us to the truth.

Meanwhile, Lila's exploration of the Bates home has, in Rothman's phrase, "taken on a life of its own" (324); more specifically, she enters and explores Norman's bedroom, even though it's empty and unlikely to yield any information about Marion. Like us, she seems determined to penetrate as much of Norman's privacy as possible.

Regarding the scene in Norman's room, probably the item most frequently discussed is the book Lila picks up and opens. Though Hitchcock's camera resolutely refuses to show what's in it, all the evidence points to pornography. In the first place, this scene in Bloch's original novel tells us that upon opening the book, Lila sees an illustration that is "almost pathologically pornographic" (143). Furthermore, Stefano's script stipulates that "her eyes go wide in shock. And then there is disgust. She slams the book closed, drops it." Durgnat also points out that she's clearly *looking* at an image, rather than reading text, because her eyes don't travel across the page. And finally, script supervisor Marshall Schlom insisted that "Hitchcock wanted to *suggest* it was a pornographic book with a slight raise of the eyebrow. It was so important to him, we shot maybe sixteen takes of Vera, which was unusual for him."

This shot, Schlom adds, was the only time in the film when Hitchcock used something other than a 50-millimeter lens; "he used to say he saved close-ups for a big emphasis — when he really wanted the audience to *know* something" (Rebello 100).

All that said, it should be pointed out that there isn't much of a raised eyebrow here, and most viewers could hardly be expected to deduce the contents of the volume this way — unless they were aware that very old pornographic books generally had blank covers.

Yet even though we might we miss this rather important revelation about Norman's character, there's plenty of other information here to help us understand his background and personality; indeed, if Mother's bedroom told a powerful story through its décor, Norman's room speaks even more evocatively. On the whole, it makes a poignant and ironic counterpoint to the last line of Norman's conversation with Sam: "My mother and I were *more* than happy," Norman insists — at which point Hitchcock cuts instantly to Lila entering the room, and we can see at once that this is not the room of a happy, healthy, well-adjusted young man. Rather, like Mom's bedroom, it too seems frozen in the past, with a curious mixture of youth and adulthood — what the script describes as "a horrible, ludicrous fantasy of childhood held beyond the point of decency."

As Lesley Brill points out, for example, the stuffed animals in Norman's room suggest that his hobby of taxidermy is merely an extension of his childhood life. In addition, the script tells us that the bed is "far too short" for Norman, "yet the rumpled covers indicate that it is in this bed that Norman sleeps." Or consider the adult-child mix of various other objects about the room: the toy car, the doll, the stuffed rabbit, and the circus wallpaper — contrasted with the "adult book" and the Beethoven symphony on Norman's record player.

One of the saddest and most significant things about the room's contents is the way they hint at Norman's desire to escape, to get away, to connect with the world at large — while also indicating the failure of these impossible yearnings: a toy car that will never leave the house; the painting of a ship trapped in its frame; a stuffed owl that cannot fly away; and a book of pornographic pictures — artificial images frozen in a simulated travesty of physical intimacy, offering no real affection, no real connection to human warmth.

Significantly, Norman has been listening to Beethoven's ninth symphony, originally dedicated to Napoleon. Since Napoleon once tried to "take over the world," this recording combines with the tiny nearby globe to suggest the truth of Norman's earlier statement to Sam: "This place happens to be my only world."

Perhaps most powerful of all are the two shots of Norman's stuffed rabbit; with its mouth turned down in a painfully forlorn and abandoned look, the rabbit conveys a sense of loneliness, sadness, and desolation that would be difficult to duplicate in a non-visual medium.

Having finished with Norman's bedroom, Lila now proceeds from the third floor to the ground floor to the basement, thus cementing what several writers have noticed about the Bates home.

> The Victorian gingerbread house on the hill with its turn-of-the-century bedroom was a physical replica of Freud's post–Victorian three-leveled theory: the superego corresponding to the upper room, with mother/son quarrels and parental prohibitions regarding women; the ego level of the ground floor, with its door opening into everyday, outer reality; and the id (or libidinal) force represented by the dark cellar of guilty secrets and subliminal attachments [Hurley 37].

Here, in this dark, dank basement, Lila at last finds exactly what she's been looking for — both Mrs. Bates, and the dreadful truth about what happened to Marion at the Bates Motel.

Our first confrontation with this truth consists of the skeleton that turns to face Lila as she taps on its shoulder. Featuring a real human skull covered with molded rubber, this remarkably realistic prop was designed with advice from a Los Angeles college of mortuary science.

Costumer Rita Riggs told Rebello that "having to go down into the set and get that dummy dressed and shoed so gave me the chills, I would actually dress her from behind" (76).

Another person on the set who didn't care much for the skeleton was

Janet Leigh. Hitchcock and his crew kept refining the figure to get it just right, and Leigh later loved to regale listeners with stories of how Hitchcock would take the latest version of the corpse and prop it up in her dressing room while she was out. In her own memoir *There Really Was a Hollywood*, she explained that the volume of her shrieks upon entering the dressing room enabled Hitchcock to determine which version of Mom's cadaver was most effective.

Another aspect of the basement scene that required extensive work for the crew: getting Mother's chair to turn properly when the skeleton swings around to face Lila.

Assistant director Hilton A. Green told Rebello, "Hitchcock wanted the dummy to turn a certain way and cock a certain way as Vera [Miles] put her hand on it." So the dummy was affixed to a swiveling camera mount, which was then turned by a prop man on the floor, below and outside the frame (126–27).

And as Lila confronts this atrocity, we find a convergence of several standard elements in horror films — including one that *Psycho* seems to have initiated.

In her 1992 book *Men, Women and Chainsaws*, Carol Clover points out that in most recent horror films, the hero who confronts and destroys the monster-murderer is usually a single woman — as happens, for example, in *Friday the 13th*, *Scream*, and even Ridley Scott's *Alien*. Robert Kolker has observed that this "final girl," such a staple in modern horror films, is a direct descendant of Lila Crane, who confronts and "undoes" the male-female "monster" in *Psycho*.

Yet just as it ushered in this new horror trend, *Psycho* ends much as older horror thrillers did. Naremore observes that as Norman's dress is ripped open and his wig falls off, he seems to disintegrate before our eyes, like Boris Karloff's mummy, or the witch in *The Wizard of Oz*.

Indeed, though Norman steps into the basement with an expression of hideous glee on his countenance, he seems to concede the struggle as soon as his disguise is penetrated — as though his own self-deception somehow depended on these external accoutrements.

Tim Dirks points out that as Norman is collapsing, Mrs. Bates seems to be in the process reviving. The script tells us that her cadaver turns "as if in response to Lila's call and touch" — and once the turn is complete, the figure jerks slightly; Mom seems to be saying, "Well, here I am! Your search is over!" (Rothman 326).

Lila then flings her hand back, striking a bare bulb that hangs from the ceiling by a single wire. As this bulb sways wildly back and forth, it yields sharp shadows that sweep across the walls, giving a surreal and dizzying feel to the scene. More than that, it enables Hitchcock to show us a shot of Mother's skull with the shadows in the eye sockets moving back and forth — as though she were alive, watching and enjoying the struggle between Sam and her unmasked son.

More than one writer has noted a similarity between this scene and the climax of Albert Lewin's 1945 version of *The Picture of Dorian Gray*—which also features a wildly swinging light bulb. This echo seems particularly fascinating since the *Gray* scene, like this one, also involves a murderer confronting a badly aged double of himself.

Fittingly, then, this is the first and only time we learn how similar Norman's name is to that of his mother. As he enters the basement room, he calls out loudly, "I am Norma Bates!"—though this line isn't particularly easy to distinguish. During that rather sustained line of dialogue, we have a clear view of Norman's face—yet we can see that he is not actually saying these words with his mouth. This may possibly be a continuity error (Perkins had asked that the scream be dubbed in later because he was rehearsing for a musical in New York and wanted to save his voice); but if so, it's a fitting error indeed. In our shocked and disoriented state, we are just as likely to believe that this scream is coming from Mother's wizened corpse.

Yet these fascinating details provide only a small part of the scene's appeal, for what makes the sequence most memorable is its triumphant blend of suspense and surprise.

Hitchcock himself was fond of observing that these two effects resulted from two different approaches to a scene, and that they could rarely occur together. In speaking on this subject to Truffaut, Hitchcock used the example of a time bomb: If two men are sitting and talking at a table, and suddenly a bomb goes off—that's surprise. If instead the filmmaker *shows* us the bomb beforehand, and lets us know what time it will go off, then we worry about the two men; that's suspense. Since the storyteller cannot both reveal something *and* keep it a secret, he must generally choose either suspense or surprise as the dominant emotion in a given scene.

But Hitchcock does indeed manage both effects at the climax of *Psycho*. In fact, he employs the two in an escalating fashion, piling surprise on surprise and suspense on suspense.

First, there is the suspense of worrying about Lila in a house where a murderer has already killed at least one victim. To heighten this, we then see Norman rushing toward the house as Lila is coming down the stairs from Norman's room. Worse yet, Lila then descends to the basement, where she finds, approaches, and actually *touches* the supposed killer.

And presto—at the moment of the very greatest suspense in the film, just as we are sure Mother will leap up and unleash on Lila the same horrors she wrought on Marion and Arbogast — at that very moment, Hitchcock piles up surprises as well: First, we learn that Mrs. Bates is really just a skeleton; then, as Norman enters, we are shocked to see that he is dressed as a woman; furthermore, since he wears a dress we've seen before, and raises a very familiar-looking knife, we also learn that he is in fact the killer; and finally, we are both surprised and relieved to see that Sam has recovered from being knocked unconscious by Norman, and has come to Lila's rescue.

This may well be *Psycho*'s greatest success — possibly even more triumphant than the shower scene. Among other things, the scene's skillful mixture of suspense and surprise probably accounts for why *Psycho* still works on horror-hardened young viewers born 30 years after it came out. Even if they haven't seen the film, they certainly know about the shower scene, and it rarely shocks them as it did viewers in the 1960s. With their smug expectations and the certainty that they've "seen it all," most of them never dream that *Psycho* still has a big surprise up its sleeve. And even if they might have considered it, Hitchcock distracts them throughout the film — with the sound of Mother's voice; with a shot of her being carried downstairs while she protests; with the terror of Lila's plight inside the house; and finally, with an actual body sitting in the basement chair — a body that yet seems alive even as it turns to reveal the truth.

Contrast Hitchcock's approach here with Robert Bloch's original novel, where Norman reveals the truth ahead of time, during his conversation with Sam in the motel office. Bloch's climax is exciting, but certainly not surprising or shocking.

That's the difference between a fairly effective little thriller and a virtually perfect film from the Master of Suspense.

And Surprise.

15

As If from a Deep Sleep

Richmond and Norman

When Hitchcock had finished shooting the psychiatrist's speech at the end of *Psycho*, he strode over to actor Simon Oakland, shook his hand, and said, "Thank you very much, Mr. Oakland. You've just saved my picture" (Rebello 128).

On the one hand, as Rebello points out in the 2008 DVD commentary, Hitchcock felt that Oakland's carefully balanced and emotionally detached presentation helped get *Psycho* past the censors — giving an air of clinical credibility to the risky and risqué material with which the film has grappled throughout.

In addition, Hitchcock had worried that the scene would be a "hat-grabber"— that is, restless viewers would be more interested in getting home than in listening to the doctor's long explanation of what they'd learned in the preceding scene.

Joseph Stefano did not share this concern. "I never believed it would be a hat-grabber," the screenwriter recalled in Janet Leigh's book on the making of the film. "Because by this time, we would need to know the *why* of Norman" (40). Hitchcock, in other words, had perhaps overestimated the amount of information viewers could receive and process during the movie's shattering climax. Still reeling from the multiple shocks piled on in the basement scene, they could hardly be expected to grasp all the implications of what they had seen.

Yet Hitchcock also recognized what many *Psycho* fans now take for granted: Oakland's presence surely helps keep viewers glued to the screen during this fuller explanation of the mystery. According to an interview in Philip J. Skerry's volume on the shower scene, Stefano himself had recommended Oakland for the part of the psychiatrist; the original script even misidentifies him as "Dr. Simon." (Perhaps such a Freudian slip is especially forgivable when dealing with the part of a psychiatrist.)

In any case, though the actual name never appears anywhere in the finished film, "Dr. Richmond" is given in virtually every credit listing for *Psycho*. It's also the appellation used when this same character appears in *Psycho IV*—which, incidentally, was scripted by Stefano.

So it's clear that Oakland—who incidentally nailed this speech in one take, and was thereafter rewarded by a round of applause from the crew—was vital to the success of this scene. More important, the sequence as written gives viewers the info they've been grasping at for nearly an hour. Indeed, one seldom notices restlessness during this speech, even among viewers who have seen the film repeatedly. Terse, clear, and nicely acted, the scene really does serve as what Durgnat calls "a *second* climax — after the *action* climax, a *moral-intellectual* one" (209).

Yet in spite of all this, many writers find the psychiatrist's explanation unsatisfactory—in part resulting from Richmond's apparent indifference to the grief and death he is describing. He seems painfully uncaring in his description of Marion's death at the hands of Norman-Mother. And as if to exacerbate this, the scene itself includes several reminders of Marion: The sink in the corner recalls the first thing we saw upon entering Marion and Sam's window in the opening scene—and the fan behind Richmond bears a striking resemblance to the background fan in the Phoenix hotel room. Thus, we may be thinking of Marion—and certainly Sam and Lila are recalling her; yet Richmond seems to have little sense that he is confirming the long-suspected but nonetheless horrific news about Lila's sister — unaware of the pain, sadness, and discomfort he causes by insisting that Norman killed Marion because "he was touched by her, aroused by her — he wanted her."

On a subtler note, we might also be puzzled by the wall calendar indicating that it's Dec. 17, which can't be right; the film began on Friday, Dec. 11, and Sam and Lila's visit to the Bates Motel takes place more than a week later — on the following Sunday; so it must be Dec. 20. Is this a mere continuity error? Or is it meant to suggest how "out of touch" the police and the psychiatrist are — how they still haven't yet "caught up" to reality...?

As Rebello points out in the DVD commentary, Richmond is another of Hitchcock's authority figures who — like the sheriff before him — "knew the facts but never actually got the whole picture."

That in fact seems to be the main problem with Richmond's explanation: It fails to account for the full reality of what has happened to the characters — especially Norman. Indeed, some might consider these final moments in the film even more intimidating to analyze and discuss than the much-more-famous shower scene. To put it plainly, the character of Norman-Mom, as revealed by the psychiatrist and by the ensuing voiceover in the detainment cell, is so complex, so baffling and enigmatic, as to defy explanation in mere words.

To begin with, several authors have suggested that we need not take Richmond's explanation at face value. Tim Dirks, for instance, makes the striking suggestion that perhaps Norman did *not* kill his mother and her lover. In other words, the sheriff's original explanation is the true one: Mother poisoned herself and her lover; then afterwards, Norman — already "dangerously disturbed" by his father's earlier death — simply assumed the guilt of killing his mother, perhaps as a way of covering up what *she* had done: Much better to be guilty himself than taint the precious purity of Mom!

Taking a different angle, several writers wonder just how accurate a portrait of Mother we actually get in her final voiceover speech. In other words, does this voice tell us what Mother was really like? Or is it merely a false representation of Mother, as recreated by Norman?

To put it more simply: Is Norman a creation of Mom, or is Mom a creation of Norman?

The question is astonishingly difficult to answer.

Writers such as Paula Marantz Cohen and James Naremore have suggested the latter — namely, that this evil, murderous woman is a personality fabricated entirely by Norman, and that the real Mrs. Bates wasn't like that at all. More specifically, Tom Bauso and William Rothman point out that Norman's actual mother, far from being a repressed prude, seems to have taken an unabashed interest in sexuality. She had, after all, not only a husband but also a lover — and at the entrance to her home stands a large statue of Cupid, which gets prominent emphasis during the visits of both Arbogast and Lila. There is also a naked Venus statue in her bedroom (visible on the left as Lila takes her first steps into the room) and what looks very much like another Cupid over the fireplace. Would the real Mrs. Bates, who decorated her domain in this fashion, have called sexuality "disgusting," as she does in her very first speech in the film?

Isn't it more likely that *Norman* was disgusted by his mother's sexuality — an Oedipal disgust, if you will, much like Hamlet's — and that he killed her in order to "keep her pure"? Rothman thinks so, and explains the subsequent murders as Norman's compulsion to "reassert" this purity every time sex rears its ugly head. In other words, perhaps the imaginary Mom — the one Norman has idealized — is so "pure" that she refuses to allow any attractive young women to remain at the motel, where they might "contaminate" the place by tempting Norman into sexual activity. Perhaps the real Mrs. Bates wasn't like this at all.

Bloch's original novel seems to supports this exoneration of Mother.

During Norman's conversation with Marion in the motel parlor, he insists, "You don't have to tell me about jealousy, possessiveness — I was worse than she could ever be. Ten times crazier..." (33).

In other words, maybe the real Mother was relatively normal; we viewers of *Psycho* have only *learned* to think of her as crazy because of the way Norman presents her to us — because of the warped and twisted personality he has projected onto her.

Indeed, using some of the material from Bloch's novel, Bauso, writing in the 1994 *Hitchcock Annual*, makes a rather convincing attempt to "resuscitate" Mom's "tainted reputation" — to "reconstruct her image along more erotic, more humane, and certainly less tyrannical lines" (4–6). Having been "murdered, buried, resurrected, stuffed, carried about the house, and spoken for," she might well be "the archetypal unacknowledged victim of American cinema" (13).

Yet on the other hand, it is equally easy to believe that Mrs. Bates really was the foul, vindictive shrew we hear so often in the film. This opposing idea — that Mom is entirely to blame for her crazed son and his murders — finds support from two important aspects of the film: First, by the end of the film, the Norman Bates we knew so well has completely vanished; and second, "Mom" really does seem to be a separate person.

Let's take a closer look at these ideas.

As for Norman's disappearance: We noted in earlier chapters that the pleasant, boyish shyness with which Norman first greeted Marion slowly erodes during the film, eventually usurped by hard-edged suspicion during his talks with Sam and Lila toward the end. Yet even in these later exchanges, there are glimpses of the old Norman: his disarming "No, that won't be necessary" when Sam wants to sign in; his frank surprise when Sam all but demands to pay beforehand. In this final scene at the police station, however, the timid and likable Norman is nowhere to be found; as Dr. Richmond puts it, "Norman Bates no longer exists." Or in the words of Robin Wood, we have witnessed "the irretrievable annihilation of a human being" (149). (This haunting disappearance, incidentally, is slyly hinted at in the name of the Fairvale deputy —*Lackman*— seen briefly on the door into the sheriff's office.)

So: Norman is gone.

And in his place sits a figure who seems very much to have a life of her own. Consider it this way: On the surface, most of us accept Richmond's thesis that Norman has a split personality; yet in reality, we really do tend to think of Mom as a separate person — not as one aspect of Norman's psyche, but rather as a distinct, fully realized individual. That's why it's possible to keep discussing "Mom" and her actions without batting an eyelash, even after we've seen the film a dozen times. Most likely the frequent references to Mother in this chapter — and indeed throughout the entire book — hardly strike readers as odd or even questionable. Of *course* she's real. It scarcely occurs to us to think otherwise. Almost subconsciously, we've come to believe that there really is a person named *Mother Bates* — an actual presence in the film, one who can think, speak, move about, and impose her will on others.

This ulterior presence may well have been conceived on the set itself; Perkins told Stephen Rebello that "the crew always referred to Mother and Norman as *totally* separate people. Mother always has her own 'backstage' persona, as it were." Most viewers, he insisted, just won't acknowledge that Mother is really Norman. "It's just not how people want to see it..." (113).

So we tend to see Mom as a separate individual — particularly because it's tough to believe that a shy and ineffectual person like the "real" Norman could ever have created such a nasty, strong-willed personality. Yet at the same time, there's no doubt whatever that Mother is dead; after all, we've seen her withered corpse in a shocking and memorable close-up. If we insist on feeling that this voice is the *real* Mother, as opposed to someone created by Norman, we shall soon be forced to believe in ghosts.

As a way of considering the difficulty and complexity of this matter, think about the intricate workings of accusation and guilt moving back and forth between these two distinct personalities:

Each of them, for instance, wanted to put the other in an institution. Norman earlier admitted to Marion that he had considered putting his mother "some place." And now in this final scene, we see that she had considered this option for him as well. She tells us she's *glad* they've locked up Norman, because she should have done it "years ago."

Each wants to make the other responsible for the crimes, perhaps as a way of eluding his or her own guilt. Perhaps, as James Naremore has written, Norman sought to make his mother share in his crimes; "he had murdered her lover, so she was made to murder his" (69). And now, having been implicated by Norman as the one ultimately responsible for the crimes, Mom has returned the favor, telling Richmond that Norman was to blame: "It's sad when a mother has to speak the words that condemn her own son." Has she *deliberately* orchestrated this scenario, cleverly setting Richmond up to conclude that Norman was to blame? And even if she has, it's nevertheless quite clear that Mom knows perfectly well who was really responsible; for although she insists that she "wouldn't even harm a fly," her knowing and sardonic grin after this line suggests that she knows she really *is* the killer — and that she has no scruples about blaming it on Norman. Indeed, she assumes that he would have ratted on her as well ("In the end he intended to tell them *I* killed those girls, and that man"). Yet in a way, he *has* blamed it on her — by creating a personality so real that we somehow believe Norman didn't really do it. Unless, of course, that personality is what Mom was really like.

See how this scene defies verbal explanation? The more we say about it, the less we understand.

The matter is further complicated by the way Hitchcock handled the voiceover in Mom's final monologue.

As we saw in Chapter 8, Mother's voicing was provided by three different performers — two female and one male — whose words were then spliced together in varying proportions. According to Rebello, Hitchcock actually had the male vocal artist — Paul Jasmin — on the set during many of the scenes with Mother, both to feed lines to Perkins during the filming, and to help Jasmin get a better feel for the scenes so he could do his later dubbing more effectively.

During the filming of Mom's concluding monologue, Jasmin stood off camera and voiced the lines so Perkins could hear them during the forward track toward his seated figure. Set decorator Robert Clatworthy told Rebello, "Even watching and listening to the scene as it was shot gave the crew goosebumps. The damn thing was so weird, so uncanny" (132).

Yet as Jasmin later explained, all the voicing that was actually *used* on the soundtrack in the final scene was female — mostly Virginia Gregg, with perhaps a little of the other female vocalist, Jeanette Nolan, spliced in. In her book on *Psycho*, Janet Leigh points out how markedly Mom's tone in this scene differs from her earlier speeches : "There is no need now for scolding or humiliating. The voice is softer, more feminine, almost seductive..." (83). So if Perkins was *acting* to the sound of a male, but the audience *hears* the sound of a female — then who is this person? Mother or Norman? Male or female?

Could s/he be some inexplicable combination of both? Indeed, as the above analysis has attempted to demonstrate, Mother seems to exist and not exist at the same time. We are looking at a person who in some ineffable way brings together a vast array of opposites: real and imaginary, physical and mental, parent and child, male and female, past and present, dead and alive.

This blend of opposites is perfectly exemplified by the now-famous superimposition of Mom's face over Norman's in the concluding moments: Just after the scene's final line ("She wouldn't even harm a fly"), and just before the dissolve to the swamp, a shot of Mother's skull appears behind Norman's visage. It's tough to see because it matches the size of Norman's head; the faint image is most noticeable in its lower hairline, large dark eye sockets, and prominent teeth. Viewers who didn't notice it at first had two excuses.

To begin with, some of the original 1960 prints did not contain this super-imposition; and second, Hitchcock insisted that it be so brief as to be almost subliminal. Script supervisor Marshall Schlom recalled, "I remember Mr. Hitchcock saying, 'It's got to be on and off that [snapping his fingers] quickly. I want the audience to say, "Did I *see* that?"'" (Rebello 135).

Nowadays, of course, it's on all the DVDs, and you can simply pause the scene for a good long look. What few folks ever mention, however, is that if you hit *pause* at precisely the right moment — just when the composite of Norman-Mom begins fading into the swamp — you will see that the chain pulling the car from the bog seems firmly attached to Mother's neck, looking uncannily like a hangman's noose!

Final shot of Norman, with Mother's skull superimposed; note her lower hairline and prominent teeth, and the chain, visible as the scene dissolves to Marion's car being pulled from the swamp. In this triple image, the chain appears as a noose at the neck of Norman and his mother. (©Universal Pictures; courtesy Universal Pictures–Photofest)

This image, of course — a mingling of the dead and living — is the culminating statement in the film's argument that the past inescapably dominates the present.

As we shall see in more detail in Chapter 17, throughout this film the past hovers over the present just as the old Bates mansion hovers over the newer motel. Sam can't escape his father's debts; Lowery's secretary is still being phoned by her mother; Marion is unable to free herself from the effects of her decision to steal the money; and for Norman, the past is one of those personal prisons he describes when talking to Marion: "We're all in our private traps — clamped in them. And none of us can ever get out." The end of the film fulfills these statements with terrifying permanence: The present has been absorbed by the past, and the world of the dead, as represented by Mother Bates, has triumphed over the world of the living.

All of this imbues *Psycho*'s ending with a sense of despair, dissonance, and confusion — a hopelessness, a profound *lack* of resolution. Not only has the whole world of the film been swallowed up by the past, but the pleasant and likable Norman has been annihilated — as have the similarly sympathetic Marion Crane and Milton Arbogast. And on top of all that, in spite of Richmond's long explanation, we still cannot tell what Mother was really like, who is actually responsible for the murders, or whom we are seeing and hearing in these final moments.

Along these same lines, we might also note the clever way *Psycho*'s last two shots *undercut* what has preceded them: First, the psychiatrist neatly explains the mystery of Norman — yet this is undercut by the frightening enigma of the figure in the chair and its baffling, disconcerting monologue. Then, Mom's insistence that she herself "wouldn't even harm a fly" gets swiftly undercut by the sight of Marion's car being pulled from the bog — clearly recalling the actual fate of Mother's victims.

*   *   *

Let's conclude our analysis of this scene by answering a question that is often asked concerning works of art such as stories, plays, and musical compositions: "How does the end reply to the beginning?"

In the case of *Psycho*, there are several answers.

Wood, for example, has pointed out that the film, with its documentary-style intro, "opens by making us aware of time and ends ... with a situation in which time (i.e., development) has ceased to exist" (143).

On a subtler note, the fly on Mom's hand was clearly intended to echo the opening hotel room scene. Although this shot didn't make it into the final film, the script stipulates that Sam and Marion's kiss in the first scene is "disturbed and finally interrupted by the buzzing closeness of an inconsiderate fly."

More substantially, *Psycho* seems to have three distinct beginnings and three endings — which mirror each other in reverse:

Very beginning: Opening titles
Beginning No. 2: Forward pan-and-zoom toward hotel
Beginning of actual story: Exposition in Sam and Marion's room

Ending of actual story: Exposition by psychiatrist
Ending No. 2: Forward track toward Norman-Mom
Very end: Car in bog, with closing title

This structure seems especially deliberate if we keep in mind that the exposition by the psychiatrist, as we have already noted, features several visual reminders of the exposition scene with Marion. And of course the "final ending" reprises the sliding horizontal bars from the opening credits, as well as an actual closing title ("The End").

Some writers — Wood, Spoto, and especially Neil Hurley — have seen the final shot of the car as liberating or therapeutic, a movement *outward*, a hint that what has been hidden will now be revealed. But for many viewers, it hardly seems long enough, or pronounced enough, to counter the forward, downward, *dark*-ward movement of the film as a whole; and in the long run, it doesn't provide an emotionally healing effect either.

On the contrary: The sight of mud slithering off the car is slightly nauseating, obscene, almost excremental — as though it would be better off left hidden than exposed to light and scrutiny. And of course, we know what lies inside that trunk: a body that is well on its way to decomposition and decay — though Hitchcock mercifully doesn't show it to us.

Like so much else in *Psycho,* it's left to our unseemly imagination.

16

Two Personalities
Psycho *and* Psycho

In the late 1990s, one young Hitchcock fan tersely summed up a central truth about the structure of Hitchcock's most famous thriller. "*Psycho*," he wrote in a student essay, "is schizophrenic. It has a split personality."

The divide, of course, occurs at the shower scene — though it's not a particularly "clean" break, because Marion's death really belongs to both halves of the film. Nevertheless, as we observed in Chapter 9, *Psycho* is a crime thriller up to that point — a melodrama keyed on such genre fixtures as stolen money, suspicious cops, illicit sex, and girls gone bad. With Marion's death it quite suddenly becomes instead a gothic horror film complete with a black bog, a huge slashing knife, a mysterious mansion, and a ghostly figure from the world of the dead.

Indeed, Hitchcock seems to have deliberately fostered this division among cast and crew as the film was being shot. In the 2008 DVD commentary, Stephen Rebello points out that the director was much friendlier with Part One's Leigh and Perkins — frequently playing word games with them during down time, for instance — than he was with Part Two's Gavin and Miles. And in his book on the film, Rebello describes "two camps" during the shoot; he also uses the phrase "a set divided," citing a "schism that Hitchcock tried to maintain between the stars of 'Part One' of the film — Janet Leigh and Tony Perkins — and 'Part Two' — Vera Miles and John Gavin." Costumer Rita Riggs recalled that the director "loved that kind of tension" (Rebello 91).

The "split" that is key to *Psycho*'s structure is presented to us visually in a number of ways throughout the film:

In the opening credits, for example, sliding white bars split up the black screen — and the credits often "fly apart" to opposite sides; in particular, the first set of vertical bars after the movie's title, as well as the last set before the fade to Phoenix, move up and down from a horizontal split across the center of the visual field.

A short time later, as the highway cop pulls up next to Marion's car, a telephone pole neatly bisects the screen. Significantly, Marion's car sits to the right of this, pointed toward the left half of the screen — where a barren wasteland portends both her future and the vacant emptiness of the Bates motel and home. The framing presents us with a swift visualization of Marion's truncated life — and perhaps, of the film's two halves.

Additionally, in the two overhead shots of the staircase inside the Bates mansion, the banister also splits the screen. And the basement of the Bates home is divided into two rooms. These two locales are particularly apt, as the scenes that take place there tend to involve both halves of Norman's personality.

Undoubtedly, however, this split is best represented by the many mirrors seen throughout the film. Hitchcock reportedly told set decorator George Milo, "Let's have lots of mirrors, old boy" (Rebello 70) — and with good reason. Noting that most of the mirrored reflections we see in the film (particularly Marion's) are incomplete, partial, or bisected, Lesley Brill observes that the many reflections point to the shattering of the characters' "personal coherence" (227). In other words, the mirrors — if you'll pardon the pun — reflect the split personalities of the film's two central characters.

Yet George Toles has noted that in spite of this, there is scarcely a moment in the film when any of the characters actually turn to look at their own reflections; perhaps they are unable to face their own potential for division and duality. And if Norman is the character least aware of his own bifurcation, that may be why we almost never see him in a mirror. This observation is from Bill Krohn, who also points out that the much more self-centered, self-aware Mother has a bedroom that's a "veritable hall of mirrors" (220).

In examining how this visual motif functions in *Psycho*, Durgnat asserts that mirrors can serve three functions: They double, they reflect, and they deepen.

Thus, in one sense, the second half of *Psycho* "doubles" or reprises the first. What we might call "Part One" — the story of Marion — ends when her car sinks into the bog. Not only is this located at the approximate midpoint of the film, but it also marks a clear emotional and narrative break: At precisely this point, the story can be neatly divided into what Durgnat calls "two long, fast, urgent 'time-runs'" separated by a week (152): Part one runs from lunchtime Friday to Saturday night; then, on the *following* Saturday, the Sam-Lila story picks up again at lunchtime and concludes on the following night. Indeed, as we noted in Chapter 11, the hardware store scene seems to start the story all over again: With Sam's letter and the discussion of money, it reprises many of the themes and issues in the opening hotel room scene. More important, the two halves lead to a similar climax and denouement: Both wind up at the Bates property, with a woman named Crane confronted by a bewigged, knife-wielding figure; both feature someone staring blankly in a white-walled room (Marion dead in the bathroom, Norman-Mother in the detention cell); and both end with a shot of Marion's car in the bog.

If we consider the film as first Marion's story and then Norman's, we can see that these two halves of the film reverse each other as well: Marion is an assertive female who takes control in the struggle with an absent male; Norman is a passive male who loses control in the struggle with an absent female.

Consider, for example, our earlier examination of two contrasting shots that occur after Marion arrives at the Bates Motel: First, upon entering the office, Norman welcomes Marion while standing at the right — and Marion stands on the left, where we can see her reflection in the mirror behind her. Later, when Norman holds the tray of food on the motel porch, Marion stands at the right — while he, on the left, is reflected in the window glass behind him.

This effect is reprised much later, when Sam and Norman face each other in the motel office — standing in the same positions Marion and Norman had assumed in their very first encounter. Tall and dark-haired, even Sam and Norman seem to double and reverse one another. To borrow Philip J. Skerry's phraseology, Sam is "a man without property but with sexuality," whereas Norman is the opposite — "a man with property but without sexuality" (124).

And thus, even as they double and reflect, the mirror images deepen as well — for each half of the pair contains some elements of the other. To use James Naremore's fascinating phrase, the film's two worlds "somehow *evoke* one another, like characters in a dream" (46).

But there is more to *Psycho*'s "split personality" than such visual cues as mirrors and divided screens. In its very tone and subject matter, *Psycho* uncannily fuses the familiar and the taboo: The seemingly ordinary, mundane world of hotels, cars, secretaries, money, and marriage collides with a taboo world of nudity, grave-robbing, incest, and murder. To borrow again from Naremore:

> The difference between these two worlds is roughly the difference between the Bates motel and the massive Gothic building behind it, or, as many critics have observed, between a film by Godard and a film by James Whale. *Psycho* is all the more remarkable for the way it plays these entirely different modes off against one another without falling apart, as if to suggest a relationship between daytime Americana and a night world of baroque terror [37].

As these comments suggest, *Psycho* yokes together a vast array of cinematic genres and traditions:

It's a Hollywood feature film with big-name stars — yet it's filmed in the quick, economical style of Hitchcock's television programs. (Skerry points out that in its two halves, it employs the two-act structure of the episodes on *Alfred Hitchcock Presents*.)

It has elements of docudramas like *The Wrong Man* (time-and-locale opening, black-and-white photography) — yet it also embraces the lurid horror of popular thrillers from such directors as Castle, Corman, and Clouzot.

Furthermore, as Naremore has observed, its morality is both old-fashioned and modern. It is, he writes,

> midway between the repressive manners of the classic Hollywood studio movie (Janet Leigh wears a bra) and the "liberated" ethos of the R-rated contemporary film (Janet Leigh is shown in bed with a man at midday). It might seem to point toward the "new" morality, but it belongs ... squarely within the traditions of the "old" morality.... In much the same way, *Psycho* stands midway between the conventional Hollywood narrative and the self-conscious style of the art film [75–76].

In the tradition of Corman and Castle, yes — but not out of place alongside such films as *Persona*, *Blow-Up*, or *My Life to Live*. Indeed, perhaps *Psycho*'s greatest triumph is the way it appeals to popular taste while also being aesthetically refined enough for scholars and intellectuals. Durgnat spells this out in considerable detail:

"It's a woman's film but with mayhem galore for the young, especially young males; it's sensitive enough for mature moviegoers; it's libidinal and intellectual; it's Gothic adapted to a psychological age; it's emotionally literate ...; it's morally serious but not obviously moralistic; it's — pleasurable and anguished" (9).

Hmmm — both enjoyable and agonizing.... It would seem that *Psycho*'s split is not merely a matter of what's on the screen, but also of what's going on within its viewers.

In one sense, the film divides viewer loyalties by asking us to identify with opposing characters — first, for example, with Marion, and then with the man disposing of her slashed-up body. Sometimes this split in viewer loyalties occurs in the very same scene — for instance, in the interview between Norman and Arbogast. On the one hand, we hope the detective will get more information, while on the other hand, we feel nervous for Norman as he struggles to keep the truth concealed.

And when a character such as Arbogast or Lila approaches the Bates home, we are torn between fear for these potential victims and a desperate desire to get inside that house. As we saw in Chapter 14, this is perhaps most apparent in that moment when Lila stands at the top of the basement stairs. Part of us is afraid she will go down there, while another part is *dying* for her to go down and help us discover the truth.

In *The Dark Side of Genius*, Donald Spoto posits that the film thus effects a split in our desires — a split "between squeamishness and curiosity that is the essence of the picture" (423). It's the essence of the picture — as it is for the horror film experience in general — because we desire to see the violence (after all, we have paid for the privilege) yet we are also afraid to watch.

Along the same lines, consider for a moment whether repeat viewers experience something similar with the shower scene. We know it's coming; we're interested in watching it again; part of us *wants* it to occur ... yet when it does, it's just as hard to watch as ever. Thus, this savage, brutal scene always seems to "punish" viewers for wanting it to happen again.

Yes, *Psycho*'s "split personality" is certainly designed to reflect the division in its characters — most notably Norman, and to some degree Marion as well. Yet at the same time, the movie locates a split in viewers too. Like the movie's characters, we also are torn in two by fear and desire.

Perhaps we are not so very different from Norman Bates.

17

Want to Check
the Picture Again?
Psycho *and Its Themes*

Merriam-Webster's 11th Collegiate Dictionary defines "motif" as "a usually recurring salient thematic element." Like most great works of art, *Psycho* offers many of these — mirrors, privacy, and the dominance of past over present, to name only a few.

A few of the more compact motifs have been highlighted and discussed in the main body of this text: verticals and horizontals (page 25); downward movement (pages 26–27); enclosed spaces (pages 62–63); privacy (page 63); paranoia and illicit activity (page 121). However, several of *Psycho's* recurring motifs are so prevalent and detailed that they seem best dealt with separately. That is the purpose of the present chapter.

These discussions will necessarily incorporate some examples already mentioned individually in the preceding chapters. However, even if it involves some repetition, grouping all of the instances together in one place will certainly help demonstrate the breadth, prominence, and complexity of these particular motifs. In addition, it will allow us to examine the ramifications of each motif in a way that would have seemed cumbersome and perhaps ill-placed in the earlier shot-by-shot analysis.

The Domination of the Past

Perhaps the single most persistent theme in American thought is the attempt to break free from the past. It runs all the way from the Pilgrims' voyage *away* from oppression in England, on through *The Scarlet Letter*, *Huckleberry Finn*, and *The Great Gatsby* — even into such comparatively recent works as *Death of a Salesman*, *A Raisin in the Sun*, and Sam Shepard's Pulitzer

Prize–winning *Buried Child.* Such optimists as Emerson and Whitman suggest that it is indeed possible to escape from the past and start all over again. The work of many less sanguine writers — Hawthorne, Arthur Miller, Tennessee Williams — seems to argue that such escape is impossible. For these more skeptical thinkers, characters often struggle to be free from *parents* (*Huckleberry Finn, Cat on a Hot Tin Roof*) or *past sins* (*The Scarlet Letter, A Streetcar Named Desire*) or, quintessentially, *past sins of parents* (*Buried Child, Death of a Salesman*).

A fundamentally *American* picture, *Psycho* uses all of these ideas to suggest that one can never escape the past — that the very attempt to do so merely leaves one more entrapped than ever.

Hitchcock announces this theme at the very beginning of the film: Immediately after the opening credits, *Psycho*'s first shot shows a modern section of downtown Phoenix, with a brand-new building under construction — but the camera swings away from this and heads toward a much older part of town. Though time is moving forward, we seem to be heading into the past.

In the ensuing hotel room scene, Marion tries to break free from her longstanding relationship with Sam — yet at the end of the scene they remain inexplicably attached. A few hours later she commits a crime that leaves her more firmly bound to him than ever.

Marion then makes the archetypal American journey — heading west, toward ostensible freedom. But instead of starting life anew, she winds up out on "the old highway," at an old motel, below an old mansion with an old woman sitting in the window. Even Marion's "new" car is old.

Though both Marion and Norman eventually find that their past sins catch up with them, *Psycho*'s fixation on the past appears more often in the form of domineering parents.

In the opening scene, for example, Sam feels unable to wed Marion because he is fettered to the debts of his dead father ("I sweat to pay off my father's debts, and he's in his grave"). At the same time, Marion wants to have Sam over for a "respectable" dinner, "with my mother's picture on the mantel" — but Sam senses the intrusiveness of this and hopes they can later "turn Mama's picture to the wall."

Equally invasive parents can be found in the real estate office, where Marion's coworker, Caroline, blithely declares that her mother phoned the office to check on whether or not Caroline's husband, Teddy, called her that day. Worse, Caroline tells us that her mother's doctor gave her tranquilizers before her wedding — and thus a dominating shadow from the past was cast across the very day on which Caroline was supposed to be separating from her parents.

And things don't look much brighter in this scene for the daughter of the rich man, Mr. Cassidy. Although he insists that "tomorrow she stands her sweet self up there and gets married away from me," he still calls her "my baby" and "my sweet little girl." Certainly she and her new husband (whom Cassidy in the script describes as a "penniless punk") will feel indebted to her father by his extravagant "free" gift of a $40,000 house — well over twice the cost of an average home in 1960.

Visually, a sense of the past hovering over the present is represented by the photo of Marion's parents that hangs on her bedroom wall, seeming to watch over her as she prepares to steal the money — and recalling Marion's statement about her mother's picture on the mantel. Much later, we see that Mrs. Bates's bedroom actually does have pictures of Norman's mother and father on the mantel. In addition, over the bed is a large and imposing portrait of a rather stern-looking matron who must certainly be one of Norman's grandparents — probably on his mother's side, since this room was occupied by Mrs. Bates during the course of two sexual relationships (first with her husband and then with her lover).

As with Marion and Sam, as well as Caroline and Teddy, the lingering presence of parents seems to intrude even upon the characters' most private and intimate liaisons.

These images of the past seem rather subtle, and they are certainly overshadowed by *Psycho*'s ultimate visual embodiment of the past's dominion over the present: the old Bates home, sitting atop its hill, usually with Mom in the window, gazing down upon the much-newer motel, and seeming to scrutinize every move.

Not only is the house architecturally older than the motel, but as we saw in Chapter 14, its interiors are steeped in the past. Norman's bedroom, with its childish toys, stuffed rabbit, tiny bed, and circus wallpaper, reflects a world frozen in the past — as does Mother's bedroom. Robert Bloch's original novel tells us that hers "was a room ... such as had not existed for the past fifty years" (144); and the script says it's filled with "furnishings and bric-a-brac of the last century." Significantly, this type of décor has begun to invade even the newer motel down below; Norman's parlor boasts Victorian lamps, quaint candlesticks, and framed paintings — all of which look like they were carried right down out of Mother's bedroom.

It's fitting, then, that many of these ideas about the past are summed up in Norman's conversation with Marion, which takes place in this antiquated setting: "We're all in our private traps, clamped in them," Norman declares. "And none of us can ever get out. We scratch and we claw, but ... we never budge an inch." He has of course very nicely described both Marion and himself: Marion's "private trap"—like Norman's—has its roots in the past, specifically with parents; in an omitted scene just before Sam and Lila arrive at the motel, Lila explains that she and Marion were orphaned, after which Marion quit college and got a job so that Lila could go to college instead. Having thus wound up in the trap of spinsterhood and a dead-end job, Marion attempts to free herself—only to find that she has stepped into the even more confining trap of larceny and fearful flight. When she then determines to step out of this new trap, she is killed. Truly, she never budged an inch.

But Marion is hardly alone in finding it impossible to escape from past crimes. The psychiatrist tells us that Norman also wanted to "erase the crime" (in this case, the "unbearable" crime of matricide) yet in doing so, he only wound up more entrapped in the past than ever, trying desperately to side-step his guilt by pretending to be his own mother and thus resurrecting the past —"probably for all time," the doctor tells us at the end.

Norman's case seems particularly hopeless, for he specifically admits that he was born in his own trap; and as much as he rails against it by arguing with Mother, befriending Marion, and spying through peepholes at naked women, he likewise never budges an inch. Norman's beautifully subtle line to Arbogast —"Old habits die hard"—seems to refer to his weekly work routine at the motel; yet considering the aged parental garb he wears during the murders, it's interesting to note that the word "habits" originally meant *clothing*. And in a broader sense, this brief but poignant line sums up the whole trajectory of Norman's life. By the end of the film, he has been completely absorbed by a past that simply refuses to die.

Notice too how the past is represented not only by parents, but also by death — for when one dies, one moves irretrievably into the past. And death keeps reasserting itself in this film, not only in the murders but also in the resurrected corpse of Mother; in long-hidden homicides being unearthed and reexamined; and particularly in the concluding moments. Here, it becomes despairingly apparent that *Psycho* is in fact a film that moves backward — toward the past, toward the dead, toward a state in which time has come to a halt. In the film's final seconds, Norman's face is haunted by the superimposed image of his Mother's skull, and this then dissolves to the emerging car, held by a chain that seems to attach itself to Norman's neck; thus the storyline arrives at last in a realm where death has triumphed over the living — a world of withered skeletons, hangman's nooses, exhumed corpses, rotting swamps, and voices speaking from beyond the grave.

For some, the concluding reemergence of Marion's car seems to suggest renewal and restoration — i.e., escape from the past. However, it can just as easily be seen as the *inevitable reappearance* of the past. Norman has tried to cover up his past crimes by sinking them in the bog, but they won't stay hidden. The car is just another image from the past that returns to convict him, like the vengeful ghost of his own mother.

As Lesley Brill has written so aptly, "Unearthing the past in *Psycho* allows us nothing more than a partial understanding of its ravages; we cannot cure or undo them" (236).

Birds

Psycho's opening moments are rich in bird imagery. Its very first shot gives us a "bird's eye view" of a cityscape, and Hitchcock's camera then begins looking around and moving forward—like a falcon zeroing in on its prey. Eventually, the hawk-eyed camera will fly us right up to the hotel building, where we seem to perch on the ledge and peer in.

But that's not all: When the very first image fades in after the credits, we can see a revolving sign on top of a building at the right; as the camera pans right and the sign revolves, it reveals an upright bird, its wings spread wide (like the eagle on the back of a quarter). Just as this bird sign is leaving the frame, the film's locale appears: Phoenix. Named for the mythological firebird that rises from its own ashes, this city name is perhaps a forerunner of the resurrected Mrs. Bates. (See page 27 for a still of this evocative shot.)

Phoenix, in fact, is the first of several names that relate to birds. For example, the appellation *Bates* suggests the way Norman captures birds—by *baiting* them. At the same time, it's an antiquated word from the now-rare sport of falconry; the *American Heritage Dictionary* tells us that it means "to flap the wings wildly or frantically." (Interestingly, it's also a short form of the verb "abate," meaning "to die down, to lessen"—which is certainly what happens to Norman's personality during the story.)

And let's not forget that Marion's surname—*Crane*—is a water bird, and thus quite suitable for someone who gets lost in the rain, killed in the shower, and buried in the swamp.

A few lines of dialogue also hint at the bird motif: Norman, for example, denounces well-meaning people who "cluck" their tongues; he also asserts that we're all stuck in traps, where we "scratch and claw" but cannot escape. This clawing and scratching is no doubt familiar to Norman through his hobby of taxidermy; he must have seen many trapped birds do just this before he killed them.

Careful observers will count at least a dozen actual stuffed birds in Norman's parlor, varying in size from two large pheasants to four or five small ones behind the phone. But by far the most noticeable of these are the owl and the crow, visible in numerous shots throughout this sequence.

Faced with the undeniable prevalence of this motif, viewers often wonder if Hitchcock was obsessed with birds; after all, his very next film (1963's *The Birds*) represents a full-blown exploration of the avian imagery laid out in *Psycho*. In any case, Hitchcock's framing in the parlor scene certainly offers at least one explanation as to why birds seem to hover so constantly over this particular film.

As we saw in Chapter 8, both the owl and the crow are associated with death: The crow, of course, feeds on carrion — and the owl is traditionally viewed as an omen of impending death (cf. Lady Macbeth, who calls it "the fatal bellman, which gives the stern'st good night" [2.2.4]). Fittingly, the crow is usually shown in the frame with Marion, and the owl is often in the frame with Norman; there's also one in his bedroom.

These two birds, then, mark out killer and corpse, particularly if we recall what several writers have already noted: *Psycho*'s killings seem markedly similar to bird attacks; Norman-Mom is like a bird of prey, swooping down on victims and "pecking" them to death — accompanied by high-pitched, bird-like shrieks.

Indeed, the script takes pains to connect both Mom and Norman to birds. We have seen, of course, that Norman's name relates to birds in two different senses. In addition, the Kandy Korn he is eating when Arbogast arrives is reminiscent of birdseed. And several writers have noted Norman's unusual appearance during one shot in the office with Arbogast: When he leans forward to look at the register, we see his neck and jaw outlined in an extraordinarily bird-like way. Furthermore, during his later exchange with Sam in the office and parlor, the script has Norman hurry up to the parlor window "as if he might fly through it" — adding that he is nonetheless "as unable to fly away as are the many still, stuffed birds." Indeed, the stuffed owls — the threatening one in the parlor and the other at rest in Norman's bedroom — clearly show us a killer who has been killed; and thus they represent Norman: both a victim (of his mother) and a victimizer (of other women).

Mother, too, can be linked to birds. In a scripted scene that didn't make the final cut, after Norman talks with the sheriff on the phone, he knocks over a "shrike-like bird which is perched on the lampshade," spilling sawdust on the floor. He then cleans this up and tucks the bird away in a drawer — after which he proceeds to the house, where he will also tuck Mother away in the basement.

In this way, Hitchcock creates grim humor in the lines that group Mother with the rest of Norman's avian victims. For example, Norman tells Marion that his mother is "as harmless as one of those stuffed birds"—a comparison echoed by Mother in the final scene: "As if I could do anything except just sit and stare, like one of his stuffed birds." These are similes, of course; but in a more literal sense—since the psychiatrist tells us the corpse has been "treated to keep it as well as it would keep"—Mom really is another of Norman's mummified trophies. Come to think of it, "bird" is also British slang for a young woman—and thus when Norman feeds Marion, she too becomes a "stuffed bird."

In one sense, Mother's stiffened, motionless corpse fulfills Norman's claim about birds in his conversation with Marion—namely, that they are "passive." Yet Mom is pretty active too—as are birds, with their pecking, swooping, flapping, flitting, and flying. We might then take a cue from Durgnat, who claims that *Psycho*'s birds present a combination of the opposing internal tendencies in many of its characters. In particular, the stuffed birds seem to embody both freedom and entrapment, wildness and control, movement and stagnation. Like so much else in Norman's world, they show us life frozen in death.

Similarly, Naremore has pointed out that these "obsessive, dream-like" objects are hard to decode; like most literary symbols, they are ambiguous, resonant, multilayered (51). "I was quite intrigued with them," Hitchcock told Truffaut. "They were like symbols.... Owls belong to the night world; they are watchers, and this appeals to Perkins' masochism. He knows the birds and he knows that they're watching him all the time. He can see his own guilt reflected in their knowing eyes" (282).

Which brings us to our next motif.

Eyes, Seeing, and Looking

When I discuss the shower scene with high school students, I begin by drawing on the board an outline of the human eye:

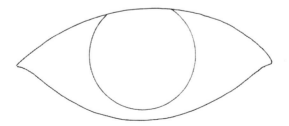

I then ask a volunteer to come up and fill in the inner circle. Almost invariably, I get something like this:

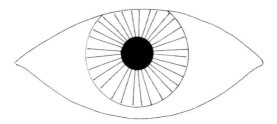

And then I erase the part I myself had drawn — leaving the following image, created by the student with little or no coaching from me:

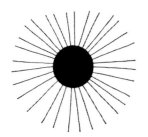

I then ask the students where this image shows up in the shower scene. Some of the kids note that it echoes Norman's peephole and the toilet bowl — part of a "circle in a circle" motif that we shall explore in more depth momentarily.

Nearly every student, however, can see that the image appears most blatantly in the head-on shot of the showerhead.

Many of them also mention the drain, with its central black hole surrounded by swirling lines. (See page 85.) Occasionally, some students object to this, crying out something like, "You're reading too much into it!" But such complaints are quickly quelled with another question: What does the shot of the drain dissolve into? Easy answer: Marion's dead eye. And thus the similarity between these images is clearly and undeniably established.

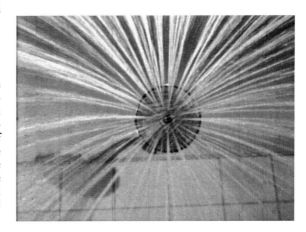

To achieve this now-famous head-on shot of the showerhead that precedes the even more famous murder, Hitchcock's crew had to block off the center holes so that the camera wouldn't get wet. Note how this image resembles the pupil of an eye. (©Universal Pictures; courtesy Universal Pictures–Photofest)

Needless to say, all of this makes an excellent starting point for discussing other examples of the eye motif.

To begin with, Janet Leigh's large, doe-like eyes get considerable emphasis in some scenes, especially in Marion's nighttime drive. In addition, Arbogast gets stabbed across the eye at the top of the stairs. On a lesser note, we might mention one of the film's few allusions — namely, Marion's early statement to Sam that "they also pay who meet in hotel rooms." Referring to a line in John Milton's sonnet "On His Blindness" ("they also serve who only stand and wait"), this paraphrase points to the group of eyes in the film that stare vacantly: Marion's dead eye, the highway cop with his creepy opaque sunglasses, Mom's eyeless skull.

But of course, in this last example, the blank-eyed gaze of the skull gets a little help from Hitchcock and his crew: The swinging basement light bulb casts curious shadows inside its empty sockets, so that it appears as though Mother does have eyes that are looking back and forth. Indeed, as the script puts it, "She appears to be watching and enjoying the fight" between Sam and her cross-dressing son.

We might include in this motif the idea that everyone is *looking* for Marion — especially the private detective. Consider how "looking" is emphasized in Arbogast's dialogue with Norman: "I'm looking for a missing person." "Do you mind if I look at your book?" "Mind looking at the picture...?" "Look at the picture, please." And when Norman denies there's someone in the window: "Sure, go ahead. Take a look."

In the same way, attentive listeners will note how much of *Psycho*'s dialogue incorporates idiomatic uses of the word "see."

Marion to Sam in the opening scene: "We can see each other."

Arbogast describing Marion's disappearance: "Someone has seen her. Someone always sees a girl with $40,000."

Sheriff Chambers, when Lila says she still feels suspicious: "I see you do."

And note the four different "sight words" when California Charlie speculates on why Marion wants to replace her old car: He says she must be "sick of the *sight* of it. Well, why don't you have a *look* around here and *see* if there's something that strikes your *eyes*."

This exchange is shortly followed by what may be the film's most evocative exchange of looks: As Marion and Charlie are walking toward the office, she looks back over her shoulder at the highway cop, who has pulled up across the street and is looking back at her; Charlie glances at Marion, sees her looking elsewhere, looks at the cop, looks back at Marion with more concern, then resumes his forward gaze just before Marion does. Taking all of three or four seconds, this brief exchange is another piece of what Durgnat has called "silent dialog" (54). Indeed, as so often in Hitchcock, it's hard to imagine how one could adequately render this moment in print; it's too nebulous, too fast, the feelings are too hard to pin down — which is probably why it doesn't appear in Stefano's script.

Of course, this brief visual exchange is only one of many scenes in which people watch or stare at one another: Cassidy gives Marion "the up and down" in the real-estate office; Lowery gapes at Marion in her car on the street in Phoenix; Norman peeps while Marion gets undressed; and of course, Norman-Mom stares out at the screen — and at viewers — in the concluding scene.

In this final example, what's even more significant is Mom's statement, "They're probably watching me." She is of course referring to the police, who would naturally be keeping an eye on this dangerous killer. Indeed, when the cop approaches Mom's room with a blanket, he gestures at some colleagues, who step off screen to what must surely be a one-way window.

But we in the audience get the uncomfortable feeling that Mom is talking about more than just the watchful eye of the law in this scene. After all, as the movie ends she is looking at *us*, as if to say, "I see you out there"— and as if to implicate us in much of the watching that occurs in *Psycho*.

In his seminal *Art of Alfred Hitchcock*, Donald Spoto was among the first to note that dialogue of this sort in the film has a self-referential character — that *Psycho*, in fact, is a movie about watching movies. When Mom, for example, says that she can't do anything "except just sit and stare," she could be referring to the viewers in their comfortable theater seats. Equally passive, we might claim a similar lack of responsibility for or power over the goings-on in the story. Consider also the way Norman describes a mental institution: "the laughing and the tears and the cruel eyes studying you"— a perfect description of a crowded movie house. And Spoto has also noted that the movie's opening entry into the hotel room parallels the viewer's experience at the beginning of a film: We go into a dark place; once we enter, we see an empty chair — at which point the camera jogs left as though it has actually assumed this seat; it then looks up — and the story begins.

This idea is corroborated by Hitchcock's insistence on shooting the entire film with a 50-millimeter lens. As Rebello puts it, "On the 35-millimeter cameras of the day, such lenses gave the closest approximation to human vision technically possible" (93).

In other words, *Psycho* is filmed as though we ourselves were present in this world as unseen watchers. The 50-millimeter lens is Hitchcock's way of playing out *Psycho*'s oft-noted theme of voyeurism — his way of suggesting that the act of watching movies is simply an act of publicly approved voyeurism, like watching a pretty lady get undressed. Or sneaking up to a window and peeking in at a half-naked couple.

We might take this one step further by recalling the shower scene's dissolve from a drain to an eye. Hitchcock seems to be suggesting that the act of watching has the quality of absorbing, of sucking down. Like the drain, our eyes are hungrily drinking in —*consuming*, if you will — the world of the film, and thus drawing it down into our beings, as though feeding some insatiable appetite.

And once again, this brings us to our next motif...

Food, Drink, and Appetite

At the risk of overkill, this section will encompass virtually all the examples of food and drink in the film — even those brief and subtle ones that tend to get overlooked. For the sake of clarity and organization, let's approach most of these in chronological order:

The film begins with the line, "Never did eat your lunch, did you?" — after which we see Marion's uneaten sandwich and a drink. Marion then returns to work from her "lunch break," only to find that her boss is still on *his* lunch break.

A short time later, when Marion sees Lowery and Cassidy crossing the street, a restaurant and candy shop are visible in the background; later, as she navigates city streets while approaching the car dealer, we can see an EAT sign along the road, as well as a placard indicating the town she is in —*Bakers*field.

Marion's arrival at the Bates Motel yields numerous salient examples. When she indicates that she's hungry, Norman mentions "a big diner" up the road; but instead of going out to eat, she accepts his dinner invitation, and we actually watch her consuming a sandwich and some milk. As she does, Norman observes, "You eat like a bird," momentarily linking these two motifs. After this exchange, Norman returns to the house and sits thoughtfully in the kitchen, where he toys briefly with a sugar bowl on the table.

In the hardware store scene after Marion's death, as Lila begins to break down in tears, Sam tells his clerk to run out and get himself some lunch. The ensuing exchange marks one of the film's few funny moments, with the clerk responding, "That's okay, Sam; I brought it with me" — to which Sam gruffly replies, "Run out and eat it."

Later, when Arbogast arrives at the motel, Norman is eating Kandy Korn; and toward the end of this scene, Arbogast uses a food-related adage to express his feeling that "something's missing": "If it doesn't jell, it isn't aspic."

Furthermore, after Arbogast's death, Norman argues with his mother over going to the fruit cellar; and when we finally get there with Lila at the end, apples are clearly visible on shelves along the wall. Incidentally, we might also note Mother's amusing reprimand in her argument with Norman: "No! I will not hide in the fruit cellar. Hah! You think I'm fruity, huh?" Of course, it's an ironic line because *Norman*, running around in a dress and wig, is actually the "fruity" one; and it's doubly ironic when we consider the kind of rotten fruit that has actually sprung from this woman's loins.

And finally, we might also mention the coffee cup sitting on the floor during the final scene in the detention cell. (This is not visible in some copies. The 1999 DVD is framed to show it, sitting near Norman's right foot at the very beginning of the shot.)

If some important examples seem to have been omitted from this chronological list, that's because the other instances are perhaps best discussed under the heading of "Why?" What, in other words, are all these examples doing in the film, and why is this motif so astonishingly prevalent?

For one likely answer, let's look at the argument between Mom and Norman — the one Marion overhears through her motel room window. In this exchange, Mom rejects Norman's idea of a hospitable meal, insisting that she won't have Marion "appeasing her ugly appetite with *my* food — or my *son!*"

In one brief line, *Psycho* thus points out that there are other kinds of appetites besides the literal hunger for food. Indeed, the many references to eating become a sort of extended metaphor for the other types of hunger we can easily find in *Psycho*'s storyline: greed (the appetite for money); lust (the appetite for sex); murder (the appetite for destruction); and curiosity (the appetite for information).

In fact, these types of hunger are often in competition with the normal human routine of eating. Made under the watchful eye of a director who was something of a connoisseur of fine foods, *Psycho* presents us with a world in which something is wrong, in which people, for the most part, do *not* eat — because they are focused on some *other* appetite.

In the opening scene, for example, Marion was too focused on her sexual appetite to bother eating lunch. Indeed, as Lesley Brill has observed, *Psycho* posits a competition between sex and food — as shown again in the opening scene when Marion urges Sam to join her and Lila for a respectable steak dinner. Sam is less interested in the meal itself than in what might happen after dinner: "Do we send Sister to the movies, turn Mama's picture to the wall?" This is echoed later when Mom assumes Norman has more in mind with Marion than merely eating: "And then what? After supper? Music? Whispers?"

But sex is not the only thing competing with food in *Psycho*. After Marion's theft, for example, her hunger for the money and for Sam trump her normal appetite for food: Not only does she refuse the car dealer's offer of coffee, but on arriving at the Bates Motel, as far as we can tell she has not eaten at all during her entire two-day trip! And then when she finally does eat, Norman doesn't join her — probably too caught up in his hunger for this beautiful woman. Arbogast also refuses Norman's offer of candy; he's too hungry for information to bother with a snack. In the same way, the sheriff's wife later asks Sam and Lila if they've had breakfast. And she invites them over to dinner as well. But their hunger for the truth about Marion is greater than their desire for either of these meals.

Time and again in *Psycho*'s warped world, the healthy act of eating is trumped by some other appetite — usually, a less healthy one. Likewise, this sense of abnormality is also reflected in the odd types of food and eating that occur. The aspic mentioned by Arbogast, for example, is rather unappetizing: a cold gelatin made from meat, fish, or tomato juice. Or consider Cassidy's opening sally on the warm Phoenix weather: "Wow! Hot as fresh milk!" An attention-getting reminder that milk doesn't come out of the cow nice and cold as it does from the fridge, the remark also serves as an oblique early reference to motherhood and breasts — perhaps a bit odd coming from a middle-aged man. Similarly, Norman's candy doesn't really count as a food — any more than the whisky in Lowery's desk drawer. In fact, Lowery and Cassidy seem to have basically drunk their lunch, and will probably do the same with dinner. Likewise, the other secretary, Caroline, swallowed a tranquilizer on her wedding day — something that probably went on to affect her wedding *night* too; as Brill points out, it's another example of ingestion competing with sex. And in one of the most subtle examples, the sheriff tells us that Norman's mother and her lover died of strychnine poisoning — an "ugly way to die." Of course, Norman must have put it in their food — a notion confirmed in Joseph Stefano's script for the "prequel" *Psycho IV*, which recounts Norman's youth: A key scene shows Norman bringing them a tray of food and drink deliberately laced with poison.

And finally, this last example shows pretty plainly how food in the film is regularly associated with death. Not only did Norma Bates and her lover die from eating, but the certainty of Marion's death was virtually determined by her decision to eat with Norman instead of heading on to Fairvale. Or consider the mechanics of the shower scene, in which the blood was represented by chocolate syrup and the stabbing by a casaba melon (or perhaps by raw meat — see Chapter 9). And of course, in both the shower murder and the basement climax, the script stipulates the use of a *bread* knife — which makes one wonder whether this was the same knife Norman used to make Marion's sandwich.

Indeed, in the world of this film, all the appetites we've discussed can be said to lead to death. Love-hunger killed Mother, greed killed Marion, and curiosity killed the private detective. Thus, appetites that are supposed to sustain the human race — particularly sex and food — are seen instead to result, ironically, in death.

Circles

The motif of circles could almost be discussed as a subset in the motif of eyes, yet it's also firmly wedded to the next motif: emptiness and absence. So let's discuss it separately, as a transition — even though it's fairly brief.

We might begin with a few minor examples that are easy to miss: the label on the record in Norman's bedroom; the circular tags on the Bates Motel room keys; the round logo on Norman's bag of Kandy Korn; and the close-up of Marion's mouth in the shower, wide open in a scream of horror. Or consider the way an "O" appears on Marion's first license plate (ANL-709) — and in the middle of such names as *Caroline* and *Arbogast*; the latter, in fact, is highlighted for us by the sheriff, when he carefully pronounces it "Arb-oh-gast."

Yet if we move on to some of the more notable instances discussed earlier — the showerhead, the drain, Marion's dead eye — we quickly see that there's more to this than just circles. Nearly every example of this motif presents us with not merely a circle, but *a circle within a circle*. The drain, eye, and showerhead all show us a darker circle within a larger, lighter one. Sometimes this pattern is reversed, as with Norman's peephole and the car roof disappearing in the bog — both of which give us a small bright spot surrounded by a pool of black.

Robert Kolker sees the "circle-in-a-circle" as one of the film's key visual images, and indeed it seems to encapsulate nearly all the other examples we can find: Watch for the double circles in the fans that appear in the opening hotel room scene and the police station at the end; in the toilet and seat; in the dial on the telephone Arbogast uses; in the circular Rolodex in the real estate office (see page 36 for a still of the opening shot in that scene; it's amazing how much this visually striking little desk device recalls both showerhead and pupil, with their round central spot and straight lines radiating outward). Even the compact Marion uses when she returns from lunch bears a decorative circular design on its round cover.

So: What do these circles mean?

In one sense, they may remind us of the seamless fluidity of the Norman-Mother persona; you cannot tell where one begins and the other ends.

In another sense, we might take a cue from *Vertigo*, where a recurrent circle motif represents the movie's circular plot as well as the dizziness implied in its title. But is this the case in *Psycho*? Certainly the plot repeats itself to some degree, but the story can hardly be called "circular"; the linear forward movement of both halves is almost palpable.

For a clue to the meaning of these circles, we need look no further than Hitchcock's previous film, *North by Northwest*—in which the main character's middle initial is "O"; when asked what it stands for, he answers, "Nothing."

Thus the circles in *Psycho*: A circle makes an empty hole that should be filled with something. What does Hitchcock fill it with? Nothing: another circle, another empty hole. Inside the emptiness is more emptiness — like a bottomless pit. The circle-in-a-circle motif thus really does mirror *Psycho*'s structure — for throughout the film we are seeking to "fill in" missing information, trying to solve a mystery. And when we reach the end, the solution to the mystery is just another mystery — the bizarre enigma of Mother-Norman, which seems even more baffling than the first mystery was. It's a hole within a hole, a circle in a circle, an emptiness filling emptiness.

And thus we arrive at our final motif...

Emptiness, Absence, and Negation

The motifs of the past, birds, eyes, and food have been discussed in such seminal works as Spoto's *Art of Alfred Hitchcock* and Wood's *Hitchcock's Films*. (Leigh's book on the film includes an especially comprehensive list of bird motifs.) A few of the examples — the old-fashioned meaning of *bates*, for example — were brought to my attention by some very observant younger viewers. And *Hitchcock's Motifs*, by Michael Walker, is an invaluable reference that helps connect *Psycho*'s motifs to the rest of Hitchcock's oeuvre.

But the final motif is one that does not seem to have been covered substantially anywhere — though it is perhaps implicit in the discussion of hunger.

It is particularly apparent at the end of Marion's drive, when — upon pulling into the motel lot, with its sign posting a "vacancy" — her headlights pick out a chair, sitting empty and forlorn in the rain. Like the chair, the motel office also contains no one. Even after Norman comes along, he stresses that the motel itself is completely empty ("Twelve cabins, twelve vacancies").

This idea is further emphasized in the parlor conversation, when Marion asks Norman if his time is really so empty — and he in turn asserts that she's probably "never had an empty moment" in her life.

The motif, of course, is emptiness: vacancy, nothingness, absence, blankness. Though not found in other analyses of *Psycho*, this may well be the film's single most pervasive motif— and one unacknowledged key to its chilling horror.

The emptiness motif is in fact so pervasive that the motel's "vacancy" notice could easily be taken as one of Hitchcock's grim private jokes, like the line about Mother not being "quite herself today." The motel itself is a locus of emptiness: Empty chairs are everywhere; the safe in Norman's parlor is empty; the stuffed birds are empty of life, and have what has often been called a "vacant stare." The motel cabins are all empty as well, as are all the closets and drawers — a fact that gets emphasis when Sam and Lila go through them one by one in the room Marion no longer occupies. The mansion likewise is empty of life; the place Mother ought to occupy is vacant — embodied and symbolized by the sockets in her skull and the empty indentation in her bed. By the end of the film, not even Norman lives here any longer; indeed, he appears entirely absent from the movie's world, leaving behind a mere empty shell.

If we broaden this idea to include things that are missing or blank, the movie yields numerous other examples: missing money; missing persons (both "young girls"); a missing shower curtain; Mother's missing corpse ("An empty coffin was buried"); and missing information ("It's not coming together," Arbogast complains; "something's missing"). Also: the blank or missing title on the book in Norman's bedroom; the blank stare of the highway cop; and the blank, backlit face of Mother as she pulls back the shower curtain and raises her knife. This last effect, as we have seen, is strikingly recreated one week later when Lila runs the length of the hardware store upon Sam's return from the motel; she too is backlit, and her shadowed face is startlingly blank.

This motif could even be extended to Hitchcock's careful use of shadows, which represent a sort of disembodied presence that isn't really alive. Indeed, a sort of lifeless absence can be found not only in the shadows but also in the paintings, sculptures, and mirror reflections that are so prominent in the film's *mise-en-scène*. Perhaps the idea could even extend to the movie's characters—figures on a screen that seem to be there but really aren't. Like Mother Bates.

When Sam complains about his dead father's debts, he says that he is "tired of sweating for people who aren't there." This action, of course, describes the lives of several people in the film — most notably Norman, who writhes in bondage to a long-dead parent. But as we viewers squirm and cover our eyes before two-dimensional images projected on a screen, we too are sweating over people who aren't really there.

Lest we get too abstract, however, let's focus briefly on an example that is clearer, more concrete, and much more striking: the third desk in the real estate office where Marion works. It sits against the wall between Marion's desk and the door to the street, yet there is no hint that Lowery employs a third secretary. Who sits here? And why is this phantom desk the last thing we see when Marion leaves the office, followed by her shadow? Has Marion begun to move into that world of vacant nonexistence represented by the Bates Motel and mansion? Or is there some significance to the fact that this empty desk is framed by a painting of a tranquil pond and forest, while the wall behind Marion's desk bears an enormous picture of a desert?

More to the point, who would hang a picture of a desert on the wall in a real estate office? Answer: Alfred Hitchcock. This desert simply mirrors the emptiness in Marion's life, as do the arid hills through which she drives and the empty flower vases that are prominent in both of the film's hotel rooms. Indeed, it would be hard to think of a simpler yet more profound and poignant symbol for Marion's life than these two vases. Quietly but clearly they speak of this single orphan's rootless, homeless, colorless life — and the lack of romance that turns her into a desperate fugitive. She too is sweating for someone or something that isn't there.

Psycho is a film of pronounced negation. Its dialogue is riddled with words like *no, not, nobody, nothing,* and *never.* Indeed, *never* is the film's first word ("Never did eat your lunch, did you?") — and it recurs frequently thereafter. Sam to Lila (speaking of the Bates Motel): "You'll never find it." Norman on our inability to get free: "We never budge an inch" and "People never run away from anything." This last is grammatically awkward but uncannily accurate: Marion isn't running away from anything; she's running from *nothing*—from the vacant emptiness of her lonely life.

Other instances of negative expressions in *Psycho*:

Mother to Norman (denying his wish to have Marion in for dinner): "No! I tell you, no!"
Cassidy's voice in Marion's head: "You checked with the bank, no? They never laid eyes on her, no?"
Lila on Arbogast's phone call: "No, no, he said he was dissatisfied.... He called when he had nothing, nothing but a dissatisfied feeling."

After returning from the motel, Sam insists that he found "no Arbogast, no Bates," and the sheriff also confirms that he found "nothing": "No woman was there." Even the name *No*rman echoes several of these negative expressions. (Bloch, in his memoir, writes that he chose the name because it suggested "neither woman nor man.")

But the densest negative dialogue in the film can be found in the interview between Arbogast and Norman. In this eight-minute scene, the word *no* recurs at least 22 times. It's most noticeable at the outset, where Arbogast insists, "No, no, no, I don't want to trouble you," and Norman replies, "No, it's no trouble." But it's similarly prominent in at least a dozen unadorned no's with which Norman responds to the questioning. The relentless denial and negation here might remind us of King Lear's anguished "Never, never, never, never, never!" (5.3.306)—perhaps the most potent expression of loss and emptiness ever penned. Or, given the prominent black bird in Norman's parlor, it might remind us of "The Raven"'s hopeless "Nevermore!"—which Edgar Allan Poe regarded as the saddest word in the English language.

The strongest negative force in the film, however, is one we've already examined at length in Chapter 15: Mother Bates. She seems to determine virtually everything that happens after Marion's arrival at the motel—including the death of Marion, Arbogast, and of course Norman (indeed, for him she is both beginning and end). Nevertheless, Mom herself doesn't actually exist. After all, what are we looking at in the final scene, and who is speaking silently in that blank-walled room, a room that the script describes as having "a quality of no-whereness"? Is it Norman? No. "Norman Bates no longer exists," to use the psychiatrist's telling phrase. Well, then, is it Norman's mother? No. The sheriff assures us that "Norman Bates's mother has been dead and buried in Greenlawn Cemetery for the past ten years." We are in fact looking at a *non*-person, a nonentity, the ultimate member of that group Sam describes as "people who aren't there."

In other words, at the heart of *Psycho* Hitchcock has placed a dizzying void—an absence, a vacuum, a black hole. And this black hole, like the swamp and the shower drain, inexorably sucks everything into itself, leaving us at last with empty eyes in an empty skull in an empty body in an empty room—a terrifying, almost apocalyptic vision.

This vision of annihilation is what the existentialists see when they look at death—or try to see; for here is an idea for which we scarcely have a label or category. It is perhaps the most alien and threatening idea we can conceive. Yet in *Psycho*, this nameless, faceless fear steps up to the screen and stares us blankly in the eye—threatening to absorb us as well.

18

The Whole Story

Psycho *and Its Moral Implications*

Alfred Hitchcock might well be described as "the Shakespeare of cinema."

The vast range, depth, and variety of his work; the readiness with which it can be sub-grouped by topic, period, genre, and theme; the sense in which he towers over virtually every other artist in his medium; his seemingly endless appeal to literary scholars together with remarkable popularity among "ordinary" viewers — all this combines to make him filmdom's most truly Shakespearean figure.

If Hitchcock is cinema's Shakespeare, then *Vertigo* is his *Hamlet*, and *Psycho* his *Macbeth*.

Indeed, there are striking parallels between "the Scottish play" and *Psycho*: the suddenness with which a relatively good person can plunge into wickedness — carefully and deliberately committing an act s/he knows is wrong; the inexorable way one murder leads to another; the overpowering sense of darkness, chaos, and claustrophobia; and the preoccupation with the effects of guilt, symbolized so vividly in Shakespeare by the bloody hands that Macbeth fears will never come clean — and in *Psycho* by Norman's similarly blood-stained hands after he moves Marion's corpse (note how hurriedly he washes in the bathroom sink, as though he fears the stain might become permanent). Indeed, we might well wonder whether the insecticide purchased in Sam's store shortly afterward — in a can labeled Spot Insect Remover — is a reference to Lady Macbeth's famous "damned" and indelible spot of blood. (On the 2008 DVD commentary, *Psycho* expert Stephen Rebello invokes Lady Macbeth when discussing this scene in which Norman washes his hands.)

But *Macbeth* is a profoundly *moral* work — with swift retribution for the crime, beginning with the guilt Macbeth feels even before he commits it, and culminating in insomnia and death for the culprits, along with restoration of order in Scotland under a stalwart, upright new king. Does *Psycho* embody a similar sense of justice? Or is it ultimately a tragic and despairing tale, without a glimmer of light or hope? Is it a moral or an immoral film?

Certainly this latter charge has been made. In his book *Hitchcock: The Making of a Reputation*, Robert E. Kapsis quotes the following letter Hitchcock received from an angry viewer:

> Acclaim is yours for presenting to humanity the lessons in crime so clearly depicted in *Psycho*:
>> You have made love without marriage in a cheap hotel room acceptable.
>> You have made respectability, responsibility, and alimony, dirty words.
>> You have made robbery forgiveable.
>> You have made murder explainable.
>> You have made matricide agreeable.
>> You have made grave-robbing plausible.
>> You have made corpse-taxidermy a national hobby.
> You have given your fellow man complete vindication for any or all such crimes [61].

Some of these charges don't deserve to be answered in detail. It seems unlikely, for example, that *Psycho* would have caused a sudden boom in American taxidermy; and students of Victorian-era body-snatching (not to mention Ed Gein) could tell you that grave-robbing was already quite "plausible" long before Hitchcock came along.

But much of the letter merits more examination.

Does *Psycho*, for instance, look favorably on premarital sex in cheap hotel rooms?

On the contrary.

In the first place, as we saw in Chapter 5, Hitchcock was frustrated by "the lack of erotic heat" between stars Janet Leigh and John Gavin (Rebello 86), and the opening hotel room tryst emerges, to use Patrick McGilligan's phraseology, as "audacious but awkward, provocative but cold, sexy with a whiff of BO" (592). In other words, it's hardly the sort of sequence that would titillate viewers into doing the same thing themselves. Even the main character isn't interested in repeating the experience.

As we have seen, Marion — with whom we sympathize increasingly throughout the scene and the film — has become uncomfortable with these illicit liaisons; she tells Sam, "I hate having to be with you in a place like this," and eventually declares that "this is the last time" they can meet in such a way. Her desperate desire for the legitimacy of marriage is something we are expected to understand — something that helps us empathize with her in everything that follows. Indeed, the desirability of "respectable" marriage for Marion is fundamental to the grip *Psycho* holds on our emotions; we wouldn't feel half so kindly disposed toward her if she'd stolen the money out of greed or ambition, as in most crime thrillers.

For these reasons, Marion's theft may seem "forgiveable"; but it is certainly not excused in the film. Nor is larceny depicted in a way that's likely to encourage similar behavior in viewers. The terror, paranoia, and guilt Marion feels from the moment she drives out of town, the squirming discomfort we experience when she is interrogated by a nosy policeman, and when she shocks the salesman by buying a used car in a matter of minutes — all this makes the theft profoundly distasteful. We know it's wrong, and so does Marion, as indicated most clearly when she finally decides to return the money. Indeed, since she's seen subtracting $700 from the figures in her bank book, she has apparently decided to return even the money she spent on her car. And of course we must bear in mind the consequences of Marion's impulsive decision — her own tragic and senseless death, exacerbated by the idea that if she had waited instead of stealing the money, Sam would eventually have committed himself to marrying her in spite of his qualms.

Donald Spoto aptly sums up the film's attitude toward illicit sex and money by insisting that in *Psycho*, "... love stolen at mid-day, like cash stolen in late afternoon, amounts to nothing" (381).

Regarding this issue of morality, Neil P. Hurley has written an entire book — 1993's *Soul in Suspense* — claiming that Hitchcock's work is founded upon, and shot through with, the Judeo-Christian principles of his Jesuit education. Among other things, Hurley writes that Hitchcock "often treats crime as a pathetic waste" (11) — and this certainly describes both Marion's death and Norman's life in *Psycho*. What sane viewer — having contemplated the labyrinth of guilt Norman is trapped in, and the final annihilation of his personhood — could possibly conclude that *Psycho* makes matricide "agreeable"?

Thus, Hurley writes, even in Hitchcock films whose protagonists do not demonstrate moral improvement (e.g., Norman Bates), there is nevertheless "a moral lesson, a spiritual insight to be gained by watching the terrible consequences of jealousy, fear, suspicion, wealth, psychic disorders, or childhood traumas" (35).

As Naremore puts it, "Hitchcock is no anarchist. His villains are often sympathetic, yet they are inevitably trapped by an unremitting, almost cosmic system of justice" (20).

Psycho, in other words, gives us a world of secretive lunchtime trysts, larceny, grave-robbing, murder, and matricide; yet these actions certainly never seem lucrative or laudable. We never want to be these people or act like them, nor would we ever want to live in their world.

It's rather surprising that the angry letter-writer failed to level at *Psycho* the one accusation that might stick — something along the lines of, "You have made voyeurism a type of entertainment." Yet even here, the film hardly seems to *condone* the act of peeping into people's lives. The ultimate result of Norman watching Marion undress is a guilt so profound that he must disguise himself as a killer and *obliterate* the object of his desire — in a vicious murder that is as much an attack on his own desires as it is on his unwilling victim. To some degree, it is also an attack on the viewers who have shared Norman's unseemly lust.

In the 1992 revised edition of his seminal *Art of Alfred Hitchcock*, Donald Spoto insists that *Psycho* is a work of "brave, uncompromising moralism" (327) — "an indictment of the viewer's capacity for voyeurism and his own potential for depravity" (314). Spoto contends that even "the audience manipulation ... has an artistic, even a moral purpose" (320); Hitchcock's film insists on "looking evil squarely in the face and calling it evil" (326). Thus, in the earlier edition of the same book, Spoto can write of our being "made aware of dark impulses" and thus "forewarned" (380): "It is only by fully confronting a reflection of ourselves that psychic healing is possible" (358). *Psycho*, in other words, is not an endorsement of crime and perversion, but a *warning* — all the more potent because it makes us feel how much we have in common with Marion and Norman, how close we are to them, how easily we could slip into their mindset and their tragic actions.

On the whole, then, the only one of the letter-writer's statements that is actually borne out in the film is that the story makes robbery seem "forgiveable." Yet if the film enables and urges us to forgive crimes, does that make it a morally corrupting work? Isn't forgiveness a virtue?

Indeed, Hurley sees this as a keystone of the film's morality, insisting repeatedly that the film "prevents condemnation and severe judgment of seemingly contemptible actions..." (14). *Psycho*, he writes, is "drenched with irony and compassion.... The director's sympathy for Marion Crane and Norman Bates is in abundant evidence.... *Psycho* brims with horror, true, but it calls for understanding, a higher consciousness — 'There, but for the grace of God, stand I!'" (27).

Psycho's morality thus results not in spite of our identification with the characters — but *because of it*. Since both Marion and Norman have so profoundly and consistently enlisted our sympathies, we are precluded from judging them too harshly. Furthermore, says Hurley, the film's final moments, with the baffling, enigmatic figure of Norman-Mom, "invite awe at the mystery of good and evil and deny the viewer grounds for judgments. These scenes brim with reverent unknowing" (75); and thus "Hitchcock seems to

point to an Absolute Judge who alone will be able to resolve these complexities" (61).

So: We have answered those who accuse *Psycho* of espousing immoral-
ity, either in its characters or its viewers. But that still leaves open the question of whether *Psycho* is a film without hope — a work of despair and
desolation that leaves viewers floundering amid lives wrecked by greed, lust,
and murder.

This charge is harder to answer.

Some writers have pointed to the ironic humor in the film: Norman saying his mother "isn't quite herself today"; the cop telling Marion she should
have stayed in a motel "just to be safe"; Lila insisting that she "can handle a
sick old woman." They see this not so much as hopefulness, but rather as a
way of helping us process the brutality and misery depicted in the story.

"The keen humor of the film," writes Spoto, "is a refusal to yield to the
horror and tyranny of those impulses which the film so relentlessly analyzes"
(381). Robin Wood adds: "No film conveys — to those not afraid to expose
themselves fully to it — a greater sense of desolation, yet it does so from an
exceptionally mature and secure emotional viewpoint. And an essential part
of this viewpoint is the detached sardonic humor. It enables the film to con-
template the ultimate horrors without hysteria, with a poised, almost serene
detachment" (151). This is certainly the case when *Psycho* is discussed with
high school students. An emphasis on Hitchcock's grim jokes — and a sardonic approach that approximates that of the director ("Uh-oh — Mother left
the bathroom a mess again!") — enables them to step back from the horror
and to grapple with the film intellectually, as a work of art rather than a gut-
wrenching rollercoaster ride.

But this scarcely enables anyone to call the film *hopeful* — especially first-
time viewers. Wholly unable to pick up the in-jokes, they are often shocked
to hear that Hitchcock considered it "a *fun* picture" (quoted in Wood 142).

More important to the question of despair vs. hope is *Psycho*'s *orderli-
ness* — its artistic rigor, its complexity, its technical and aesthetic excellence.
Psycho's storyline may depict a world of chaos, but — as in the shower scene,
for example — it does so in a carefully crafted form, with a meticulous director imposing his vision on every frame — exerting his control, as it were, over
the mayhem and disorder he presents. Indeed, as in most great art, there is
vivid hopefulness inherent in the very act of constructing such an intricate,
rich, and *symmetrical* work — the hopefulness of ideas, of creation, of artistic
beauty, of communicating to fellow human beings. If Hitchcock really felt
that the world was a place of hopeless tragedy, negation, and despair, why
would he — why would any artist, for that matter — bother to make so many

fine and enduring masterpieces? The fiction writer Flannery O'Connor, in her collection of essays entitled *Mystery and Manners*, puts it more succinctly: "People are always complaining that the modern novelist has no hope and that the picture he paints of the world is unbearable. The only answer to this is that people without hope do not write novels" (77).

Or make films.

O'Connor, with whom Hitchcock shares a Catholic upbringing, has several insights on this matter. Frequently questioned as to how a Catholic writer, interested in morality and goodness, could write such violent and depressing stories, O'Connor quotes Wyndham Lewis's introduction to his own story collection called *Rotting Hill*: "If I write about a hill that is rotting, it is because I despise rot" (31). In other words, a story that depicts the kinds of horrors found in *Psycho* does so not because it relishes the horrors, but rather as an act of protest against them — and sometimes, to make the good look better in comparison. "Often, the nature of grace can be made plain only by describing its absence," writes O'Connor (204) — using a phrase that makes an almost perfect summary of *Psycho*'s approach, especially when it is compared with Hitchcock's other work.

Indeed, to resolve this matter of *Psycho*'s moral stance we need to look ultimately to Lesley Brill, whose landmark 1988 book *The Hitchcock Romance* asserts that Hitchcock's worldview is *not* principally one of macabre despair and horror, as is so often assumed. Brill insists that films such as *Vertigo* and *Psycho* are *exceptions* among Hitchcock's films, most of which feature "the conventions of happy fairy tales" and "conclusions in which central lovers live more or less happily ever after." Focusing on movies such as *To Catch a Thief* (1955), *The Trouble with Harry* (1955), and especially *North by Northwest* (1959), Brill finds that most of Hitchcock's work offers "an affectionate, profoundly hopeful view of fallen human nature and the redemptive possibilities of love between women and men" (xiii). *Psycho*, in other words, needs to be seen in the context of Hitchcock's vast oeuvre, a body of work replete with romance, comedy, colorful adventure, and upbeat resolutions — to be seen, perhaps, as the exception that proves the rule. Consider it this way: If we refuse to accept the happy, hopeful world of films like *North by Northwest* and *Family Plot*, then the horrific, despairing world of *Psycho* is our only alternative. As James Naremore puts it, Hitchcock "is a brilliant satirist who is fully aware of the tenuousness and occasional absurdity of civilization, but for him there is nothing but chaos and nihilism to offer in its place" (17).

Brill's eye-opening book is subtitled *Love and Irony in Hitchcock's Films* — by which he means to indicate that most Hitchcock films emphasize love, whereas a few of them — *Vertigo* and *Psycho* especially — are ironic. Truly, if we consider *Psycho* not a "depressing" film but rather an *ironic* one, we can get a firmer grasp on what it has to offer. For irony, like sarcasm and satire, always implies a positive; it serves to provide a bracing and attention-getting contrast between good and bad.

As an example of how this works, let's briefly consider the deeply ironic short story "The Interlopers," written in 1919 by H. H. Munro, under the pen name Saki. This may be one of the five or ten greatest short stories ever written — absolutely flawless in its pace, setting, characterization, and storyline. In fact, it's such a masterpiece that those not familiar with it should stop right here and spend a few minutes reading Saki's little gem before proceeding further; full texts can be found online using these URLs:

http://www.readbookonline.net/readOnLine/925/
http://www.horrormasters.com/Text/a1262.pdf
http://www.fullbooks.com/The-Toys-of-Peace2.html

Or of course, you can just try googling *Saki Interlopers text*.

The original print version is found in Saki's collection *The Toys of Peace and Other Papers* (Viking, 1926) and reprinted in *The Collected Short Stories of Saki* (Wordsworth, 1993).

If you haven't read this story, please read it now; you're in for a treat.

For those who have read it, here is a recap: "The Interlopers" concerns a longstanding feud between two rural families somewhere in Eastern Europe. The feud concerns a disputed strip of land which is currently owned by the von Gradwitz family, whose leader, Ulrich, is patrolling the contested woodland as the story begins. Von Gradwitz is certain that "trespassers" from the other family, the Znaeyms, are poaching on the land, and he has brought a group of men out to seek them on a windy night. As Ulrich wanders away from his party and begins to search alone, he suddenly comes face to face with Georg Znaeym, the leader of the opposing family and the man whom Ulrich hates most in the world.

Before either of them can act, a nearby tree is felled by the storm, landing on both of them. Pinned helplessly to the ground and barely able to move, the two begin hurling curses and abuse, each threatening the other with death if his own fellow-foresters happen to arrive first on the scene. But after a drink of wine from a pocket flask he's able to reach, Ulrich has a change of heart and offers a drink to Georg. With some hesitation, the two men become friends and decide to put their quarrel behind them. After happily discussing the amazement their reconciliation will excite in family members and local villagers, they agree to begin calling for help, each hoping that his own men will be the first to arrive. Before long, Ulrich is able to see figures moving toward them through the woods. The two call louder for a few moments, and then Ulrich suddenly laughs as though "unstrung with hideous fear." When Georg questions him, he explains that the figures they have seen are actually wolves.

On the surface, "The Interlopers" seems to bear little resemblance to *Psycho*—but notice particularly the open-ended hopelessness of the story. Notice how it enlists our sympathy for a character engaged in a highly questionable activity—in this case, hunting down a fellow human being; it then puts him into a trap of sorts, from which he determines to free himself by making a morally laudable resolution. Yet like Marion's decision to return the money, his hopeful action is suddenly and brutally cut off by a horrific, senseless death. Not only will both men die painfully, but no one will ever know they became friends—just as no one will ever know that Marion planned to return the stolen money.

This would seem to make "The Interlopers" a work of hopeless despair and negation; yet the horror and sorrow we feel at the end are possible only because we recognize the value of life, the preciousness of reconciliation, the wondrous possibilities of the future these men glimpsed for just a moment. As so often in ironic stories—consider "The Necklace" or "The Gift of the Magi" as other examples—the irony derives not merely from the *bad* thing that happens, but from the vast *discrepancy* we feel between the good and the bad. Like *Psycho*, such ironic tales make us painfully aware of evil, tragedy, and despair—but they are able to do so largely by counting on the reader's innate sense of goodness, victory, and hope. In this way, they may ultimately end up reemphasizing and reestablishing the very things they seem to negate.

Only by fully grasping the atrocities of oppression, exploitation, and infanticide, for instance, are we able to understand Swift's essay "A Modest Proposal." Only because we know the horrors of atomic bombings are we able to process Stanley Kubrick's black comedy *Dr. Strangelove*. Only because we understand the absurdity of "honor above all" are we able to laugh at the ridiculous Black Knight in *Monty Python and the Holy Grail*. By being entirely *negative*, these satirical and ironic attacks force us back to the *positive* virtues of compassion, moderation, and humility.

Thus with *Psycho*—which "affirms by indirection," as Spoto puts it in his revised edition (326). The film, in other words, counts on our ideas of normalcy, happiness, love, fulfillment. If we did not bring these ideas to the film, it would have no power to shock or horrify us; it would leave us cold, unaffected, indifferent. In fact, our reaction of horror, alarm, revulsion—like our initial reaction to Swift's "proposal"—serves to rouse our attention, to point to our underlying assumptions about the world, to counsel us about what is truly right, good, and worthy, to challenge us about how firmly we believe these things. And the greater the horror — that is, the greater the discrepancy between what happens in the film and our cherished hopes and dreams — then the greater our outrage, and the greater emphasis on our sense of right and wrong. *Psycho* is a protest film; and those who protest its horrors simply fail to consider that the film itself is protesting them, too.

Brill concludes:

"The grief at the center of such films as *Vertigo* and *Psycho* ... shows that Hitchcock, like his characters, cannot reconcile himself to the inevitability of a long, meaningless spiral into oblivion. Even in Hitchcock's uncompromisingly ironic works, the quest for rebirth, or innocence, and for a better, more whole self realized in love, remains enormously powerful" (237).

Part 3.
And That Still
Wasn't Enough:
Aftermath

19

They'll See and They'll Know
Psycho *and Its Viewers*

In an audio recording included in *Psycho*'s publicity kit, Hitchcock himself instructed theater owners on what to do once the movie had ended:

> Close your house curtains over the screen after the end-titles of the picture, and keep the theater dark for ½ minute. During these thirty seconds of stygian blackness, the suspense of *Psycho* is indelibly engraved in the mind of the audience, later to be discussed among gaping friends and relations. You will then bring up houselights of a greenish hue, and shine spotlights of this ominous hue across the faces of your departing patrons. Never, never, never will I permit *Psycho* to be followed immediately by a short subject or newsreel [quoted in Rebello 151].

These precise stipulations represent only one of the many tactics used in preparing and publicizing what would turn out to be Alfred Hitchcock's most successful film.

The careful handling of *Psycho* began during the actual shoot, when Hitchcock strove to maintain absolute secrecy about the storyline. Of course, anyone who read the book would know the truth about Marion's demise — not to mention Norman and his mother. And so, to discourage folks from seeking answers in Bloch's novel (which of course bore the same title), the film was sometimes referred to not as *Psycho* but as "Wimpy" — possibly from second-unit cameraman Rex Wimpy, whose name appeared on some clapboards and production sheets.

In addition, Hitchcock strictly monitored publicity stills for the film — to such a degree that Paramount's publicity department complained about not being able to take pictures on the set. And indeed, most of the film's publicity shots — even those taken later, after the shoot was done — do not reflect events in the actual film. They show a screaming Janet Leigh — fully clothed! Others depict Leigh standing near an empty rocking chair; John Gavin in the same stance; Gavin and Vera Miles snuggling and smiling; Gavin protectively embracing a frightened Miles and Leigh. Needless to say, none of these poses show up in the film itself— though they are readily available in the bonus features on the 1999 Collector's Edition of *Psycho* on DVD. (Several of these shots, however, have been inexplicably omitted from the extras on the 2008 Legacy Edition.)

Hitchcock was especially careful about not revealing the true identity of Mother. At one point during the production, he put out word that he was looking for an older actress to play this role; Helen Hayes and Judith Anderson were supposedly among his top candidates. Furthermore, art director Robert Clatworthy told Rebello that throughout the shoot, Hitchcock had, in prominent view on the set, a director's chair with "Mrs. Bates" written on the back. One afternoon, Hitchcock even allowed himself to be photographed in this chair — partly to appease studio publicists.

More from Rebello:

"Aside from Hitchcock's hype to the press about secrecy, many in the cast and crew did not know the ending. 'Mr. Hitchcock held up the last few pages of the script — and rightly so,' noted wardrobe supervisor Rita Riggs. 'When we started to work,' observed actress Vera Miles, 'we all had to raise our right hands and promise not to divulge one word of the story'" (81).

In her book on *Psycho*, Leigh noted, "Hitchcock didn't want Tony [Perkins] or me to make the usual rounds of television, radio, and print interviews, because we might have spilled the beans about the contents of the plot" (95).

However, the film's most famous trailer suggests that Hitchcock himself had fewer scruples about "spilling the beans" — at least in terms of the two murders. Scripted by James Allardice — who wrote most of Hitchcock's droll intros for *Alfred Hitchcock Presents* — this trailer features the director taking viewers on a six-and-a-half-minute tour of the Bates Motel and mansion. As Hitchcock deadpans his way around the premises, he indicates teasingly but quite clearly where the two murders would occur: "Well, they've cleaned all this up now," he says in the bathroom of Cabin 1. "You should have seen the blood. The whole place was — well, it's, it's too horrible to describe."

Later, standing at the bottom of the stairs in the Bates house, he recounts Arbogast's demise with surprisingly precise detail: "Now it was at the top of the stairs that the second murder took place. She came out of the door there, and met the victim at the top. Of course in a flash, there was the knife, and in no time the victim tumbled and fell with a horrible crash."

Following the approach Hitchcock took with publicity stills, the trailer contains no actual footage from the film. The woman screaming in the shower stall at the very end is Miles — in a wig!

As with most of the publicity stills, this trailer can be seen in its entirety on the 1999 DVD of *Psycho* and on the 2008 Legacy Edition as well.

Despite all these preliminary maneuvers, the key factor in Hitchcock's brilliant publicity campaign was his insistence that no one be admitted to the theater after the film had started.

This was not what viewers were used to. Throughout the preceding decades, as Rebello describes it, movie theaters opened at 10 A.M. and ran a continuous program well into the evening — a mix of previews, newsreels, shorts, cartoons, and double features. Moviegoers would arrive and leave whenever they wished; if they came in halfway through the feature, they could stay till it started again and watch the portion they'd missed earlier, after which they felt free to leave — resulting in the once-common idiom, "This is where I came in."

Two years before *Psycho*, Hitchcock had advised theater managers against admitting viewers during the last ten minutes of *Vertigo*. Now, however, it was not merely a matter of advice; rather, he "*insisted* that theater owners follow his decree against admitting patrons once the picture began." He also demanded that this decree be rigorously enforced — "as a contractual prerequisite for any theater exhibitor who booked the film" (Rebello 149).

Realizing that this new policy would meet with considerable resistance, Hitchcock organized a massive publicity kit for theater owners: two 20-page manuals; a series of filmed interviews with exhibitors testifying to the effectiveness of the no-early-admissions policy; and 40" × 60" standees of Hitchcock. These last items were to accompany recorded messages from the master himself, addressed to outgoing audiences and urging them not to reveal the ending.

The kit further advised theaters to hire Pinkerton guards to control crowds, and contained a tongue-in-cheek recorded message in which Hitchcock spoke to those waiting in line: "The manager of this theater has been instructed, at the risk of his life, not to admit to the theater any persons after the picture starts. Any spurious attempts to enter by side doors, fire escapes, or ventilating shafts will be met by force" (quoted in Rebello 151). One lobby poster shows Hitchcock glaring outward and pointing significantly at his watch — accompanied by the all-caps statement, "IT IS *REQUIRED* THAT YOU SEE *PSYCHO* FROM THE VERY BEGINNING!" Paramount publicity materials — available as an extra on the 2008 DVD release — show a snappily dressed Pinkerton guard pointing out a placard in front of one theater. Having insisted that patrons will not be admitted after the film begins, the pronouncement on the plaque concludes rather firmly, "We say no one — and we mean no one — not even the manager's brother, the President of the United States, or the Queen of England (God bless her)!"

These same materials show massive lines stretching around the block outside Manhattan's De Mille theater — while a public-address system airs the following message from Hitchcock: "This queuing up and standing about is good for you. It will make you appreciate the seats inside. It will also make you appreciate *Psycho*."

Hitchcock assistant Peggy Robertson said that this "see-it-from-the-start" policy was at first designed with Janet Leigh's leading role in mind. Hitchcock knew that this well-known star would draw viewers to the film — and he didn't want them coming in after Marion had died, and then spending the next 50 minutes wondering why she wasn't onscreen.

But whether it was this, or concern about the surprise ending, Hitchcock's controversial policy extended even to film critics, who were accustomed to private preliminary screenings that enabled reviews to appear on the day a film was released.

Instead, for fear that reviews would reveal too much, critics were forced to attend the film along with the rest of the viewing public — which may account for the initial drubbing the movie received.

Time magazine called it "a spectacle of stomach-churning horror"; *The Nation*'s Robert Hatch was "offended and disgusted"; and perhaps most famously, Dwight Macdonald, writing for *Esquire*, said the film reflected "a most unpleasant mind, a mean, sly, sadistic little mind."

England was similarly hostile: British censors gave the picture an X rating; the *Daily Express* said *Psycho* was "one of the most vile and disgusting films ever made." And *Observer* film critic C. A. Lejeune promised not to reveal the ending — because she had walked out! According to a 1998 story in the *Evening Standard*, Lejeune was so offended by the film that she promptly resigned her post.

Among the few who praised the picture were V. F. Perkins ("immeasurably rewarding"); the French magazine *Cahiers du cinema* (which hailed its precision, its efficacy, and its "beauty"); and Andrew Sarris, who in his *Village Voice* review called *Psycho* "the first American movie since *Touch of Evil* to stand in the same creative rank as the great European films."

New York Times critic Bosley Crowther initially called the film "a blot on an honorable career"; later, having watched it a second time to see if he could figure out what all the fuss was about, Crowther put it on his list of the year's best films. *Time* also reconsidered, later calling it "superlative" and "masterly."

This was the sort of thing that prompted Hitchcock to say, "My movies go from failures to masterpieces without ever being successes!" (quoted in Rebello 164).

But whatever the critics may have felt, Hitchcock's policy was an unqualified success with the general public. *Psycho* opened on June 16, 1960, initially playing only at the De Mille and Baronet in Manhattan; lines began forming at 8 A.M. and continued till the final show that evening. And as the film went nationwide in the following weeks, fans around the country proved surprisingly willing to wait in line, many of them doing so for the very first time — often regardless of the weather. Paramount publicity material tells of 1100 people waiting in line in Wildwood, New Jersey, despite warnings of torrential downpours and possible tornadoes. Police were called to direct knotted traffic at drive-ins (one New Jersey venue reported a three-mile line of cars) — and some drive-in managers used golf carts to deliver concessions to those waiting in the automotive queues. One impatient crowd waiting in the rain in Chicago prompted the manager to phone Paramount, where Hitchcock himself finally told the man, "Buy them umbrellas" — which he did.

But some of the phone calls coming in to Paramount were not about the lines; instead, they reported patrons passing out as the picture was being shown. Indeed, though Hitchcock and Paramount had been uncertain about the film's chances of success, *Psycho* was quickly causing a national sensation — not because of the lines, but simply because it was scaring people half to death: Numerous reports of fainting. People shrieking. Covering their eyes. Yelling at the characters onscreen. Running up and down the aisles. Writer Joseph Stefano told Rebello that at one screening, "I saw people grabbing each other, howling, screaming, reacting like six-year-olds at a Saturday matinee" (163).

Audience reactions were indeed so violent that Hitchcock considered remixing the sound on the film, particularly during the two hardware store scenes. Coming on the heels of the nerve-wracking swamp sequence and the shocking death of Arbogast, these two scenes proved virtually inaudible behind the storm of discussion and nervous laughter in crowded movie houses.

If younger fans of more recent horror films have trouble understanding this, they'd do well to find a grandparent and ask about the first time he or she saw this film. Stories of *Psycho*'s initial impact are now so legendary that they've inspired a BBC television special, "*Psycho* — The First Time"; Philip J. Skerry's book on the film includes 36 pages of personal reminiscences about initial viewings; and Leigh, in her own volume on *Psycho*, recounts a number of similar anecdotes — admitting that even she herself was "stupefied and electrified" the first time she saw the completed film (89).

One woman wrote to Leigh:

> I was six months pregnant with my son when I went to see *Psycho*. When the murder in the shower began, I started to hyperventilate, and I rushed out to the lobby, as I was afraid I might go into false labor or something. After a while I felt better,

but I didn't go back to see the rest of the picture.... The funny thing is, my son Tim, who is now thirty-four, has never been able to watch scary movies of any kind. Is it possible *Psycho* frightened him prenatally?! [170]

Documentary filmmaker Fred Simon told Skerry about seeing the film with a friend at age 14: "Leaving the theater, we of course were shaken.... We had to walk several long blocks.... Every shadow was menacing, every person a demon.... Each darkened doorway a threat.... I had no idea what Jay was feeling, because we didn't talk. Not a word. Neither of us.... Not all the way home" (360).

Among the many other stories, perhaps the most representative is one from retired attorney Don Heiser, who gave Skerry the following account of seeing the movie in his late teens:

When the knifing occurred, I was completely unprepared.... I bolted upright. I was terrified. I had never before, and never since, witnessed a movie scene as surprising and shocking. For a split second, and only a split second, the audience was quiet. Then there was an eruption of shrill screams, held breaths released and "oh my gods." ... When the show emptied out, people were wandering around with eyes wide open, still unbelieving what they saw.... I am starting to shake just writing this letter [366–67].

Rodney Easton, a retired airline worker, relates yet another fairly representative experience with *Psycho*:

I think I was 13 years old when I first saw *Psycho*. It was in one of those cavernous theaters on Main Street in downtown Buffalo. My buddy and I caught the bus on Route 5 in Hamburg one summer afternoon and rode right into downtown Buffalo. The Greyhound station was only about half a block away from the theater.... We heard that *Psycho* was really scary, but I don't think we knew much more than that. For a boy heavy into puberty, when Norman looked at Ms. Crane through the peephole in the wall, I knew I was in for a pretty good time. Little did I know what was to follow.... It sure scared the ever-livin' crap out of me. That "scree-scree-scree" noise that Hitchcock used during the infamous shower scene. I had no clue that Mother and Norman were the same person. Now when the movie comes on, it seems so obvious....

Horror director Wes Craven — who has himself had plenty of success scaring modern teens in such films as *Scream* and *Nightmare on Elm Street* — told Skerry that coming out of *Psycho* was "like getting off the most shattering roller coaster imaginable" (361); and in this he agrees with writer Linda Williams, who observes in her essay "Discipline and Fun" that "traditional roller coasters have become more like the movies; and movies, in turn, have become more like roller coasters" (175).

As proof for the first half of Williams's assertion — that thrill rides have

Shot of a 1960 audience reacting to *Psycho*. They look scared, but at least they're still in their seats. Many early screenings had patrons running from the theater in terror, which didn't stop others from queuing up in unprecedented lines for the next show. (Photofest)

become like movies — consider the "Dark Knight Coaster" that opened in 2008 at Six Flags in New Jersey and Chicago. Or "Batman: The Ride" at numerous Six Flags venues across the country.

Or, slightly closer to home for *Psycho*, the Universal Studios theme parks in Hollywood and Orlando, which feature actual rides reenacting scenes from such hit movies as *Men in Black*, *Twister*, and *Terminator 2*. (The *Jurassic Park* phenomenon is especially appropriate in this regard; the movie is *about* a theme park, its action simulates theme park thrills, and it has in turn inspired a raft ride at Universal's theme parks.)

The Universal experience also includes an extensive studio tour that began in 1964; even today it takes patrons past the famous Bates mansion, though the aging house has been moved more than once and considerably refurbished over the years. (Among other things, it was built for *Psycho* with only two walls — the left and the front — but now has all four.) In fact, for several years in the 1990s, Universal-Orlando included a pavilion devoted entirely to Hitchcock; one of its attractions was a live restaging of the shower scene from *Psycho*, in which participants were chosen from park patrons to play both Mother and Marion. The all-new house and motel used for filming *Psycho IV* were erected at the park in Orlando so that they could be included in the studio tour there as well. Unfortunately, both the Hitchcock pavilion and the Bates home in the park have since been torn down.

Dr. Matthew A. Reitz, a public school administrator in Pennsylvania, was able to provide a detailed firsthand account of participating in the shower scene reenactment in 1992 at Universal in Orlando:

On the day we visited Universal Studios and began seeking out the various attractions, we immediately became aware of the Hitchcock Pavilion. Apparently, it was a popular attraction, as it lured people in with its daunting exterior design and interesting audio that pumped eerie music in and around crowds as they approached the attraction. A group of us entered and began waiting in the long line. While we waited, a producer of the Hitchcock show was walking within and among the crowd of people. He began to approach a few individuals within the crowd and, for whatever reason, approached me. He quickly informed me that they were looking for actors to act a couple of roles of a scene in *Psycho*, and I recall him saying that I had the right build and demeanor for one of the characters they needed. I had no idea what it entailed, and it was hard for me to refuse since everyone around me was coaxing and urging me to do so. So, away we went through a side door and into the building that housed the set of the recreation of *Psycho*.

Once inside, I was approached by set folks who quickly told me that they needed me to act the role of Norman during one of the scenes in which he becomes Mother — namely, the shower scene. I recalled becoming immediately sick to the stomach as they began to apply makeup, dress me in an actual replica of the dress, and hand me a very real-looking rubber knife. They whisked me onto the actual set, and began to provide me with instruction as to where I should rock in the rocker on a porch, stand near the shower, how I should stand, and how I should actually plunge the knife into Janet Leigh's character as she showered.

I think I practiced several times, but recall feeling a very strange rush, not only by the actual feat of acting onstage but at the act of actually performing a murder. It all happened very quickly. I remember my interaction with set crew and production assistants, the bright lights when the curtain opened at a particular moment, rocking in the rocking chair on the front porch, performing the actual "murder," and the large number of folks in the audience who were actually watching me perform this role, and the curtain closing in traditional Hitchcock fashion. As for the woman who was chosen to play Janet Leigh's character — she and I rehearsed separately, and I never got a look at her until I pulled back the shower curtain. She wasn't naked, of course, but I don't remember what they had her wearing for the scene.

It was very exciting and surreal — the kind of thing people may get a chance to experience only once in a lifetime. Overall, the reenactment went off without a "hitch," and I was again whisked off the stage, undressed by staff, and thanked for my performance.

It's clear, then, that Hitchcock's film seems to have established something of an amusement park mentality in its viewers and fans — as further evidenced by the "Bates Motel haunted house ride" that is part of a theme park in Glen Mills, Pennsylvania. Additionally, according to Charles Winecoff's biography of Anthony Perkins, the original treatment for *Psycho IV* saw the Bates Motel turned into a tourist attraction where the murders were regularly re-enacted. (Plans for this follow-up, which would have starred Perkins, were scrapped after *Psycho III* proved a box-office failure — though Showtime eventually produced a third sequel along very different lines; see Chapter 20.)

As for the second half of Williams's assertion — that movies have become more like rollercoasters — one has only to watch the action climaxes of *Star Wars, Mission: Impossible, Speed,* or *Indiana Jones and the Temple of Doom* to note how cinema seeks to imitate amusement park thrills. Or consider the phenomenally successful *Pirates of the Caribbean* franchise — three lengthy movies all based on a popular Disneyland park ride.

According to Williams, *Psycho* is the film that initiated this so-called "roller-coaster concept to the phenomenon of film viewing. For *Psycho* the ride began, like the rides at Disneyland, with the line and its anticipation of terror. It continued in the film proper with an unprecedented experience of disorientation, destabilization, and terror." With *Psycho*, she writes, "audiences could, for the first time in mainstream motion picture history, take pleasure in losing ... control, mastery, and forward momentum..." (175–76). Speaking of *Psycho*, Hitchcock himself said that "the processes through which we take the audience" were "rather like taking them through the haunted house at the fairground or on the roller-coaster" (quoted in Sarris, *Interviews* 245).

This "thrill ride" aspect of viewing *Psycho* was no doubt one of the factors in its astonishing financial success. The film broke box-office records in North and South America, as well as China, Britain, Portugal, France, Japan, Italy, and Germany — undoubtedly boosted by Hitchcock's whirlwind publicity tour, which included stops in America, Europe, Asia, and Australia. In 1960 alone, the film netted $9 million in the U.S. and another $6 million overseas. It was second only to *Ben-Hur* that year — but since *Ben-Hur*'s budget was more than 13 times that of *Psycho*, Hitchcock's film was actually the year's most profitable movie. In his book on Hitchcock's public reputation, Robert E. Kapsis hypothesizes that *Psycho* vaulted to box-office success by appealing to a broad age range. The director's visible presence on marquees and in lobby displays helped lure older fans of his earlier films, while for younger viewers the film, with its frank sexuality and violence, "came to be perceived as a major social event not to be missed" (62).

Psycho was re-released theatrically several times in the 1960s — yet despite its popularity, the film was never shown on network television. CBS reportedly paid nearly $450,000 to air it during the 1966 season; but three days before the scheduled broadcast, the 21-year-old daughter of an Illinois Senatorial candidate was brutally stabbed to death at her home in a Chicago suburb. Responding to multiple requests, CBS agreed to postpone the airing. (Ultimately, the film never ran on CBS.) It went into syndication in 1970 and has since become a staple for local stations and cable networks.

So it's easy to see why networks never got to run the film — but a good deal harder to understand its poor performance in the 1960 Oscar race. *Psycho* received only four nominations: Best Director, Best Cinematography (Black and White), Best Supporting Actress (Leigh), and Best Set Decoration-Art Direction (Black and White). Not only did it fail to get a Best Picture nod, but Perkins also was overlooked (Hitchcock wired him, "I am ashamed of your fellow actors" [quoted in Rebello 179]); and perhaps most surprisingly, Bernard Herrmann's legendary score did not receive a nomination, either. When the dust had cleared, Hitchcock's masterpiece failed to win a single Academy Award. Leigh lost to Shirley Jones (*Elmer Gantry*); designers Joseph Hurley and Robert Clatworthy lost to the designers of *The Apartment*; photographer John L. Russell lost to Freddie Francis (*Sons and Lovers*); and Hitchcock lost to Billy Wilder — also for *The Apartment*. Having been nominated five times (*Rebecca, Lifeboat, Spellbound, Rear Window,* and *Psycho*), Hitchcock eventually received the Academy's Irving G. Thalberg Memorial Award, but he never won a Best Director Oscar.

20

After the Murder, Norman Returned

Sequels and Spin-Offs

In her book on the making of *Psycho*, Janet Leigh describes the effect this film had on those who were involved in making it. Leigh, for example, carefully avoided showers for the rest of her life — and even in the 1990s she was still receiving "kooky mail and phone calls." (One sample: "Hello, is Norman there? This *is* the Bates Motel, isn't it?") (134). Hitchcock, on the other hand, became a multimillionaire, and the film cemented his reputation as the grand master of cinematic thrills. Likewise, later obits for such figures as writer Robert Bloch and actors John Anderson and Simon Oakland always keyed on the fact that they had been associated with the world-famous thriller.

But perhaps the career most profoundly affected was that of Anthony Perkins.

Though he had been chosen for *Psycho* precisely because of his boyish charm and good looks, Perkins was forever afterward associated with murderers, lunatics, and perverts; his few "normal" roles following *Psycho* — e.g., *The Trial* (1962), *Catch-22* (1970), *Play It As It Lays* (1972) — are overshadowed by psychotic roles in such films as *Pretty Poison* (1968), *Mahogany* (1975), Ken Russell's *Crimes of Passion* (1984) and, of course, three sequels to *Psycho*.

Though Bloch penned two follow-ups — *Psycho II* (1982) and *Psycho House* (1991) — these built on his own 1959 novel and not on the world of the film. Of considerably greater interest to the Hitchcock fan is Richard Franklin's 1983 sequel.

Psycho II (1983)

This first and best of *Psycho*'s successors shares a number of interesting items with Hitchcock's masterpiece. Though many *Psycho* fans don't care for it much, it's certainly worth watching; in fact, readers who haven't seen it should certainly do so before taking up the ensuing material — which will necessarily divulge most of the surprises in the movie's clever, twisty plot.

Psycho II begins 22 years after its predecessor, with Perkins again playing Norman Bates. Declared sane and released to resume residence at the Bates home, Norman inspires the wrath of one "Lila Loomis" — played by original *Psycho* star Vera Miles. The film makes it clear that Lila wound up wedding Marion's former boyfriend, Sam Loomis — who has since passed away. (Very convenient, this; if Sam *had* been a character in this film, he couldn't have been played by *Psycho*'s John Gavin, who was then serving as ambassador to Mexico under President Reagan.)

The psychiatrist helping with Norman's readjustment is "Dr. Raymond"—perhaps a tribute to *Psycho*'s Dr. Richmond. He is played by Robert Loggia, who had been briefly considered for the role of Sam in the original *Psycho*. Loggia brings a nice conviction to the somewhat outlandish proceedings in this film.

Hitchcock had died in 1980, but *Psycho*'s assistant director, Hilton A. Green, served as producer on this film as well as *III* and *IV*. And for the off-screen voice of Mother, *II* and *III* also brought back Virginia Gregg, who had done voicing for Mom in the original.

Like Hitchcock's film, *Psycho II* features a number of self-referential in-jokes and allusions. For example, Norman's new friend and coworker Mary (nicely played by Meg Tilly) stays overnight at the Bates mansion, where she is seen reading Jack Henry Abbott's *In the Belly of the Beast*—a book about prison, written by a man who had stabbed someone to death a short time before the film came out. A few others: Director Franklin makes a Hitchcock-style cameo playing a video game in the diner where Norman works; one store in Fairvale — "Polito's Sundries" — is named for *Psycho II* set decorator Jennifer Polito; Perkins's son Osgood — who would grow up to be a successful actor in such films as *Legally Blonde* and *Secretary*—plays Norman as a child in one scene; and *Psycho II* script writer Tom Holland appears briefly as a deputy sheriff.

For most *Psycho* fans, Franklin's sequel comes across as a lame attempt to capitalize on the first film's success. Yet if we grant the impossibility of duplicating *Psycho*, we can at least see that *Psycho II*'s producers certainly "wish to acknowledge their debt to Sir Alfred Hitchcock" — as the closing credits state. Franklin, after all, had studied film at USC, organized a major retrospective on Hitchcock, and actually met the director, who invited him onto the set of *Topaz*. So it shouldn't be surprising that Franklin and his crew pay tribute to Hitchcock and *Psycho* in a variety of clever ways.

Psycho II opens with the old-fashioned black-and-white Universal logo, then moves straight to the original shower scene from *Psycho*. Slightly edited, this version is missing the toilet and the drain and eye shots; and it includes remixed sound (one can hear, for instance, Marion's nails scraping the wall — a noise not present in the original film). Franklin told Philip J. Skerry that he wanted viewers to see this famous scene as it had originally looked on the big screen. *Psycho II* also includes its own little shower scene. Though no one dies, Franklin carefully reprises some of Hitchcock's shots — notably, the woman stepping into the tub; her body seen vaguely behind the opaque curtain; and of course, a head-on shot of the showerhead.

In addition to the shower scene, Franklin and Holland pay tribute to *Psycho*'s food and bird motifs: Norman works at a diner; the sheriff spends much time focusing on his lunch; and Norman makes dinner for Mary at the house. During the latter sequence, as in the first film, he refuses to join her in the actual meal, and even quotes from the *Psycho* script when serving the food: "It's just sandwiches and milk." (There's another quote from the original film when Norman shows Mary around the house: "The, uh ..." — a line which his female companion, like Marion before her, finishes for him: "The bathroom.")

Regarding the bird motif: When Norman cuts Mary's sandwich, we can see that the knife bears some sort of bird logo; the soundtrack foregrounds cawing and chirping; and Mom's bedroom has two bird pictures that look remarkably similar to those next to Cabin 1's bathroom in the Hitchcock original.

As a further tribute to its predecessor, *II* has Tilly's character conceal her identity by using the last name "Samuels" — making her "Mary Samuels" and recalling the pseudonym ("Marie Samuels") that Marion used when signing the motel registration book in *Psycho*. And as in Hitchcock's film, it is raining when this young woman first arrives at the motel.

Structurally, *II* takes a cue from Hitchcock and Stefano in that the first murder does not occur until 40 minutes in. Similarly, the sequel, like its forbear, takes a big twist at the halfway point, when we learn that the friendly Mary Samuels is actually the niece of Marion Crane — and that she and her mother (Marion's sister, Lila) have been scheming to get Norman recommitted. As in *Psycho*, the sequel's climax concludes with a shot of Mom's wig on the floor, which then dissolves to the front of a courthouse; this is followed by a long verbal explanation of what was really going on. That explanation is then undercut by a chilling coda — a coda that includes, incidentally, an overhead shot of Norman carrying his mother's body *up* the staircase.

Perhaps most cleverly, when Mary and Norman first go into Mom's long-unused bedroom, we can see Hitchcock's famous silhouette in shadow on the far right wall, just before they turn on the light.

However, the most notable Hitchcock tribute in *Psycho II* is its meticulous visual scheme. Norman's parlor and the interiors of the Bates home — especially Mom's bedroom — are letter-perfect; and Franklin hired veteran matte artist Albert Whitlock to supervise visual effects. Whitlock had worked on eight Hitchcock films (including *The Lady Vanishes, Frenzy,* and *Topaz*), and his matte work in *II* is gorgeous, almost spooky in the way it evokes the *mise-en-scène* of Hitchcock in the 1960s — especially *The Birds, Marnie,* and *Torn Curtain,* all of which also featured Whitlock's work.

Particularly noteworthy in this respect are two splendid shots during the second murder scene. This begins with Norman in the attic: We see him in a medium shot, looking out the small round window at the top of the house; the camera pulls away from the window, slides along the shingles, peeks over the edge of the roof, and looks down at the ground, where two teens are approaching the house. The camera then descends the full height of the house to join them at ground level — a consummately Hitchcockian shot. Later, after one teen has been killed, we get an astonishing wide-angle process shot from the very top of the house: At screen left is the house, angling vertiginously downward, and to the right we see sparsely grassed ground with the surviving teen running across it. Looking much like something out of *Vertigo* or *North by Northwest,* it's a breathtaking moment. Try pausing the film at this spot to relish how perfectly it recaptures Hitchcock's milieu.

These careful and often clever tributes are one reason why some Hitchcock fans enjoy *Psycho II* in spite of its shortcomings. Another is Jerry Goldsmith's brilliant score.

Psycho's original composer, Bernard Herrmann, died in 1975 (his last two scores were for Martin Scorsese's *Taxi Driver* and Brian De Palma's Hitchcock tribute *Obsession*); but even Herrmann might have had trouble matching his own famous work in *Psycho*. Goldsmith — who died in 2004 after penning more than 200 scores — wisely chose not to go louder or more strident than Herrmann. Though his music for the murders includes a jolting, percussive, hammer-like sound, most of *II*'s score is notably subdued, particularly the main theme, an elegant and simple melody played on a mournful electronic keyboard. Elegiac, romantic, even haunting, this theme goes a long way toward creating the potent sense of loss that pervades this film. As Franklin himself observed in the album's liner notes, "Jerry's score is the heart of *Psycho II.*"

While no one would claim that *II* comes anywhere near the brilliance of its predecessor, it's a fairly successful film in its own right, and an intelligent contrast to the many mindless slasher films that predominated American screens in the 1970s and 1980s.

Though violent in spots, the film places emphasis not so much on gore and death as on the character of Norman, who is portrayed with remarkable sympathy. We see him playing a lovely version of "Moonlight Sonata," and we cheer for him when he fires the sleazy manager, who has turned the Bates Motel into a party palace for illicit sex and drugs.

When Norman first returns to the Bates home, accompanied by his coworker, Mary, he begs her to stay with him because he is scared. Eventually, Mary urges Lila to abandon their attempts at driving Norman over the edge: "He isn't like that any more…. He's trying so very hard to do what's right, to keep his sanity." Thanks to Perkins's nuanced performance, it's easy to believe this — and concomitantly distressing to watch Norman slowly cracking up ("Just don't let them send me back to the institution, all right?" he begs). At the end, his likable persona has once again vanished; and every other character we liked is gone, too — including Mary, and Norman's affable doctor as well. Like its predecessor, *Psycho II* ends by leaving us with no one to care about. Its overall effect is both sad and chilling.

Nevertheless, most critics were harsh, objecting to the graphic murder scenes, which they compared unfavorably to the restraint of Hitchcock's original work. But Robert E. Kapsis has pointed out the irony of these claims: Originally, the press had lambasted Hitchcock's *Psycho* for being too shocking and horrific; now critics were praising it as a model of restraint and good taste.

Psycho II, in fact, could hardly have been a true sequel had it not included at least a few genuine shocks — specifically, a brief but brutal murder in which the knife plunges into an open mouth and comes out the back of the neck. There's also a squirm-inducing scene in which Norman grabs the blade of a knife, which is then pulled away, slicing both his hands. Yet Franklin told Kapsis that he tried to maintain an element of surprise by holding off these horrors till the end of the film. Indeed, the early murders *are* quite restrained, and the blood doesn't really start flowing till the movie's last 20 minutes.

Regardless of what critics felt, *Psycho II* was a financial success. It was perhaps helped by a clever marketing campaign that ran with one of two taglines. The better-known one is still used on some of the DVD packaging: "It's 22 years later, and Norman Bates is coming home."

The lesser-known version is a good deal cleverer: Piggybacking on the tag for the recent *Jaws 2* ("Just when you thought it was safe to go back in the water"), *Psycho II* jested, "Just when you thought it was safe to go back in the shower."

Modestly budgeted at $4 million, *Psycho II* wound up netting nearly $35 million, just breaking the top 20 for 1983.

Psycho III (1986)

There's a thin line between paying homage to a great work of art and ripping it off. Hitchcock "tributes" such as *Dressed to Kill* and *Obsession* make many viewers feel that director Brian De Palma crossed this line — though *Obsession* has some ardent fans.

Psycho III not only crosses the line, it doesn't seem to know that there *is* one. In fact, having watched and disliked the film once on its initial release, I could barely bring myself to finish it a second time in preparation for this book.

Along with a couple of minor characters from *Psycho II*, the film once again stars Perkins — who also directed it. Besides *Psycho* assistant director Hilton A. Green (who produced this film) and Virginia Gregg (who again supplies Mother's voice), the film's only other Hitchcock associate is Oscar-winning production designer Henry Bumstead, who died in 2006 at the age of 91, having worked on dozens of films, including *To Kill a Mockingbird*, *Unforgiven*, *The Sting*, and — for Hitchcock — *Vertigo*, *Topaz*, and *The Man Who Knew Too Much* (1956).

It's odd that *III* fails so badly, because it does — or tries to do — many of the same things Franklin and Holland achieved in *Psycho II*.

There are, for example, numerous references to Hitchcock and *Psycho*: A car trip in the rain; a bell-tower scene, complete with matte work and process shots, looking a bit too much like *Vertigo* (indeed, *Vertigo* is actually quoted when Maureen Coyle — whose initials match those of Marion in *Psycho* — asks if Norman likes her only "Because I remind you of her?").

Birds and food are everywhere in *III* (we see Norman trapping and stuffing birds, and he offers some of his famous Kandy Korn to the new motel manager); and in addition to including some clips from Hitchcock's shower scene, *III* quotes from the *Psycho* script ("We all go a little mad sometimes"; "Mother! Oh God, Mother! Blood! Blood!").

Among the film's few successes are its Hitchcock-style in-jokes; for example, when Norman's new manager says he won't be staying at the motel very long, Norman replies calmly, "No one ever does." Perhaps the wittiest occurs after Maureen has attempted to commit suicide by slitting her wrists during a bath in Cabin 1. Recovering later, she tells Norman apologetically, "I guess I did leave the bathroom a mess" — to which Norman deadpans, "I've seen it worse."

Though these two gags work reasonably well, they're both a trifle overstated; one feels almost subconsciously that Hitchcock himself would never have been so obvious. And that's where *III* stumbles and falls. Everything is over the top, obliterating any sense of Hitchcockian subtlety and ambiguity. The color scheme is glaring green or neon-pink in many scenes; a woman has her neck slashed open while sitting on the toilet; Norman kisses the corpse of one murder victim; we actually see Norman speaking in Mom's voice (it's amazing how poorly this works); and the film offers a discomfiting muddle of deranged religious ideas (its opening line is "There is no God!"— and the dying Maureen sees Norman-Mom as the Virgin Mary, holding a crucifix instead of a knife!).

In addition, the film's appalling dialogue serves mostly to highlight the way original *Psycho* writer Joseph Stefano could make common, idiomatic speech sound both ordinary and profound: "You can't buy off unhappiness with pills"; "People never run away from anything"; "Sometimes we deliberately step into those traps." In *III*, by contrast, we get trite, flat lines like "I'll get you for this, Mother — I'll get you for this!"; "You dumb, stupid, naïve girl"; and "It's just that sometimes the despair, it's just so overwhelming that all you want is, you just want it to stop."

The acting is similarly stiff, awkward, and unconvincing. Even Perkins, who did quite well in *Psycho II*, seems artificial, mannered, almost robotic in several spots.

The whole exercise recalls the comment Mark Twain is reported to have made when his wife attempted to swear the way he did: "You got the words right, Livy, but you don't know the tune."

If *Psycho II* is but a shadow of its predecessor, *III* is a shadow of a shadow. It isn't worth seeing.

The Bates Motel (1987)

In 1987, NBC aired a 90-minute movie called *The Bates Motel*— the pilot for a proposed TV series of the same name. In the film, Bud Cort (star of the 1971 cult classic *Harold and Maude*) plays Alex West, a young man who had been committed to an institution after murdering his abusive stepfather. While in the institution, West befriended Norman Bates — here played by Kurt Paul, Perkins's stunt double from *Psycho II* and *III*. As the story begins, Bates has died, leaving his estate to West; West is discharged and makes his way to his new property, where — of course — strange events begin once again happening.

On a personal note, I tried watching it one afternoon on cable but turned it off when West comes face to face with someone dressed as a chicken inside the Bates home.

The pilot, in other words, has virtually no connection to Hitchcock's original film. It did not succeed in launching a television show and it is not commercially available — which is probably a good thing.

Psycho IV (1990)

Psycho IV should be of considerable interest to Hitchcock fans — largely because it was penned by *Psycho*'s original screenwriter, Joseph Stefano.

Stefano, Perkins, and producer Hilton A. Green represent the only personnel connections to *Psycho* on this film, which was made for Showtime and not released theatrically.

It is set several years after *II* and *III* and makes passing reference to those films (Norman admits to having killed "damn near a dozen people") — but in general, it prefers to ignore them. Indeed, the grisly knifings in *Psycho III* would certainly have put Norman away for life, negating the setup of *IV*, which features a married and largely recuperated Norman phoning in to a radio talk show about "boys who kill their mothers." Subtitled "The Beginning," *Psycho IV* has Norman describing his childhood in flashbacks — specifically, what his mother was really like, how he killed her, and the story behind the two other women he murdered before Marion Crane. Listening to much of Norman's confession is radio talk show guest Dr. Leo Richmond — the psychiatrist who appears at the end of *Psycho*.

Young Norman is played by Henry Thomas, who had starred in *E.T.* eight years earlier; Mrs. Bates is played by Olivia Hussey, who had the female lead in Franco Zeffirelli's *Romeo and Juliet* (1968).

Psycho IV's music consists almost entirely of cues from Bernard Herrmann's original score, and Stefano quotes liberally from his own earlier script (Marion's early line "Not inordinately" gets repeated three times). He includes a few other in-jokes — most notably the name Norman gives when making his call-in. Wishing to remain anonymous, he identifies himself as "Ed" — recalling the famed mother-obsessed serial killer Ed Gein. Thus, in this final installment, Stefano brings us full circle, back to Robert Bloch's original 1959 novel, which itself was inspired by Gein's grisly deeds (see Chapter 1).

The name Ed, of course, also suggests Oedipus, which might seem to read too much into the script — except that Stefano here plays up the Oedipal aspects of Norman's tale. He even includes an uncomfortable scene in which Norman unwillingly gets an erection after his mother demands that he climb in bed and hold her during a thunderstorm. While this certainly lets us know the background Stefano had in mind when he wrote the first film for Hitchcock, we might take it with a grain of salt—because in writing this script 30 years later, Stefano gets some of the details wrong. In particular, the Bates Motel has already been built when Norman's mother takes her lover (whereas in *Psycho*, Norman tells us that the boyfriend "talked her into building this motel"). And if Norman's mother and her lover were indeed found "dead together, in bed"—as *Psycho*'s Mrs. Chambers claims—then it's worrisome that *IV* places their deaths in the basement. (Admittedly, it's possible Norman carried them both upstairs.)

In any case, what *Psycho IV* does unequivocally is remove the ambiguity regarding the real Mrs. Bates. As we saw in Chapter 15, Hitchcock's film leaves us wondering whether Mom's witch-like persona reflects what Mrs. Bates was really like, or is merely as a product of Norman's tortured imagination. *Psycho IV* hews firmly toward the first interpretation, making Norman's mother out to be a volatile shrew who, for example, tickles him during his father's funeral and then scolds him for laughing. In two key scenes, she deliberately flirts with him, then torments him for becoming aroused, eventually making him wear makeup and a dress so that he'll reject his own male identity.

How Hitchcock would have felt about all this will forever remain unknown.

Indeed, where Hitchcock preferred ambiguity in so many aspects of his films, *Psycho IV* has the same basic problem as *II* and *III:* There are too many easy answers, and everything is SPELLED OUT IN CAPITAL LETTERS.

In fairness, we should note that Stefano works hard to make Norman's mother fully rounded; indeed, the film's one claim to greatness occurs in a flashback to Norman's early youth—say age seven or eight—when he picnics with her. As rain erupts, she laughs merrily and the two begin dancing in the downpour. Given what is to happen later, it's a hauntingly bittersweet moment—one of the only scenes that make *IV* seem like its own motion picture, rather than a halfhearted attempt to recapture fading glory.

The only other moment that feels somewhat three-dimensional is the ending. Norman sets fire to the Bates mansion and escapes into the arms of his wife, and the final shot shows the basement doors closing on an empty rocking chair. In other words, Norman quite literally slams the door on his past, determining to go forward with his new marriage and family. This runs directly counter to the original film's tone of hopeless entrapment in the past—but it suggests that Stefano, who was in therapy at the time he wrote *Psycho* and drew on that experience for the script, had finally put his own troubles to rest when he penned *IV* 30 years later.

Yet once the doors have slammed shut, the screen goes black, and we hear a newborn infant howling — clearly Norman's baby, which had been the subject of much discussion earlier in the film (he didn't want to have a child for fear that it would turn out like him). On the one hand, this ending seems hopeful, since new life is emerging from the shadow of death; on the other hand, the screaming noise is so painfully unpleasant that one must really wonder what the new child will be like. Will he grow up to become another Norman, thus spawning *Psycho V, VI,* and *VII?*

Let's hope we never find out.

Psycho (1998)

For a film that is so widely detested, Gus Van Sant's 1998 remake of *Psycho* has generated an enormous volume of critical response and analysis.

Using Stefano's original screenplay, Van Sant set the tale in 1998 and filmed in color; other than that, the production was billed as a shot-for-shot, line-for-line remake that would essentially replicate its predecessor — including the music, the dialogue, the cuts, and even the camera angles.

In some ways, Van Sant shows an almost obsessive fixation with the original film, duplicating the tiniest details: the number on the door of the Phoenix hotel room; the license plates on both of Marion's cars; the headline on the newspaper she buys; the name above Marion's in the Bates Motel registration book. He was even able to use some props from the original film — the stuffed owl from Norman's parlor and the same bronze hands Hitchcock used in Mom's bedroom. And for the scene with the highway cop, he and his crew found the exact same physical locale along the highway near Gorman, California — even the same telephone pole, as he claims in the DVD commentary.

On the other hand, Van Sant makes so many changes that Hitchcock scholar Thomas Leitch has written an article entitled "101 Ways to Tell Hitchcock's *Psycho* from Van Sant's." He points out, for instance, that Van Sant has added music to the scene where the car sinks into the bog; that Norman and Lila wink at each other in the motel office; and that the record in Norman's room is now a country-and-western single rather than Beethoven's Eroica symphony. More substantially, Van Sant omits quite a lot: the scene at Fairvale Church; much of the opening dialogue between Marion and Sam; and some of the psychiatrist's concluding monologue — particularly the exchange about "unsolved missing persons cases" (thus we lose the important information that Norman has killed before). The omissions are in fact so substantial that Van Sant's version is fully 10 minutes shorter than its predecessor. Technically, the 1998 version runs 103 minutes — compared to Hitchcock's 109; but four minutes of Van Sant's film are closing credits — which are not present in the original.

Indeed, the 1998 remake is a curious amalgam of faithfulness to Hitchcock mixed with idiosyncratic, often nonsensical changes. On the one hand, the precise replication forces Van Sant into several disorienting anachronisms: Arbogast's old-fashioned hat; the fact that he still exits his car on the passenger side; the telephone operator who must "connect" the sheriff with Norman; odd lines of dialogue such as Sam's "You'll swing" in the opening scene. And would any grown man in 1998 still get hung up over saying the word "bathroom" in front of a woman?

Yet on the other hand, Van Sant proves perfectly willing to update certain aspects of the film: Arbogast's line about aspic becomes, "If it don't jell, it ain't Jell-O"; Lila is tougher, and actually kicks Norman in the final basement scene; and various outdated lines are omitted — most notably, the concluding exchange about Norman being a "transvestite" and Sam's early line about married couples deliberately spending "an occasional night in a cheap hotel."

Along these same lines, one of the main problems in Van Sant's version is that the story's motivations, and its aura of sexual repression, don't work well in the modern time period. As Mark Carpenter points out in his online article "Rip in the Curtain," the characters and their actions "spring all-too clearly from an earlier era, before motiveless, pathologically-driven killing became an American commonplace." Similarly, the film feels suffused with a postmodern lack of seriousness, a certain distance from the people and problems. Sam, for instance, is much more laid-back — and Marion seems considerably less nervous during her car trip with the stolen money. On the DVD commentary, Van Sant explains that Anne Heche, playing Marion Crane, kept laughing during the shoot in her mock-up car, and that he deliberately yet somewhat whimsically included a clip in which Heche is about to burst into laughter — even though she's supposedly imagining horrific scenarios in her head. It's impossible to imagine Hitchcock working in this inexplicably haphazard manner.

In a meticulously attentive article in the 2001–02 *Hitchcock Annual*, Sam Ishii-Gonzales shows how Van Sant has destroyed the careful structure of Hitchcock's parlor scene by making many small changes, particularly in the editing, framing, and camerawork. And James Naremore, in his piece on the film, has pointed out that Van Sant's version — especially in the parlor scene — lacks the deep focus of Hitchcock's original, leaving "very little sense of how characters are related to objects in the background" (392).

Similar changes by Van Sant virtually wreck two other vital scenes — the opening hotel room tryst and the famous shower scene.

Van Sant's hotel room scene is considerably shorter than Hitchcock's (3:26 as opposed to 4:39) largely because two huge portions of dialogue are excised. Sam's ode to hard work is removed ("it requires patience, temperance — and a lot of sweating out"); worse, the scene also omits Marion's early declaration that "this is the last time" the two of them can meet like this. The absence of such a firm determination from Marion removes all the groundwork for their ensuing conversation, in which Marion and Sam try to work out the future of their relationship; and thus Marion's overt and impassioned demand for marriage ("Oh, Sam, let's get married") becomes, in Van Sant's film, almost flippant ("So let's get married!"). Likewise, Marion's line about how she is willing to "lick the stamps" loses its passionate desperation; and at this line, Van Sant already has Sam on the other side of the room — whereas in Hitchcock, Sam walks away from Marion on this line, leaving her painfully alone in the frame. Also omitted are Sam's complaints about his ex-wife and his father, thus jettisoning the initial salvo in Hitchcock's reflection on the dominance of the past.

Again in the shower scene, small changes become big ones: The showerhead is now octagonal, rather than circular, and thus it no longer resembles an eye — nor can it be so readily included with the film's recurring motif of circles. Similarly, the shower curtain is now stippled with a pattern of triangular shapes, thus eclipsing Hitchcock's careful parallel between the shower curtain and the movie screen. Three times in the DVD commentary, it is pointed out that the buttons on Marion's dress were carefully chosen to match this shower curtain — but *why*? As in the scene where Marion nearly laughs in the car, Van Sant has clearly made careful and deliberate choices — but there seems to be no underlying rationale.

More on the shower scene:

As we saw in Chapter 9, Hitchcock's original version had failed to show Marion's pupil properly dilated in death. Van Sant attempts to remedy this but fails: Specifically, he inserts an extreme close-up of the pupil dilating; but — since this is followed by her act of grabbing the shower curtain — the dilation occurs before Marion is actually dead! Worse yet, in the subsequent tracking shot away from her eye, the pupil is once again constricted.

In this reverse track, Van Sant used computer-generated imagery to extend the spiraling camera movement, so that the image turns one and a half times in the frame, rather than one-quarter turn as in Hitchcock's; Van Sant also manages to include an impressive tear-like drop running down Marion's check. But on the whole, the eye shot — like so much else in his film — looks curiously artificial, plastic, unreal.

During the shower murder, Van Sant also inserts two quick shots of fleeting clouds as Marion dies. Possibly, these show us what Marion sees as she is dying — or they're meant to connect the shower to the earlier rainstorm; but in any case, the shots don't work. As James MacDowell observes in his online essay, these cloud shots "simply break the intensity and terrifying claustrophobia of a moment that so relies on close-ups for its violent effect."

Van Sant does the same thing in the second murder: As Arbogast is being stabbed, we see fleeting and inexplicable shots of a cow on a rain-swept highway and a woman in a G-string. Carpenter asserts that these jarring inserts are "rips in the fabric of the original film": "Where Hitchcock withholds, Van Sant shows, doing a violence to the original that momentarily mirrors the violence done by Norman to Marion, as if his ferocious attack is rupturing Hitchcock's frame itself."

Indeed, Van Sant's shower scene, though similarly shot and edited, is much gorier and harder to watch than Hitchcock's. Unlike Hitchcock, Van Sant repeatedly shows blood *on* Marion's body, as well as a lake of blood in which she wades while being stabbed. The sound of the stabbing becomes a ghastly crunch of bone and gristle, and although Van Sant includes the snippet Hitchcock had to omit — an overhead of Marion lying over the tub with her buttocks exposed — he garnishes her back with knife wounds, ruining the heartbreaking sadness that screenwriter Stefano said he wanted in this shot.

But of all the changes Van Sant initiated here, probably the most hotly contested occurs just before the actual shower scene, when Norman is peeping in on Marion. To begin with, Van Sant changes the painting Norman removes (in Hitchcock it was a rendering of the story of Susannah and the elders from the Old Testament Apocrypha; in Van Sant, it's Titian's "Venus with a Mirror"); worse, he also has Norman masturbate while watching Marion undress.

In an interview with Philip Skerry, Stefano argued against this offensive change, insisting that by this act, Van Sant's Norman "discharges the anxiety and tension," and would therefore not go on to commit the rape-like murder of Marion (80). However, in one of the few insightful moments on the Van Sant DVD commentary, actor Vince Vaughn (who plays Norman here) said he felt Norman's action produced much "shame and guilt" — which in turn led to the murder.

The idea of masturbation is lightly hinted at in Norman's last name (original *Psycho* author Robert Bloch, in his memoir, gently jests about this in explaining how he came up with the name). Nevertheless, most viewers find it disgusting and unnecessary. In his review of the movie, critic Roger Ebert went so far as to suggest that it's a sort of metaphor for what Van Sant is doing in this film — efficient, but soulless, solitary, and utterly lacking genuine passion.

The whole episode falls in with Van Sant's more graphic violence and sexuality (e.g., Sam is nude in the opening scene; Norman has porn magazines in his room rather than the ambiguously blank book in Hitchcock's film). It's one more instance of Van Sant "showing" what Hitchcock "withheld" — a tendency that puts the 1998 version in the same boat with *Psycho III* and *IV*—too much information!

Likewise, the dubiousness of Van Sant's decision to shoot in color is exacerbated by the film's palette of bright pastel orange and green. Often garishly lit, it creates a world so far removed from Hitchcock's as to be virtually unrecognizable. One wonders how the film might have looked if Van Sant had used black and white, and kept the 1960 timeframe (though it seems unlikely the studio would have given him the money to set the film 38 years in the past).

More generally, if Van Sant was going to make *some* changes — using color, showing more blood, inserting odd shots — then why not go the whole nine yards and be really creative, do some things that modern technology has now made possible, that perhaps Hitchcock couldn't manage back in 1960? Why not film the shower scene in some radical way that would be as disorienting to us as the original sequence was to its 1960 viewers? How about this: Film the entire shower scene with the camera circling in a bird's-eye view. That is, at the moment Mom rips back the curtain, cut to a high angle, directly overhead, and begin to rotate the camera counterclockwise — slowly at first, as the stabbing begins, and then faster and faster throughout the slaying until the images are almost a blur. As this continues, move the camera forward and down so that (still spinning dizzily) it passes Marion and zooms in on the drain, where the spinning — which now matches the movement of the water — slowly comes to a stop on a close-up of the drain; and the spinning then reverses as the shot dissolves to Marion's eye and the camera pulls back across the room. Hard to film, yes. Hard to watch, too. And harder to describe. But of course, these phrases apply to Hitchcock's original scene as well.

And for the second murder, instead of using, as Van Sant does, the awkward rear-projection that now looks so bizarre and fake — why not take original art director Robert Clatworthy's initial suggestion: He wanted to put the camera inside a large medicine ball, with the lens sticking out of an opening, and then roll it down the stairs, creating a whizzing, unnerving whirl of images that would duplicate what Arbogast sees as he falls to his death. Again — probably next to impossible in 1960; but certainly feasible nowadays.

Surely if Hitchcock were still alive he would have been the first to seize on the opportunities technology afforded him, the first to push this new envelope as far as it would go. In fact, when he did remake one of his own films — 1934's *The Man Who Knew Too Much*, remade in 1956 — he had no hesitation about changing nearly everything in the story: the setting, the photography (the new one is in color), the storyline, even the length. In other words, if Van Sant really wanted to pay homage to the master, he would have felt freer to experiment and revise in a more radical way — as Hitchcock himself would have, and did.

As for Van Sant's cast: Heche does a pretty good job of making Marion an ordinary working woman with whom we can identify and empathize — though Naremore points out that this Marion lacks "Janet Leigh's hard-boiled intelligence and mounting neurosis" (391). In this regard, Heche's remarks on the DVD commentary are revealing: She says that in the brief scene in Marion's home — where the money lies waiting on the bed — she was "trying to give Marion a little more sense of excitement and enthusiasm that she'd taken the money." This may be more in line with contemporary mores, but it certainly isn't Hitchcock's Marion.

As for the smaller roles: Julianne Moore says she chose to play Lila as a lesbian, though this is scarcely apparent in the actual film — nor does there seem to be any good reason for this particular decision. James LeGros and James Remar are effective as, respectively, California Charlie and the highway cop.

Vince Vaughn as Norman, however, is a nightmare. Several writers have noted that Vaughn has a larger, stockier build than Anthony Perkins, making his Norman much more threatening — "a full-back wearing a fright wig," in James Naremore's memorable phrase (391). Vaughn's visible distress is oddly effective during the cleanup of the bathroom; but in general his Norman is a creepy and unsettling figure from the moment he appears. We never feel for him any of the sympathy inspired by Perkins's boyish charm. And as Thomas Leitch has pointed out, Vaughn lacks the existing screen persona that "made Anthony Perkins such a deceptive choice to play Norman Bates."

Clearly, the major complaint against Van Sant's *Psycho* is not that it fails to be as good as Hitchcock's film, but that it generally fails to *be* Hitchcock's film. As James MacDowell suggests, Van Sant has put his own authorial stamp on the film, and thus the film is not truly a "copy" of its predecessor. Van Sant wants to have both Hitchcock's film and his own — yet he somehow winds up with neither.

Vince Vaughn as Norman Bates in Gus Van Sant's 1998 color remake of *Psycho*. With a build much stockier than that of Anthony Perkins, Vaughn has been described in this film as "a fullback wearing a fright wig." Note as well the much-less-creepy Bates house behind him, yet another reason why this version doesn't work very well. (©MCA/Universal; courtesy MCA/Universal-Photofest)

Indeed, to take this a step further, the 1998 version not only fails to be Hitchcock's film; in many ways, it fails to be much of a film at all. The whole thing has a curiously artificial feel — somehow synthetic, removed from reality — which certainly cannot be said of the 1960 version. This is exacerbated by Van Sant's decision to use process shots wherever they occur in the original film (e.g., virtually all the scenes in Marion's car). Hitchcock, of course, was putting up his own money for *Psycho* and wished to cut costs wherever possible; but the process shots seem wholly unnecessary in 1998. Most viewers are likely to cut some slack to the visuals in an older film; in other words, we're more willing to suspend our disbelief for a movie that's 40 or 50 years old — whereas in a contemporary film, we demand authenticity and first-rate effects. In any case, Van Sant's process work in the highway cop scene is considerably less convincing than Hitchcock's.

Yet in spite of all the contempt that has been so widely heaped on this film, Van Sant's version is well worth watching once or twice, if only because it does a number of things exceptionally well.

The new film, for example, is especially attentive to Hitchcock's bird motif: The soundtrack is rife with chirpings and cawings; there are birds in the designs on Marion's suitcase, Mr. Lowery's tie, and the back of Sam's jacket; and we can also see live birds in the bushes outside Marion's bedroom window as she's preparing to leave. (On the downside, the final cellar scene, with its cages of live birds, feels like a case of overkill.)

The new film's handling of Hitchcock's cameo seems unusually inspired. In approaching this moment, Van Sant must have wondered which director should appear: Should he simply use a stand-in who resembles Hitchcock — or instead put himself in the shot, since he's the actual director of the new film? His solution is elegant and simple: Put them both in. As the shot of Sam in the hotel room dissolves to the real estate office, we can indeed see a cowboy-hatted Hitchcock lookalike on the sidewalk outside; watch closely and you'll see that this figure (with his back to the camera, as in Hitchcock's film) is gesticulating and lecturing a younger man — who just happens to be Gus Van Sant.

The 1998 version also does a very nice job with the superimposition of Mom's face over Norman's at the end. Using modern-day technology to maximum effect, the shot is somehow both subtle and vivid — easy to miss, but deliciously creepy when you catch it.

But of all the nice touches in Van Sant's film, perhaps the most effective appear at the very beginning and the very end.

As we saw in Chapter 4, Hitchcock wanted *Psycho*'s opening to be one continuous shot from high above Phoenix, moving right up to and then into the hotel room window; however, it was impossible to achieve, because cameras during that time weren't steady enough to shoot comfortably from a helicopter — and thus *Psycho*'s introduction features several zoom shots cut together.

In 1998, of course, Van Sant was able to accomplish this beautifully: The shot starts out above Phoenix, swings gracefully around a tall building, and heads toward the hotel — gradually moving right up to the window, then in through it and across the room till it's only a foot above Marion and Sam. Van Sant shot some of it from a helicopter, and some using a crane with a studio mock-up of wall, window, and room. He then used computer-generated imagery to join the footage — producing a continuous shot so seamless that it's impossible to tell where the blend occurs.

As for the ending, Hitchcock's film contains no closing credits — simply "The End," after which horizontal bars slide on (as in the opening credits), and the screen goes black. Van Sant instead holds on the pulling of Marion's car from the bog, and about four minutes of credits roll while the camera gradually pulls back to show us the police working around the site and then, one by one, driving off. As the credits end, the police cars are all gone, and the camera has pulled so far back that we are looking at a vast landscape behind the bog, with arid terrain rolling off towards highway and horizon. The scene is lit with a hazy, dream-like aura that recalls the work of Hitchcock's 1950s cameraman Robert Burks — and the shot holds onscreen for nearly 20 seconds. It's a bold, unusual ending, probably watched by only a few theater patrons (I can testify that by this point I was alone in the theater at both of the screenings I attended). In his online article "*Psycho* Redux," Donald Totaro asserts that this shot, instead of keeping us in the world of Norman Bates, "places the threat back into the anonymity of the everyday." Like the famous dolly shot down the stairs and out the front door during the second murder in Hitchcock's *Frenzy*, it perfectly encapsulates the Master's perennial theme of horror in ordinary, mundane settings.

As an added bonus, the initial moments of the closing credits feature the song "Weepy Donuts," in which Bill Frisell and Wayne Horvitz reprise and reinterpret some of Herrmann's *Psycho* themes — on electric guitar!

But whether we are looking at good points or bad in Van Sant's film, we are constantly comparing Van Sant's version with Hitchcock's; thus, as several critics have observed, watching the 1998 version is really like watching *two* films at once. In a fascinating essay for the 2001–02 *Hitchcock Annual*, Paula Marantz Cohen asserts that this sort of imitation serves as an homage, and thus Van Sant's film merges criticism with art. She sees the 1998 film as a tribute to Hitchcock, "a mechanism for catalyzing homage, as ingeniously designed to draw admiring attention to the original as anything Hitchcock himself might have come up with" (131).

In conclusion, Van Sant's film, if nothing else, suggests something quite intriguing about Hitchcock's work: The director repeatedly boasted about how he always laid out all his scenes in advance, with every shot and angle predetermined — to such a degree that he sometimes found the actual filming anticlimactic, even dreary and disappointing. The 1998 *Psycho* demonstrates how misleading this is. If any filmmaker ever had things mapped out for him beforehand, it would certainly be a man who was remaking an existing film shot for shot. That this experiment fails so badly only proves the vitality of the creative moment, the necessity of spontaneous cooperation, of actors and technicians working together in real time — under the active hand of cinema's greatest mastermind.

Alfred Hitchcock and the Making of Psycho

In October 2007, while promoting his own film *Slipstream*, Sir Anthony Hopkins appeared on *MTV Movies* announcing that he had been signed to play Hitchcock in a feature film about the making of *Psycho*. As of late 2008, the Internet Movie Database (www.imdb.com) showed the project bearing the same title as Stephen Rebello's book: *Alfred Hitchcock and the Making of Psycho*. At the time of the Hopkins interview, various websites — including Rotten Tomatoes and Hollywood Elsewhere — were giving the somewhat more likely-sounding title *Alfred Hitchcock Presents*. However, in a personal e-mail to this author, Rebello — who is co-writing the screenplay — calmly insisted that neither of these titles would be used.

Director on the project is Ryan Murphy, who also helmed 2006's *Running with Scissors*, as well as several episodes of TV's *Nip/Tuck*.

Hopkins's actual comments, taken from a short video interview that has been widely circulated on the Internet, indicate that the film is to begin with the story of serial killer Ed Gein, the original inspiration for Norman Bates (see Chapter 1):

> It starts off with these two brothers digging in the soil around this place on the farm, and one says to the Gaines guy [sic], "You're just a mommy's boy." And suddenly this shovel hits him on the back of the head, BANG, and kills him. The camera pans to Hitchcock standing there in the middle of the field having a cup of tea: "Good evening. I hope you didn't miss that shot. Without that we wouldn't have a film."

Hopkins, of course, goes into full Hitchcock mode during the final quote, sounding much like the director did in his droll intros to the television shows that ran from 1955 to 1965.

Some of Hopkins's other comments on Hitchcock ("he was quite a difficult man"; "he had strange relationships with actresses") suggest that the script may attempt to exaggerate or over-dramatize the director's personal quirks, which have sometimes been overemphasized in print as well. If this is the case, the film is liable to raise objections from the Hitchcock estate.

On the other hand, Rebello — a supremely well-informed and level-headed Hitchcock expert — seems unlikely to let matters get out of hand.

Indeed, with Rebello on board, we have every reason to hope that this unlikely but exciting project will serve as a fitting tribute to the legacy of the greatest film director who ever lived.

Appendix:
Cast and Credits

Psycho
1960, Paramount, B&W, 109 minutes

Cast

Norman Bates	Anthony Perkins
Lila Crane	Vera Miles
Sam Loomis	John Gavin
Milton Arbogast	Martin Balsam
Sheriff Al Chambers	John McIntire
Dr. Richmond	Simon Oakland
Tom Cassidy	Frank Albertson
Caroline	Pat Hitchcock
George Lowery	Vaughn Taylor
Mrs. Chambers	Lurene Tuttle
California Charlie	John Anderson
Highway Patrolman	Mort Mills
Voice of Mother	Virginia Gregg, Jeanette Nolan, Paul Jasmin
Marion Crane	Janet Leigh

Screenplay by Joseph Stefano
Based on the novel by Robert Bloch
Director of photography: John L. Russell, A.S.C.
Art directors: Joseph Hurley & Robert Clatworthy
Set decorator: George Milo
Unit manager: Lew Leary
Titles designer–Pictorial consultant: Saul Bass
Editor: George Tomasini, A.C.E.
Costume supervisor: Helen Colvig

Wardrobe designer: Rita Riggs
Makeup supervisors: Jack Barron & Robert Dawn
Hair stylist: Florence Bush
Special effects: Clarence Champagne
Sound recording by Waldon O. Watson & William Russell
Assistant director: Hilton A. Green
Script supervisor: Marshall Schlom
Music by Bernard Herrmann

Produced and directed by
Sir Alfred Joseph Hitchcock (1899–1980)

Sources

Rather than scrupulous, point-by-point footnotes, I have cited only quoted passages in the text.

The opening quote in Chapter 1 is from Robert Bloch's memoir *Once Around the Bloch*; other material in Chapter 1 is taken from Rebello, from Bloch's autobiography and his essay "The Shambles of Ed Gein," from Christopher Nickens's prologue to Janet Leigh's book on *Psycho*, and from the terrific online article by Rachael Bell and Marilyn Bardsley. I also referenced a *Chicago Sun–Times* article ("Owner of Gein's land") and the 1991 *People* piece by Mark Goodman.

The material in Chapter 2 on Hitchcock's troubles with Paramount and on the development of the script is taken from Rebello, from McGilligan, from Spoto's *Dark Side*, and from the featurette "The Making of *Psycho*" that accompanies the 1999 collector's edition of the *Psycho* DVD, as well as the Legacy Edition released on October 7, 2008. The entire *Psycho* shooting script has never been published in print but it is available at the website The Daily Script, using the URL under Stefano below.

Preproduction info in Chapter 3 is from Krohn, Leigh (*Psycho*), McGilligan, Rebello, Spoto (*Dark Side*), and Taylor. Brown's essay in Kolker is an excellent reference on Herrmann's score.

Chapters 4 through 18 build on the work of such Hitchcock pioneers as Wood, Spoto, Brill, Naremore, Durgnat, Truffaut, and Rothman — all of whom taught me how to think about Hitchcock, and whose works are strongly recommended for those desiring more detail on this masterpiece. Points made by numerous writers are generally not credited in my text; likewise, I did not feel obligated to mention another author if I myself had made a similar observation before reading it in someone else's book. This is especially the case with the material on motifs in Chapter 17; though the motifs are covered elsewhere by numerous writers, nearly everything here stems from many years of discussion and analysis with high school students of various ages.

In chapters 4 through 18, unless otherwise noted, quotes from Leitch are from *Find the Director*, those from Leigh are from her book on the film, those from

Naremore are from *Filmguide*, and those from Spoto are from the first edition of *The Art of Alfred Hitchcock* (1976).

Audio excerpts from Truffaut's interviews with Hitchcock are available as an extra on the 2008 Legacy Edition of *Psycho* on DVD.

The material in Chapter 19 concerning *Psycho*'s sensational effect on the public relies heavily on Rebello, McGilligan, and Leigh, whose memoir on *Psycho* contains reproductions of Paramount's publicity material on the film. Extensive newsreel footage on the publicity campaign is available as an extra on the 2008 DVD. Reviews of *Psycho* —both favorable and vicious — are quoted in Leigh, McGilligan, Rebello, and Wells.

In Chapter 20, all references to Leitch and Naremore are to, respectively, "101 Ways" and "Remaking *Psycho.*"

Bibliography

"AFI's 100 Years ... 100 Thrills." June 13, 2001. *American Film Institute*. July 12, 2007 <http://www.afi.com/tvevents/100 years/thrills.aspx>.

Anobile, Richard J., ed. *Alfred Hitchcock's* Psycho. London: Picador, 1974.

Bauso, Tom. "Mother Knows Best: The Voices of Mrs. Bates in *Psycho*." *Hitchcock Annual* 1994: 3–17.

Bell, Rachael, and Marilyn Bardsley. "Eddie Gein." *Crime Library: Criminal Minds and Methods. TruTV.com*. January 2, 2009 <http://www.trutv.com/library/crime/serial_killers/notorious/gein/bill_1.html>.

Bellour, Raymond. "Psychosis, Neurosis, Perversion." In Deutelbaum and Poague: 311–31.

Biodrowski, Steve. "*Psycho* Screenwriter." 2005. *Hollywood Gothique*. July 18, 2007 <http://www.hollywoodgothique.com/stefano.html>.

Bloch, Robert. *Once Around the Bloch: An Unauthorized Autobiography*. New York: Tor, 1993.

_____. *Psycho*. Greenwich: Fawcett, 1960.

_____. "The Shambles of Ed Gein." In *The Quality of Murder*. Ed. Anthony Boucher. New York: Dutton, 1962: 216–24.

Brill, Lesley. *The Hitchcock Romance: Love and Irony in Hitchcock's Films*. Princeton University Press, 1988.

Brown, Royal S. "Herrmann, Hitchcock and the Music of the Irrational." In Kolker: 102–17.

Carpenter, Mark. "Rip in the Curtain: Gus Van Sant's *Psycho*." January 31, 2004. *Offscreen*. March 11, 2008 <http://www.horschamp.qc.ca/new_offscreen/van_psycho.html>.

Chandler, Charlotte. *It's Only a Movie: Alfred Hitchcock, A Personal Biography*. New York: Simon, 2005.

Cohen, Paula Marantz. *Alfred Hitchcock: The Legacy of Victorianism*. Lexington: University Press of Kentucky, 1995.

_____. "The Artist Pays Homage." *Hitchcock Annual* 2001–02: 126–32.

Condon, Paul, and Jim Sangster. *The Complete Hitchcock*. London: Virgin, 1999.

Conrad, Peter. *The Hitchcock Murders*. London: Faber, 2000.

Deutelbaum, Marshall, and Leland Poague, eds. *A Hitchcock Reader*. Ames: Iowa State University Press, 1986.

Dirks, Tim. "*Psycho* (1960)." 2006. "100 Greatest Films." *Filmsite*. March 28, 2006 <www.filmsite.org/psych.html>.

Dufreigne, Jean-Pierre. *Hitchcock Style*. New York: Assouline, 2004.

Durgnat, Raymond. *A Long Hard Look at* Psycho. London: BFI, 2002.

Goodman, Mark. "Cops, Killers & Cannibals." *People Weekly*. March 1991: 62–70.

Gottlieb, Sidney, ed. *Hitchcock on Hitchcock: Selected Writings and Interviews*. Berkeley: University of California Press, 1995.

Haeffner, Nicholas. *Alfred Hitchcock*. Harlow: Pearson, 2005.

Hendershot, Cyndy. "The Cold War Horror Film: Taboo and Transgression in *The*

Bad Seed, The Fly, and *Psycho." Journal of Popular Film and Television.* Spring 2001. *FindArticles.com.* July 20, 2007 <http://findarticles.com/p/articles/mi_m0412/is_1_29/ai_73036226>.

Humphries, Patrick. *The Films of Alfred Hitchcock.* New York: Crescent, 1986.

Hurley, Neil P. *Soul in Suspense: Hitchcock's Fright and Delight.* Metuchen: Scarecrow, 1993.

Ishii-Gonzales, Sam. "An Analysis of the Parlor Scene in *Psycho* x 2." *Hitchcock Annual* 2001–02: 149–54.

Kapsis, Robert E. *Hitchcock: The Making of a Reputation.* University of Chicago Press, 1992.

Katz, Ephraim. *The Film Encyclopedia.* Third edition, revised by Fred Klein and Ronald Dean Nolan. New York: Harper, 1998.

Klinger, Barbara. "*Psycho*: The Institution of Female Sexuality." In Deutelbaum and Poague: 332–39.

Kolker, Robert, ed. *Alfred Hitchcock's Psycho: A Casebook.* Oxford University Press, 2004.

_____. "The Form, Structure, and Influence of *Psycho.*" In Kolker: 206–55.

Krohn, Bill. *Hitchcock at Work.* London: Phaidon, 2000.

Leigh, Janet. *There Really Was a Hollywood.* New York: Jove-Doubleday, 1985.

_____, with Christopher Nickens. Psycho: *Behind the Scenes of the Classic Thriller.* New York: Harmony, 1995.

Leitch, Thomas M. *The Encyclopedia of Alfred Hitchcock.* New York: Checkmark–Facts on File, 2002.

_____. *Find the Director and Other Hitchcock Games.* Athens: University of Georgia Press, 1991.

_____. "101 Ways to Tell Hitchcock's *Psycho* from Gus Van Sant's." *Literature Film Quarterly* 2000. *FindArticles.com.* March 11, 2008 <http://findarticles.com/p/articles/mi_qa3768/is_200001/ai_n8878520>.

MacDowell, James. "What Value Is There in Gus Van Sant's *Psycho.*" July 31, 2005. *Offscreen.* March 11, 2008 <http://www.offscreen.com/biblio/phile/essays/value_psycho/>.

"The Making of *Psycho.*" Dir. Laurent Bouzereau. On *Psycho* DVD. Universal, 1999 and 2008.

McGilligan, Patrick. *Alfred Hitchcock: A Life in Darkness and Light.* New York: Regan-Harper, 2004.

Mogg, Ken. *The Alfred Hitchcock Story.* Dallas: Taylor, 1999.

Naremore, James. *Filmguide to* Psycho. Bloomington: Indiana University Press, 1973.

_____. "Remaking *Psycho.*" In *Framing Hitchcock: Selected Essays from the* Hitchcock Annual. Ed. Sidney Gottlieb and Christopher Brookhouse. Detroit: Wayne State University Press, 2002: 387–95.

O'Connor, Flannery. *Mystery and Manners: Occasional Prose.* Ed. Sally and Robert Fitzgerald. New York: Farrar, 1974.

"The 100 Greatest Movie Moments 1950–2000." *EW.com.* September 24, 1999. July 14, 2007 <http://www.ew.com/ew/article/0,,270803,00.html>.

"Owner of Gein's land receives 1 bid." *Chicago Sun–Times* April 11, 2006. *Findarticles.com.* July 1, 2006 <www.findarticles.com/p/articles/mi_-qn4155/is_20060411/ai_n1617935>.

Peary, Danny. *Cult Movies: The Classics, the Sleepers, the Weird and the Wonderful.* New York: Dell, 1981.

Perry, Dennis R. *Hitchcock and Poe: The Legacy of Delight and Terror.* Lanham: Scarecrow, 2003.

Phillips, Gene D. *Alfred Hitchcock.* Boston: Twayne, 1984.

Poague, Leland. "Links in a Chain: *Psycho* and Film Classicism." In Deutelbaum and Poague: 340–49.

"*Psycho* Voted Best Movie Death Ever." May 20, 2004. *CBS News.* July 12, 2007 <http://www.cbsnews.com/stories/2004/05/20>.

Rebello, Stephen. *Alfred Hitchcock and the Making of* Psycho. New York: Dembner, 1990.

Rohmer, Eric, and Claude Chabrol. *Hitchcock: The First Forty-Four Films.* New York: Ungar, 1979.

Rothman, William. *Hitchcock —The Murderous Gaze.* Cambridge: Harvard University Press, 1982.

Saney, Daniel. "*Psycho* Shower Scene Tops Poll." July 29, 2005. *Digital Spy.* July 12, 2007 <http://www.digitalspy.co.uk/movies/a23047/psycho-shower-scene-tops-poll.html>.

Sarris, Andrew. *The American Cinema: Directors and Directions, 1929–1968.* New York: Dutton, 1968.

_____, ed. *Interviews with Film Directors.* New York: Discus-Avon, 1967.

Schechter, Harold. *Deviant: The Shocking True Story of Ed Gein, the Original "Psycho."* New York: Pocket, 1989.

Schneider, Steven Jay. "Preface." In Skerry: iv–v.

Sharff, Stefan. *The Elements of Cinema: Toward a Theory of Cinesthetic Impact.* New York: Columbia University Press, 1982.

Sinyard, Neil. *The Films of Alfred Hitchcock.* New York: Gallery-Smith, 1986.

Skerry, Philip J. *The Shower Scene in Hitchcock's* Psycho: *Creating Cinematic Suspense and Terror.* Lewiston: Mellen, 2005.

Spoto, Donald. *The Art of Alfred Hitchcock: Fifty Years of His Motion Pictures.* Garden City: Dolphin-Doubleday, 1976.

_____. *The Art of Alfred Hitchcock: Fifty Years of His Motion Pictures.* Revised edition. New York: Anchor-Random, 1992.

_____. *The Dark Side of Genius: The Life of Alfred Hitchcock.* Boston: Little, 1983.

Stefano, Joseph. *Psycho.* Revised December 1, 1959. *The Daily Script.* July 11, 2006 <http://www.dailyscript.com/scripts/psycho_revised.html>.

Sterritt, David. *The Films of Alfred Hitchcock.* Cambridge University Press, 1993.

Taylor, John Russell. *Hitch: The Life and Times of Alfred Hitchcock.* New York: Da Capo, 1996.

Toles, George. "'If Thine Eye Offend Thee...': *Psycho* and the Art of Infection." In Kolker: 120–45.

Totaro, Donato. "*Psycho* Redux." January 31, 2004. *Offscreen.* March 11, 2008 <http://www.horschamp.qc.ca/new_offscreen/psycho_van.html>.

Truffaut, François, with Helen G. Scott. *Hitchcock.* Revised edition. New York: Simon, 1984.

Walker, Michael. *Hitchcock's Motifs.* Amsterdam University Press, 2005.

Wells, Amanda Sheehan. Psycho: *Director: Alfred Hitchcock.* Longman-York, 2001.

Williams, Linda. "Discipline and Fun: *Psycho* and Postmodern Cinema." In Kolker: 164–204.

Winecoff, Charles. *Split Image: The Life of Anthony Perkins.* New York: Dutton, 1996.

Wood, Robin. *Hitchcock's Films Revisited.* New York: Columbia University Press, 1989.

Index

Numbers in **bold italic** indicate pages with illustrations.